FASHIONING
POSTFEMINISM

DISSIDENT FEMINISMS

Elora Halim Chowdhury, Editor

A list of books in the series appears at the end of this book.

FASHIONING POSTFEMINISM

SPECTACULAR FEMININITY AND TRANSNATIONAL CULTURE

SIMIDELE DOSEKUN

UNIVERSITY OF ILLINOIS PRESS
Urbana, Chicago, and Springfield

Publication of this book was supported by funding from the
London School of Economics and Political Science Department
of Media and Communications.

Library of Congress Cataloging-in-Publication Data
Names: Dosekun, Simidele, author.
Title: Fashioning postfeminism : spectacular femininity and
    transnational culture / Simidele Dosekun.
Other titles: Dissident feminisms.
Description: Urbana : University of Illinois Press, 2020. | Series:
    Dissident feminisms | Includes bibliographical references
    and index. | Identifiers: LCCN 2020005468 (print) | LCCN
    2020005469 (ebook) | ISBN 9780252043215 (hardcover) | ISBN
    9780252085086 (paperback) | ISBN 9780252052095 (ebook)
Subjects: LCSH: Women —Nigeria —Lagos —Social conditions. |
    Feminine beauty (Aesthetics) —Nigeria —Lagos. | Feminism
    —Nigeria —Lagos.
Classification: LCC HQ1815.5.Z9 L343 2020 (print) | LCC
    HQ1815.5.Z9 (ebook) | DDC 305.42096691 —dc23
LC record available at https://lccn.loc.gov/2020005468
LC ebook record available at https://lccn.loc.gov/2020005469

For my parents, Kaine and Akinsan,
and in memory of Grandma

CONTENTS

ACKNOWLEDGMENTS

Nineteen women in Lagos gave freely and generously of their time, insights, and experiences for me to write this book. I am grateful to them all.

When I was working on my PhD, I was lucky to be supervised by Rosalind Gill. In addition to brilliant intellectual guidance, she offered me warmth, kindness, and enthusiasm every step of the way and ever since. Christina Scharff was also a steadfast supporter and was in many ways an example to me. A piece of advice that she shared as I went on to the job market stuck, saving me a lot of angst. I am grateful also for the encouraging feedback that both she and Joanne Entwistle offered on an early draft of a section of this book project. Shirley Tate and Sarah Banet-Weiser were enthusiastic and generous in their reading of my work and continue to support my career. I also studied under Jane Bennett at the African Gender Institute at the University of Cape Town, and her imprint on me remains. Thank you all.

As a PhD student, I found myself part of a friendly and feminist cohort in the Department of Culture, Media, and Creative Industries at King's College London. Ana Sofia Elias, Laura Speers, Rachel O'Neill, Sara de Benedictis, Natalie Wreyford, Laura García-Favaro, and B. McClure helped and encouraged me in countless ways over the years—above all, in sharing the experience. Rachel and I are in constant conversation, and when I was struggling with the book her belief in me was a great boost. She also shared her own work in progress for what became her brilliant book, *Seduction*, so that I could see how she had dealt with various things, and read and commented on mine. She got me, quite literally, over the final hump in concluding the book. Robtel Pailey is another steadfast friend from my PhD days. We shared many an adventure in London, usually revolving around Ethiopian food on Caledonian Road, and continue to have long conversations about everything and read and support each other's work.

For the supportive environment that they provided when I was just starting to teach and working on this book, I must thank my former colleagues in the Department of Methodology at the London School of Economics and Political Science, especially my awesome office mate, Ben Wilson. The bulk of the work on this manuscript was done in the years that I was a lecturer in the School of Media, Film, and Music at the University of Sussex. I cannot imagine a more collegial or warm environment in which to work and am grateful to everyone there for making it so. My special thanks to Caroline Bassett, Michael Bull, Munira Cheema, Sally Chen, Cecile Chevalier, Katherine Farrimond, Ben Highmore, Malcolm James, Margaretta Jolly, Tanya Kant, Kate Lacey, Alisa Lebow, Eleftheria Lekakis, Sarah Maltby, JoAnn McGregor, Kate O'Riordan, Naaz Rashid, Althea Rivas, Pollyanna Ruiz, and Alban Webb, for community and conviviality. Eleftheria, Sally, the two Kates, Pollyanna, and Caroline kindly read and commented on a draft of the introduction. Eleftheria is a dear friend to me and a reliable source of freshly baked goods both at work and in her home. Malcolm put up with ceaseless questions and interruptions as my official mentor, but really as a friend. Thanks to Mehita Iqani for providing me with several opportunities to share from this work at Wits in Johannesburg and for inviting me to collaborate on a new project, and for being the most easygoing collaborator too!

It has been a pleasure to work on the book with Dawn Durante at the University of Illinois Press. Although we have never met in person, I feel like I know her, and her enthusiasm for the project comes through. My thanks to her for detailed feedback and editorial advice, likewise to Elora Chowdhury as the editor of the Dissident Feminisms series, and to the anonymous reviewers who commented on the manuscript at different stages.

More friends from my life outside academia than I can name here bolstered and encouraged me over the many years that I was working on this project, and I am grateful to them all. Special thanks to those who helped to link me with potential research participants in Lagos. Although we do not live on the same continent, Yewande Omotoso, Yinka Ibukun, and Papa Omotayo have been unfailingly present for me and have felt close by. Yehoda Martei has continued to make me laugh, also from thousands of miles away. Tumi Makgetla took the time to read a section of the book when I was stuck, even though it was far removed from her own field. Abisodun Soetan has continued to check up on me, and be happy for me, even in the hardest of times. Thank you, Abis; you are a faithful friend. Tolu and Lola Ogunsanya, and their girls, welcomed and supported me like family when I moved to Brighton.

Finally, my family. My parents have given me so much and are at the foundation of everything worthwhile that I might do. Thank you, Mum and Dad, for your unequivocal love and support and faith in me, as well as your many sacrifices for me and Lamide over the years. I dedicate this work to you, with my love and appreciation. The work is also dedicated to the memory of my dear Grandma Katie. She was, quite simply, the best person I have ever known. She also nurtured my love of books and words. My stepmother and godmother, Auntie Audrey, has always taken selfless care of me—indeed of everyone. Thank you to my sister, Lamide, for always believing in me and celebrating my achievements, and also for subsidizing me when I was a not-so-flush PhD student in London! I am grateful also to her partner, Lennard van Otterloo, for all his practical help, from making sure my furniture was soundly assembled and my shower did not leak to helping to cart my belongings around.

For their love and support, I appreciate the wider Dosekun and Oruwariye families. Special thanks to Uncle Rotimi and Auntie Kofo for contributing toward my upkeep during the first year of my PhD and to Auntie Efunbo, Uncle Ekine, and Auntie Val for also seeing to my care and well-being when I first left home to study abroad, many years earlier. A special shout-out to Tosin Southey-Cole for her practical and moral support during my fieldwork in Lagos and to Mike O., my *aburo* and "personal person." I am fortunate to count Amina Mama as not only an African feminist interlocutor but an "aunt" too. She has shown me so much love and solidarity since my time in Cape Town. It is, in many ways, her early work on black women's subjectivity that set me on my present intellectual path, and I am grateful, too, that she drew me into her African feminist community. Margo Okazawa-Rey is also a dear aunt to me and believes in me. So, too, does Uncle Sam Oni, with whom I have always had a special bond and who continues to take pride in my accomplishments. Thank you all.

The research in this book was partly funded by a scholarship from King's College London, while my upkeep was supported with a small grant from the Sir Richard Stapley Educational Trust. The publication of the book was supported by a subvention from the Department of Media and Communications at the London School of Economics and Political Science. Part of the introductory chapter appeared in *Feminist Media Studies* 15, no. 6 (2015): 960–75. Part of chapter 3 appeared in the collection *Aesthetic Labour: Rethinking Beauty Politics in Neoliberalism*, edited by Ana Sofia Elias, Rosalind Gill, and Christina Scharff (2017).

FASHIONING
POSTFEMINISM

INTRODUCTION

A NEW STYLE OF FEMININITY

This is a book about women who wear, to extravagant degree and in extravagant combination, weaves and wigs, false eyelashes and false nails, heavy and immaculate makeup, and the highest of heels. Visually, materially, and symbolically, the style of dress in question is spectacular. It is ornate, flamboyant, conspicuous, "fabulous." It stands out, and it draws the eye, all the more so in a place like Lagos, Nigeria, where poverty dominates the social landscape. In Lagos and beyond, the style is also highly spectacularized—that is, put on display, to be looked at in and by media.[1] It is increasingly the image, indeed sign, of female celebrity in Nollywood, Bollywood, and Hollywood, with all that celebrity variously connotes, from glamour to aspiration.[2] The meanings of women's appearance in the style are myriad—they are the concern of this book—but *femininity* is communicated quite conspicuously, the style being made up of normative accoutrements, technologies, and signifiers of this embodied subject position.

There is a feminist theoretical tradition ready to see women's hyperfeminine stylization as "masquerade," in the sense of artifice and dissimulation, and with this to presume to already know or recognize the woman who masquerades, the "type." In some formulations, the masquerade is an utter dupe, eagerly falling into patriarchal traps; in others, she is a stealthily subversive agent, undermining patriarchy through its very own guises.[3] Eschewing any notion that subjectivity can be gleaned from the surface, that we can read a woman from her looks, this book takes a view of what I call *spectacularly feminine style* as performative. A gendered style of dressing up, the spectacularly feminine is also a style of doing gender itself, a fashion of inaugurating and materializing gendered subjects. In the ritualized donning of makeup, heels, weaves, and so on, in the attendant development of a *sens pratique* for these dress technologies, in the very recognizing and desiring of self in their normative representation and address, women are made. The question at the heart of the book is women of what kind.

Asked of class-privileged young Nigerian women who dress and appear habitually in spectacularly feminine style, I contend that they are fashioning postfeminist selves. There are differing understandings and uses of the concept and language of postfeminism in feminist scholarship, the content and implications of the "post" being debated. In this book, I join a body of feminist media and cultural scholars who understand postfeminism as a popular cultural formation and sensibility concerning the putative pastness of feminism, rather than a distinct historical period or state after feminism, or an epistemological shift within it.[4] Postfeminism is a temporalizing sensibility that makes claims about the times that are present because of the feminist activism, often called "second wave," that went before, thanks to which women gained a host of political, social, and sexual rights—particular kinds of women, to be sure. Aging feminism and representing it as a spent and outmoded force whose aims have been achieved, postfeminism declares women "empowered," able to have and do and be it all—again, women of certain sorts. It is effectively a co-optation and commodification of the language and principles of liberal feminism, telling women, *selling* to them, that they have equality and freedom, or enough, at least, to go forth on their own terms.[5] All this is a cheery fiction. A fundamentally neoliberal sensibility—"a distinctive kind of gendered neoliberalism," Rosalind Gill calls it[6]—postfeminism individualizes and thereby downplays and depoliticizes the fact that, across the board, women continue to face systemic gendered inequalities, exclusions, and violence. In place of structural and politicized critique and resistance, it offers the rationalities and vocabularies of personal empowerment, personal choice, personal responsibility, and, it follows, personal failure.

Also on offer is a celebratory, markedly consumerist reclamation of "all things feminine," from domesticity to white weddings to fashion and beauty.[7] This is packaged as part of women's new freedoms and choices, even as what we could call the new feminine, especially its embodiment, is subject to heightened regulatory standards and expectations, to a measure that Angela McRobbie calls "the perfect."[8] Starting with McRobbie's theoretical typology of the figure that she names the "postfeminist masquerade," a figure said to be "triumphantly re-instating the spectacle of excessive femininity," appearing, say, in "the silly hat, the too short skirt, the too high heels," and behind "the mask of make-up," it has been noted in the literature on postfeminism that spectacularly feminine dress and appearance constitute one modality and site of new and "perfect" self-making that the culture suggests to women.[9] Much has been said of this as mediated image, interpellation, even imperative; *Fashioning Postfeminism* explores how it is lived and inhabited in the flesh.

The spectacularly feminine is full of promise, according to the women with whom I spoke in Lagos. Individually and in combination, makeup, heels, weaves, and the other elements of the look promise to armor, to bolster, to undergird; they promise to prepare and support a woman to face the world. The style demands much, in turn. Intricate, expensive, physically, and also psychically risky to embody, it calls for material resources, technical and bodily skill, sheer labor, and mental vigilance and calculation. Not just any woman can pull it off. As told by the women in this book who can and do, their mode of dress is at once a source, practice, effect, and sign of their empowerment. Theirs is an empowered style of femininity and an empowering style of femininity. And it is good fun, to boot! Distinct pleasures are to be had in the processes of getting done up in the style and in the glow of its attainment. *Fashioning Postfeminism* critically excavates these "happy" positions, logics, and affects and turns up their manifold contradictions and omissions—indeed, the forms of *un*happiness that they conceal. Elucidated so sharply by Sara Ahmed is the notion that happiness is a disciplinary biopolitical technology.[10] A promise of living and orienting "the right way," it binds subjects and coheres worlds, papering over the cracks. It aligns subjects with power, inviting them to get along, to not make critical-political trouble, to not "kill the joy." That postfeminism promises feminine happiness, in the present, moreover, is one of the book's urgent insights, as is the further specification of this promise as, in fact, "cruel" because it demands attachment to compromised if not actively detrimental ways of being.[11] What postfeminism offers to women in the name of feminine happiness and empowerment, I argue, is new styles of continued subjection to patriarchy.

Subjection is a paradoxical and dual affair. It is in being subjected to power, pressed upon by it, that the subject is formed, or subjectified.[12] Subjectification is the process by which subjects come into being by taking up (even if to promptly reject) the names and terms by which they are hailed, by working with the styles and technologies of self that they find available to them, by coming to desire and be moved in some ways and stuck in others, by power itself. It is the process by which the subject steps constitutively into meaning, into language and practice. This discursive-material process is the necessary condition as well as the very means for the subject to think of, act upon, and account for itself. It is, in short, the condition and means for the subject to constitute and convey its subjectivity. *Fashioning Postfeminism* is about how a set of women do as much in the terms proffered by postfeminist media, consumer, and commodity culture. Among what is only a handful of book-length ethnographic inquiries into what it means and looks and feels like to be a woman in postfeminist times, the work is unique in broaching these questions through the medium of dress and, quite crucially, in posing them beyond the West or global North.[13]

Indeed, that Lagos—Nigeria, Africa—is the scene of subjectification, that Nigerian women are the subjects, extends the book's concerns beyond the matter of how postfeminist selves are made to questions of where and when. These scenes and subjects being little associated with feminism (a dissociation I challenge in the next chapter), to speak of them in terms of *post*feminism may seem incoherent, or plain incorrect. Certainly, I have been challenged on such scores by both scholars of Africa and Western scholars of postfeminism, accused variously of conceptual naïveté and conceptual imperialism, as well as ahistoricism. It is obvious that Nigerian and other African women do not share the particular Western feminist histories upon which the analytic concept and language of postfeminism are premised. But in my experience and opinion, there tends also to be a presumption that, culturally and materially speaking, African women are, *must be*, worlds removed from the content of any such thing as "postfeminism." The book demonstrates that this is not the case for women like its subjects. This matters, but it is neither the core imperative nor the core contribution of the book. These lie, rather, in the close excavation and theorizing of a new kind of feminine subjectivity and embodiment, a contemporary mode of doing and performing womanhood. If postfeminism constitutes "an undoing of feminism,"[14] if it amounts to a retreat from politics by way of an enticement to women to be happy, or just fake it, when there remains so much to protest and decry, understanding the contours of how, and again where and when, this culture subjectifies and seduces becomes vital for feminist intellectual and activist praxis at this historical juncture. But to get to this in a project about black African women, *in* Africa for that matter, demands consideration of how we can speak at all of postfeminism here and whether it is analytically and politically sound to do so.

At issue, effectively, is who gets to be or become a postfeminist subject, including if not most centrally in feminist scholarly imaginations, which is also a question of the very nature, time, and place of postfeminism and, by implication, feminism, too. These are crucial questions glossed over in the critical literature. Almost exclusively produced by white feminist scholars about white women, the literature on postfeminism tends to proceed with ultimately Eurocentric presuppositions that the culture and its styles of subjectivity and embodiment are Western and more specifically white, or at least "properly" so. There has been a relative failure to look and think across dominant lines and categories of difference and to take globalization into account. The book interrupts and challenges these privileged inattentions, and this becomes its second realm of particular contribution and significance. Bridging African and black feminist insights and concerns, postcolonial and transnational feminist analytic and methodological impulses, and feminist poststructuralist views of the gendered subject, the book elaborates a new conceptual and methodological view of postfeminism as a culture that circulates both performatively and transnationally. Postfeminism, I contend, hails and welcomes into its fold diverse and distanciated subjects who have the material, discursive, and imaginative capital *to buy into it*—subjects like the women in this book.

These women continue long traditions of black African presence and participation in transnational fashion, consumer, and media cultures. In fact, I will insist that these traditions are constitutive, that they enter into the very meanings and makings of "Africanness." Africans cannot but style their— our—bodies and selves in "the linkages between local and transnational circulations of images, objects, events, and discourses."[15] *Per force* it is "in the interstices of multiple cultural and socioeconomic grammars—colonial, local, global, and neocolonial"—that we self-fashion.[16] This is our historical and structural condition. We can see it particularly clearly from a place like Lagos, the largest city in Africa, and one built, quite literally, as a site of commercial and so, ineluctably, cultural exchange and extraversion. Lagos, as I elaborate in the next chapter, also happens to be a city with "a rich and colourful social history that revolves around fashion and style,"[17] where the mere fact of the appearance of a new feminine (or masculine) fashion is not only unremarkable but esteemed as a practice of distinction and worldly sophistication. Thus, in looking at one such new fashion in Lagos, this book is not concerned with, or already seeing, a loss or rejection of putatively authentic or necessary ways of being in or from this place. Quite the contrary. Precisely as any such thing is always co-constituted by and colocated within the "multiple elsewheres of which [Africa] actually speaks,"[18] *Fashioning Postfeminism* is resolutely about a new African—Nigerian, Lagosian—femininity.

WHEN DOES A NIGERIAN WOMAN BECOME POSTFEMINIST?

In an article titled "Towards an Ethics of Transnational Encounter; or, 'When' Does a 'Chinese' Woman Become a 'Feminist'?" postcolonial feminist scholar Shu-mei Shih offers an incisive critique of a certain inability, or perhaps disinclination, of the Western feminist to see the "Other feminist" as a coeval subject and, indeed, as a feminist in her own right, on nonreductive and non-assimilative terms. Instead, Western feminists tend to gloss over the Other's variously constituted and imagined difference with a "reified absolutism or a been there, done that superiority complex." As Chandra Mohanty has detailed, the Western feminist also has the power to invoke the Other for self-referential and self-confirmatory purposes.[19] I argue that it such historicized and also invested epistemological positions that play a part in the literature on postfeminism in rendering women like my research participants—both black and African, neither white nor Western—virtually unseeable. Proceeding by way of critique of these dominant blind spots, my argument is that we can see postfeminism instead as not "for white girls *really*" and not "for Western girls only," as I put it heuristically in the discussion below. My contention that postfeminism can include black African women as well might appear itself assimilative or mimetic, as I have already suggested has been sometimes the reading of it. Shih's problematization of transnational feminist encounters extends to the non-Western feminist scholar, as I am, who, in effectively seeking to establish that "we too are like you," falls into what she deems the Western traps of coevality and of perpetuating Western discursive hegemony.[20] Mindful of these traps, but also seeing them as part of the logics, workings, and also violences of globalization of concern in this book, I end the discussion on postfeminism as performative and transnational culture with a brief reflection on the intellectual politics of my decision to stick with the concept and language of postfeminism to say something about Nigerian women, versus ceding it as "not for the likes of us."

FOR WHITE GIRLS *REALLY?*

Postfeminism is figured overwhelmingly on and through white female bodies in Western popular media texts. A glance at this media reveals as much, from *Sex and the City* to *Girls*. This whiteness is widely noted, and problematized as exclusionary, in the literature. Angela McRobbie, for instance, writes that the luminous figure of the postfeminist masquerade is "unapologetically and invariably white" and leaves out "non-white femininities from [its] rigid repertoire of self-styling." Karen Wilkes sees postfeminism in like terms. It promotes a "privileged white aesthetic," she states, and its happy representations of autonomous and agentic professionally successful femininities are "taken for granted as a preserve of whiteness, an unspoken entitlement to privilege." Yvonne Tasker and Diane Negra begin to point to the structural foundation of this whiteness when they describe postfeminism as "white and middle class by default, [being] anchored in consumption as a strategy (and leisure as a site) for the production of the self." The question I want to pose is where all this leaves black and other minoritized women (in the West), those, say, whose style of dress and comportment quite resemble the postfeminist masquerade, or the many who also excel academically and professionally, or those for whom privileged consumerism is also a way of life. As Jess Butler has argued, the notion that women of color are excluded from postfeminism is "an apparently obvious, but rarely examined, conclusion" in the literature, and on examination, it is revealed to be both "overly simplistic and empirically unfounded."[21] Calling for a more intersectional analytic approach to postfeminism, to more fully explore and account for its racialization, Butler starts by directing our attention to the fact that women of color *do* appear in postfeminist media. She cites a host of African American examples, including figures like Beyoncé and Nicki Minaj who, to my eye at least, appear *hyper*visible, begging the question of why they were not seen previously.

What might begin in the literature as an empiricist observation or noticing of the predominant whiteness of postfeminism seems to morph fairly quickly into both implicit or explicit views of postfeminism itself *as* white, a white thing. The dominant, normative, and representational are conflated with the ontological, and what I would agree with Negra and Tasker is structural slips into a relative essentialism. This kind of slippage is most evident in the few attempts to think about how women of color are or might be included. Jess Butler, for instance, suggests that by expanding our empirical gaze beyond white women, we can see that "there is no shortage of women of colour who appear to be *appropriating* the language of postfeminism in *unexpected* . . . ways," women who are "*in a unique position to disrupt*, at least symbolically, the whiteness of postfeminism." She makes clear, repeating, that whatever inclusion of these women does occur is "in specific and limited ways" and "narrowly circumscribed."[22] Yes, but surely it is because postfeminism itself is specific, limited, and narrowly circumscribed? It is also widely noted in the literature, and empirically obvious, that in addition to being white, the dominant figuration or representation of the postfeminist subject is of a young, thin, able-bodied, conventionally attractive, heterosexual, middle- or upper-class, educated, and upwardly mobile woman! Dayna Chatman is also tentative and overqualifying in her move to read Beyoncé as a postfeminist figure.[23] Having started by acknowledging that the subject of postfeminism has been classified in the literature as "exclusively white," Chatman's aim does not seem to be to question or trouble this claim but to merely append it, to note examples of black women—"*certain*" black women, she stresses—whom postfeminism also hails.[24]

In variously seeing postfeminist figurations and performances of women of color as appropriative, disruptive, surprising, or highly exceptional—and this when they are seen at all—the whiteness of postfeminism is reified. White women are (re)centered as not merely the most visible or materially likely postfeminist subjects, but as constitutive of and hence necessary to the thing itself: part of the very definition, content, sense, and sign of postfeminism, relative to which nonwhite, postfeminist femininities then become something else, something not quite. McRobbie is also centering white women constitutively but drawing the implications in an alternate direction when she notes that what she has already called the white stylization of the postfeminist masquerade *can* include black women, in practice, "but only on condition that there is a subsuming of difference (into Western glamour)" and only if they accept "the option of mimicry, accommodation, adjustment and modification . . . negating modes of style and beauty associated with blackness, with cultural diversity and with ethnic difference."[25] I would question the unmarked elision of "Western glamour" with whiteness here and would suggest that it is possible to do or envision spectacular postfeminist femininity in a "black style" like an Afro, say. My more fundamental and theoretical point of contention, though, is with the proprietary mode of thinking and attendant presumption of proper or authentic subjects that implicitly undergird such claims and conclusions and that render postfeminism if not strictly for white women alone, then still for them *really*.

Part of the problem, I have already suggested, is that exactly what postfeminism is and exactly how it subjectifies are undertheorized considerations. One of the contributions of this book is to elaborate an understanding of postfeminism as making a peformative address, or what I will call an attempted performative, such that we can understand its subjects are performatively constituted, made, and remade. This theoretical view is neither new nor uniquely mine. McRobbie and Gill suggest it in their foundational writings on postfeminist culture, but perhaps because their concern is with mediated representations rather than empirical subjects, they do not draw out some of the implications that I propose here.[26] To understand postfeminism as an attempted performative is to understand it as not only a cultural construct or set of discursive meanings, but also one that attempts or moves to engender that which it appears to be merely naming or pointing out. Declaring that a new gendered time and state are here, postfeminism invites women to concur, to see and feel and experience that the said time and state have indeed arrived, and to think of and conduct themselves accordingly, as women who indeed can and do have it all and so on.[27] Thus, postfeminism does not simply identify or name its subjects but interpellates them. "The mark interpellation makes is not descriptive, but inaugurative. It seeks to introduce a reality rather than report on an existing one."[28] Per Gill's crucial typology,[29] the new cultural "reality" that postfeminism seeks to introduce is characterized by elements such as an emphasis on femininity as a bodily property; a growing imperative for women to (hetero)sexually self-objectify, in the name of self-empowerment; women's hyperdisciplinary consumption of fashion and beauty as part of "a new regime of self-perfectability";[30] and an insistent casting of all the above and more as freely chosen, knowing, and self-pleasing. Women are hailed to see and style themselves in such ways so as to be or become postfeminist. The postfeminist subject, then, is one who *can and does*.

There are myriad reasons—material and structural, cultural and representational, political and ideological—that, in the West, this subject is most likely to be white, although I would caution that these reasons should not be presumed conclusively but closely explored. Nonetheless, these barriers to postfeminism, if we may call them that, are not at the level of the ontological or necessary such that a postfeminist woman of color becomes an impossible or derivative sight. Mobile, adoptable, and adaptable, styles and technologies of the self move between subjects, bodies, and sites, including racialized ones.[31] To call postfeminism "a white style," which, to be clear, I do think it is, is therefore to reference a performative cultural fiction and therefore always to speak of something that may also be or become other than white, which I also think is the case with postfeminism. I would hope that these theoretical contentions become the more compelling, if not obvious, if we remind ourselves here what constitutive postfeminist practices of the feminine self look like. To paraphrase Jess Butler, we are talking here about things like embracing feminine consumption, espousing ideologies of individualist choice and empowerment, and performing agentic heterosexuality.[32] Or, to conjure up the image of McRobbie's postfeminist masquerade, we are talking about practices like dressing in short skirts and spindly heels, with a fully made-up face.[33] It is obvious that it is not only white women who can, may, or in actuality do such things.

My point here is not that postfeminism is "postracial," although it is also popularly represented and packaged as such.[34] In the dominant representational whiteness of postfeminism, of postfeminist popular media texts and advertising especially, what we can see is the continued construction and deployment of whiteness as most recognizable, consumable, and desirable by white and other women, that is, most salable, to put it a little bluntly. It is the white supremacist construction of whiteness as universal and unmarked, not particular or exclusive, that is at work.[35] Thus, while postfeminism is not for white girls only, or for white girls really, we can say that it works through them in particular kinds of ways. But that said, nonwhite postfeminist figurations also do a particular work, including for white supremacy. They work differently and, I would venture, more efficaciously, for the cheery neoliberal picture of the West as a place of equal individual opportunity and mobility. A spectacularly successful black feminine figure like Beyoncé or Tyra Banks, for example, can look like proof that sexism *and* racism are past, or surmountable.[36] It becomes all the more crucial to understand postfeminism as making a multiracial and multiethnic interpellation in the West, if made particularly through whiteness or via proximity to it, to see that it is the West itself that is being constructed as postfeminist versus "the rest."[37] The core promises of the West to those who do or would come from elsewhere (and "assimilate") are precisely "freedom," "equality," and so on, a leaving behind of the confines and strictures and spatiotemporalities of "tradition."[38] For women, the promise is centrally one of "movement from incarceration within a patriarchal culture to freedom . . . from being a victim to having more 'choices.'"[39] It is the promise of postfeminism, or moving toward it. But is this then to say that postfeminism is delimited to the West or for Western girls alone?

FOR WESTERN GIRLS ONLY?

Having long been imagined, represented, and approached as passive victims of patriarchal tradition and poverty, girls and women of the global South or developing world have been recast in recent years as latent resources for development who, grateful, disciplined, and industrious, will yield great returns for themselves and their communities—from local to global—if invested in, if brought forward. This can be understood as a historicist versioning, and biopolitical tempering, for the developing world of the postfeminist insistence on women's agency. In other words, while the logic of "girl power" makes celebratory claims about the already present and unleashed (and "sexy") in the global North, it differentiates and distances the South by gesturing toward an ideal and strictly respectable future to be achieved there via intervention on behalf of subjects now figured as "girls *to be empowered*."[40] Heather Switzer terms this a "(post)feminist development fable."[41] What girls and women of the global South are to be brought forward from is, in short, poverty, disease, and their lack of education, (micro)capital, and control over their reproductive capacities. What they are to be empowered to and for is formal participation in the global neoliberal economy. The modus of empowerment on offer, the "gift of quickened time,"[42] is programmatic, economistic, and integrative. It is the "smart economics" of gender equality, as the World Bank has sloganed it, not feminism as, say, "a refusal of oppression, and a commitment to struggling for women's liberation from all forms of oppression—internal, external, psychological and emotional, socio-economic, political and philosophical."[43]

As with older constructions and representations of the need to rescue what I will designate heuristically as the "global South girl," this more recent neoliberal and postfeminist version continues to function by ignoring and obscuring the immense plurality of the subjects in question. The Zimbabwean feminist activist Everjoice Win speaks to these points in a chapter provocatively entitled "Not Very Poor, Powerless or Pregnant: The African Woman Forgotten by Development," where she notes that "the middle-class [African] woman is completely silenced and erased from the images of development and rights work."[44] Also still ignored is the possibility that, like Win, global South girls may be feminist in their own right or have local feminist histories, referents, and strategies. The notion that they may be *post*feminist in the style and temper of Western girls is impossible, out of sync—and undesirable. Some attention to this possibility can be found in the critical literature on postfeminism, however. In her foundational typology of new postfeminist figures, including the hyperfeminine masquerade, McRobbie briefly suggests that, via global consumer culture, a postfeminism of the Western flavor gets to the global South. She does so in reference to a figure that she calls "the global girl" (and "global girl factory worker," in one instance).[45] This is the non-Western woman already incorporated into the circuits of global capital as a laboring subject. Not of the putative type awaiting rescue or empowerment then, according to McRobbie the global girl is "independent, hard working, motivated, ambitious, and [for all this] able to enjoy at least some of the rewards of the feminine consumer culture which in turn becomes a defining feature of her citizenship and identity."[46]

Earning minimal wages that grant her equally minimal means to consume, she is placated, we are told. Not of the type striving to migrate to the West, she will "stay put and yearn for the fashion and beauty products associated with Western femininity and sexuality."[47] In a nutshell, the suggestion here is that postfeminism manifests in the global South, again via the market, as a tame and derivative version of that which we see in the West. "Postfeminism proper" thus remains the province of Western girls.

The women in this book are decidedly not global southern subjects of this imagined type: women naively content to play dress-up with scarce resources, women lapping up the crumbs from the consumerist bounties of the West, women longing for better elsewheres and "elsewhens," from Africa, in their case. Schematic, heuristic, and even metaphorical though it may be, even as a re-presentation of popular representations, McRobbie's figuration of the global girl can be problematized on intersecting counts well established in postcolonial feminist critiques of Western feminist and Western state and institutional representations of gendered global difference, some of which I have already begun to reference. As with the new figure of the global South girl to be empowered by development industry intervention, McRobbie's figuration continues to locate fullest feminine subjectivity, agency, and self-reflexivity in the West—as properties of white women especially, we may well wonder—continuing, then, the same old Eurocentric ideologies of differential and teleological progress. It is premised upon an epistemologically and empirically insufficient binary of "affluent West" and "poor rest," ignoring that class and material privilege quite obviously do not hew to geopolitical borders. In a related vein, it ignores differences between women in the global South, which is the kernel of Mohanty's now thirty-year-old critique of Western feminist scholarship in her influential article "Under Western Eyes." With all these historicized blind spots, we simply could not see the kinds of women in this book. By global standards, not just local, these women are ultraprivileged. Let me give a snapshot of their spectacular fashion and beauty consumption, which the ensuing chapters detail: fifteen hundred dollars on the finest of human hair extensions, about the same on Christian Louboutin heels and Chanel handbags, and multiple visits to the hair salon each month. Based in Lagos, these women travel with ease, physically, culturally, and imaginatively. They are in the world, and they know it. They follow and assume themselves included in the latest transnational trends in femininity, not least because they are actively invited to.

In terms of postfeminism specifically, the invitation is to join "a global sisterhood of chic, empowered, consumerist and individualistically minded women who find freedom through consumption."[48] Like Eva Chen, who writes the foregoing of elite women in China, a small but growing number of feminist cultural scholars concerned with global southern and other non-Western contexts are proceeding with the analytic concept and language of postfeminism tout court, seeing, as I do, what quite looks and sounds like the culture and its stylistics on the ground: in Singapore, Japan, Russia, India, Kenya, and South Africa, for instance.[49] The mere existence of this emergent body of work is important and telling for my purposes in this book, even as I differ or diverge in some of the detail.[50] However, what it does not offer is much theoretical or methodological attention to how we can understand postfeminism's travels, or its sense, that is, what the "post-" means, in places where a certain history and putative pastness of feminism do not apply. My position on these questions is closest to that of Michelle Lazar, who researches Singapore.[51] Lazar locates the historical origins of postfeminism in Western media and popular culture, but states that the culture has been since circulated further afield by this and other media, as well as by being packaged and sold as "global," which is to say as something that is or can be for women across multiple lines and zones of difference. Lazar states rather than demonstrates these points, however, and does so in a mere few lines, which continues to render a fuller accounting necessary. Class is also completely absent in her admittedly brief remarks, whereas it is utterly central to my view of postfeminism as "transnational," as I prefer to term it.

I understand and use the term *transnational* to designate that which exceeds and traverses but does thereby negate boundaries of nation-state and region; it is a complexly layered space constituted by heterogeneous and historicized "connectivities," such as media networks, commodity circuits, and migratory movements, through which meanings, people, practices, capital, and so on travel.[52] As concept, heuristic, and terminology, transnational implies and allows for asymmetries and incompleteness, flows not fixity, and cross-cutting rather than unidirectional linkages. It is more nimble and less all encompassing than notions of the "global," then, and also opens up a methodological and analytic approach that we could summarize as "thinking transnationally." Per Caren Kaplan and Inderpal Grewal's proposed designation of the subfield of transnational feminist cultural studies, thinking transnationally involves "articulating *links* between the diverse, unequal, and uneven relations of historically constituted subjects," work that "can and must articulate differentials of power and participation . . . and can and must trace the connections between seemingly disparate elements." Thinking transnationally means thinking of "scattered hegemonies," that is, the lines and clusters of power that do not respect local, national, or regional borders but crisscross them and thereby come to constitute other kinds of boundaries and belongings.[53] It means thinking "about women in similar contexts across the world in different geographical spaces."[54] Thinking in this way, the argument in *Fashioning Postfeminism* is not that postfeminism is simply or inexorably everywhere, a cultural formation available to, or possible for, every single woman on the globe. Rather, my argument is that postfeminism and its subjects are "scattered" or dispersed.

POSTFEMINISM AS TRANSNATIONAL CULTURE

A highly mediated, commodified, and consumerist entanglement of meanings, representations, sensibilities, practices, and goods and services, postfeminism does not only cross national and other geopolitical borders, which are, of course, often also borders of culture and history. It does so readily and easily. To put the point conversely, postfeminism is transnationalized or rendered transnational culture readily and easily via the media, commodity, consumer, migratory, and other connectivities that today crisscross the world more widely, more densely, and more rapidly than ever before. From "Beyoncé" to "boob jobs" to "Brazilian waxes," it sells around the world. All this is an effect, and instantiation, of the fundamental proliferative logic of the political economic and corporate capitalist processes that constitute globalization. The media systems and representations that the forces of globalization consolidate and distribute, for instance, "circuitry that transport modalities of power" across borders,[55] engender new sensibilities, affects, and desires and provide disparate and, again, geographically distant subjects with discursive and ideological resources for the imagination and construction of new selves.[56] They also place subjects in new imagined "webs of relationality" and "interpretive communities,"[57] such as the cosmopolitan postfeminist sisterhood that Chen references from China.[58] Whether limited to learning, seeing, and perhaps fantasizing about new goods, services, and signs, or whether it extends to their material acquisition and use, the increasingly inevitable consumption of other transnationalized commodities and content functions likewise.

But let me again emphasize that—ready and internally consistent with the forces and structures of globalization though it may be—the transnationalization of postfeminism through the kinds of mechanisms that I have sketched above is highly structured and exclusionary. Consumption is structured most fundamentally by material means. Mere access to various kinds

of transnational media and technologies, and thus to their new interpellations, cultural resources, and values, is also structured. Even the "imaginative travel engendered by media is . . . inflected by relations of power. Our
capacity to imagine, even to fantasise, is shaped by our structural locations
in social fields."[59] Also structured and unequal are the origins, directions, and
availability of different media and other consumer content. That it is "Western culture" that dominates the transnational, that most travels or moves,
that hails most widely, is clear. Cautioning against easy talk and metaphors
of globalization as flow, Shih reminds us that "flow is always affected by topography—it must follow specific contours, layouts and routes," all of which
are "historically marked."[60] The transnational is an exceedingly asymmetric
space, in short. However, cultural scholars of globalization are now widely
agreed that Western dominance of this space does not simply amount to the
loss of ostensibly pure and oppositional local cultures, or to Western cultural
imperialism, or to a "uniform global condition of '[Western culture]' writ
large," to transpose Aihwa Ong's closely related point about what it means
to posit neoliberalism as a transnationally migrating rationality.[61] Rather, we
understand globalization and the transnational as engendering new localized
and hybrid—but not therefore posthegemonic—cultures, interpretations, and
subject positions, most centrally by articulating and coming to make new
and variable sense with that which it finds on the ground.[62]

Thus, originating in Western popular culture from about the 1980s, postfeminism is Western culture but not essentially or exclusively and not when
it travels or arrives elsewhere. It rearticulates across time and space, including
within the West.[63] Noting along the same lines that postfeminism is "marked
by a number of characteristics that are not unique to Western cultures," Joel
Gwynne goes on to suggest that we might be able to delimit the culture's
terrain and purchase otherwise: "While it would be a mistake to assert that
postfeminism as a cultural sensibility may operate in any society across the
globe, it is perhaps accurate to suggest that it more commonly operates in
economically prosperous neoliberal nations, regardless of their geographical
location. Postfeminism is, after all, strongly implicated in neoliberal governance and citizenship . . . and should be understood as imbricated with
global neoliberal ideologies that serve not only to affirm the individualistic
values of late-capitalist culture, but also function to position feminism as
redundant within democratic and ostensibly egalitarian societies."[64] I cite
Gwynne at length here, as his contentions are useful to offset and thereby
clarify the detail of mine. I would draw Gwynne's insights about the economic
structuration of postfeminism, the fact that one needs a relative degree of

disposable income to perform it, to the very opposite conclusion than he does. It is exactly because postfeminism is a neoliberal, individualistic, and consumerist culture we may find its sensibilities and practices not only in developed or rapidly developing national contexts but in places like Nigeria as well. First, neoliberalism is increasingly hegemonic worldwide.[65] Second, as I have already flagged earlier, there is immense class inequality and private (or privatized) wealth in the global South, and hence subjects able to partake of the kinds of expensive lifestyles that postfeminism trucks.

The predominance of postfeminism in any given society may require the kinds of political, economic, and cultural conditions that Gwynne outlines, but their absence does not render its presence therefore impossible, unable to find ground or make sense. The culture may yet be found in elite pockets. In fact, as I argue in relation to the women in this book, elitism may be key to postfeminism's local sense and possibility in certain places. It is in a similar vein that I would also dispute the suggestion that postfeminism requires the positioning of feminism as no longer locally relevant such that it can be meaningful only in "ostensibly egalitarian societies"—in Japan versus India or Nigeria, say. The positioning of feminism as redundant for some women can very well include the presumed continued need for it or the need for the now more dominant, neoliberal, and technocratic variant of "women's empowerment," *for local others*. In one of the interviews conducted for this book, for instance, the participant suggested that by patronizing fashion and beauty services in Nigeria, she played a role in economically empowering and uplifting the working-class women who labor in these sectors—women who still needed empowerment, unlike her, being the suggestion.

In societies that do not or cannot even pretend to be egalitarian, of which Nigeria is indubitably one, the imagined existence of what I earlier termed "girls to be empowered" can meaningfully coexist with and, again, lend further sense and force to a postfeminist sense of self for those who occupy vastly divergent social, economic, and cultural positions. I will go further to argue that this bifurcation is actually encouraged by the manner in which the "neoliberal gender equality rationale" has come to be framed and mobilized in these societies by the development industry, by corporate social responsibility initiatives, by governments, and so on.[66] If women's empowerment is constructed, represented, and mapped in terms of their distance from gendered resource poverty, as is increasingly the case in the global South, it becomes a thoroughly classed matter and state. It becomes "poor women" still in need of empowerment, and, however indirectly, this positions their class-privileged counterparts as past or post the mark. Chen gets at this point regarding India when she says that because "feminist work to improve women's political and legal rights has been conducted mostly at the [rural and] grassroots level," it seems to enable urban middle- and upper-class women "to bypass feminism altogether," to take up the commodified emancipations of postfeminism.[67] The notion and imagery of "feminism bypassed" are very useful for my present argument, if they may be shed of any possible Eurocentric suggestion that a particular feminism would need to, or should, proceed postfeminism in the non-West as in the Western historical case, as if the West is the teleological template for the rest of us. Globalization "plays havoc with the hegemony of Eurochronology."[68] It produces "new spatialities and temporalities" and also disproves any notion that the nation (or region) is or ever was "a unified spatiotemporality."[69] It makes clearer that Nigerians, say, all 170 million plus of us, are not in the exact same time and place, or even in the same complex intersections, juxtapositions, or disjunctures thereof.[70] We never were.

So, as to the question of when a Nigerian woman becomes postfeminist, the answer is that it depends utterly on which of the many kinds of Nigerian woman we are asking after. For some, like the privileged, cosmopolitan, self-spectacularized kinds from whom we hear in this book, the answer is now; the time is already here. "Empowered *already*" is how these women see themselves, I will argue, and this also spatiotemporalized formulation becomes another way in which the book conceptualizes postfeminism and therein contributes to advancing critical feminist insights into how the culture works to undermine feminism—to bypass, short-circuit, undo, preempt, weaken—despite the fact that, whether in the global South or North, we are still, all, in patriarchal times.

*   *   *

In addition to the critical analytic work that *postfeminism* does as concept, sheer word, and rhetorical formulation to encapsulate and elucidate the concerns of this book, there is an intellectual politics to what is ultimately my choice to write about Nigerian women in Nigeria, or African women in Africa, with what is a quite particular historicized and historicizing term. The term is conspicuously absent in an important body of transnational feminist scholarship on new femininities elsewhere in the global South that has directly and considerably influenced my thinking, for instance, and that I read as being substantively about much the same kinds of new, gendered transnational phenomena, processes, and subjects as *Fashioning Postfeminism* and as the Western-focused literature on postfeminism.[71] Scholars like Inderpal Grewal and Radhika Parameswaran conceptualize new and variously spectacular femininities in India in terms of "neoliberal feminism," "consumer feminism," and "cosmopolitan feminism," for example, but not "postfeminism."[72] Without presuming to impute this view to this literature as a whole, Pamela Butler and Jigna Desai suggest that the latter concept does not well serve transnational feminist cultural critique, as, reflecting and refracting the limitations of the dominant Western (specifically U.S.) feminist scholarship from which it emerges, it ignores questions of "race, nation, empire, and political economy."[73] While clearly reading and critical of these omissions in much of the literature on postfeminism myself, my position is not to therefore discard it but to put it in close conversation with African, black, and transnational feminist scholarship, where I very much situate this book, to problematize, at once provincialize and deprovincialize, and, I hope, expand and enrich it.

If, as has been said, the view in the book is not of postfeminism as a universal culture, the analytic and political intent is equally not for a universalizing of the concept and language or for their unthinking exportation "from West to rest." The aim is to think postfeminism *with* globalization, a thinking that strikes me as utterly indispensable. Raka Shome and Radha Hegde warn that we must keep up with the conceptual challenges, even trickery and surprises of globalization, or "be left wandering in situations of theoretical stasis," reliant on old, insufficient maps of culture, identity, and difference that little resemble those that "are emerging through and in the global and that are exploding and imploding in unexpected ways, often indiscernible—at least to much of our established theoretical eye."[74] I attempt in this work to do this kind of keeping up. I endeavor to enact the different kind of seeing that Shome and Hegde go on to propose, a seeing transnationally, to show in terms of new spectacularly feminine styles that clear connectivities, continuities, and conversations exist across forms and sites of difference that tend to be prefigured as unrelated, or incommensurable, even oppositional, of which "Africa"—so often imagined as "epitomizing the intractable, the mute, the abject, the other-worldly"[75]—effectively represents the limit case. The starting point of my engagement in this work was my own being in Lagos, namely, home, and noticing that a new feminine fashion was appearing around me and that it was one that I had also seen when I was away. Thus, the concerns and contributions of this book stem from the crisscrossing, constituted locations from which we may see and look to inquire in the first place. Of a transnational cultural formation as it becomes deeply personal, the view in this book is offered from postcolonial, urban black Africa, a vantage still too little seen or heard from in feminist cultural and media studies, particularly for *theorizing*.

Yet I do so in terms of "postfeminism," a term that unabashedly declares its baggage and announces its historicity and in all this its apparent "not for us," as I called it. I recognize that to continue to expound why, to justify, twist, and turn where other scholars may just proceed, breathes further life into the very metaphysics of "African difference" that I seek to resist and critique in this book. But to just proceed also does not evade or resolve the issue. To briefly continue to expound, then, my motivation for thinking and working with the concept and language of postfeminism is not to achieve "theoretical coevalness," a motive of which Shih is rightly wary. It is not for an a priori investment in, or seduction by, "vocabulary and terminologies that are current and therefore appear to confer power."[76] That I nonetheless end up making an argument for theoretical coevalness, for the applicability and purchase and above all analytic value of a conceptual framework not outlined for women like my research participants, follows from my fundamental contention, and as far as this book goes my findings in the field, that black African women in Africa are necessarily in "shared presents,"[77] in the world and in time alongside others, in and through our diverse practices of self, and therein subjectified.[78] That I chose to call the present in question postfeminist—although I do not mean this in a totalizing way, as if the current time is only postfeminist—reflects that it is not neutral or equal or apolitical. It marks a certain violence. The world in which black African women find and fashion ourselves *is* structured by Western dominance, past, continued, anew. Eurocentric temporal frames *are* elevated over others. To disavow or cede the conceptual framework of "postfeminism" so as not to contribute to perpetuating this dominance is a possible and valid strategy, but would at the same time contribute to validating that certain, and ready, racism or nativism (or both) that imagines and purports African alterity. These are only some of the intellectual traps and trade-offs facing the postcolonial scholar. What I have attempted to do here is to "clear a politically framed theoretical space" in which the book proceeds.[79]

"HEY, YOU STYLIZED WOMAN THERE . . .": BRIEF METHODOLOGICAL NOTES

Who is the spectacularly feminine Lagos woman, performatively and subjectively? What type of subject does she desire to be, including as read and recognized by others? How does she envision the appearance of her subjectivity?[80] These are the questions that *Fashioning Postfeminism* poses and approaches via theoretical and analytic concern with the discursive subject positions, the "broad cultural slots or locations" from which it is possible to be, speak, experience, feel, and so on,[81] that eighteen spectacularly stylized women in Lagos variously took up, rejected, or resignified in interviews about their dress practice. The book ranges from consideration of why these women dress and appear as they do (chapter 2), to how they manage to achieve and afford their fashion (chapter 3), to questions and contestations over its "authenticity" and "appropriateness" (chapters 4 and 5), to the moral and social risks of misapprehension that they face and fear (chapters 4 and 5).

At the time of the interviews, in 2013, the women were undergraduate and postgraduate students; media professionals, including a Nollywood actress and a television presenter; professionals in fields such as public relations and banking; and entrepreneurs. Six identified or were seen by me as "celebrities" in that they had some degree of mediated public visibility and recognizability in Lagos. Per the criteria for participation that I devised, in addition to recognizing their habitual style of dress in my written, heuristic description of the spectacularly feminine, all the women were between the ages of eighteen and thirty-five, had lived in Lagos for at least two years at the time of the interview, and had either completed or were in the process of pursuing tertiary education. I used higher education as a broad index of high socioeconomic status in Nigeria. In practice, because of the networks and spaces through which I found and recruited the women, the majority belonged to the most privileged strata of Nigerian society.

To recruit interviewees, I first disseminated a written call for participants via e-mail and social media, but this gained little traction. Via mutual friends, I purposely approached acquaintances whose style of dress I was already familiar with and, with the help of contacts in the Nigerian music industry, reached out to a number of celebrities whose look I had seen in the media. I also went out and about in Lagos to physically look for, approach, and invite women who appeared to meet the stylistic and social criteria for participation. For this I visited spaces ranging from the city's most expensive malls to pop-up lifestyle events to the main university campus and the parking lot of an elite primary school after the morning drop-off. As friends and others with whom I discussed the project informally repeatedly named and proposed potential participants who they thought fit the bill, I also asked some to put me in touch with these women, with the women's permission.

All these methods of recruiting participants later produced a series of "uncomfortable" realizations for me.[82] For instance, I came to see that by encouraging others to seriously propose potential participants to me, I was effectively asking them to dissect, classify, and objectify women's looks on my behalf. Here and more generally, I see more clearly when looking back that, however much I conceptualized and in this book and elsewhere frame the research and its analytic and political impulses as "feminist," the "spaces of constructed visibility and incitements to see" that rendered my research questions both conceivable and empirically practicable are also very much patriarchal and sexist.[83] The fact that the research concerns women's embodied appearances means that feminist analytic incitements to see, question, and critique readily combine with mundane sexist ones. Certainly, it became evident to me during my time in the field how readily the mere fact that the research was being done (and with formal academic backing) could be joined to the "citational chain" of sexist discourses that equate women's desires for beauty and fashion with their moral and intellectual deficiency.[84] I found that this was how my project was understood by many nonparticipants with whom I spoke about it. To summarize comments that friends and family made to me on hearing what I was doing, for example, the project was essentially about "Lagos babes," "superficial women," "runs girls"—local slang for young women believed to rely on transactional heterosexual relationships to fund consumerist lifestyles. Often a related assumption was that my necessary intent as researcher was to mock and judge the women who would consent—be so hapless as to consent—to participate.[85]

Not only are the women whom I interviewed in Lagos far from hapless or helpless in person, including in their "taking up and rendering specific of a set of historical possibilities" of styling their bodies and selves, they are also agentic for both the fact and the manner of their being in the interviews and, eventually, in this book.[86] My point here is not to exculpate myself from responsibility for how I proceed to parse and represent these women's positions on the pages to come. It is to posit the act and scene of recruiting research participants as one of interpellation, and thus premised upon and inviting participants' agency. Figuratively, the act of research recruitment entails calling out to passersby to see or recognize themselves as the sort of subjects that the research concerns and to therefore turn in agreement to participate. As Judith Butler argues, accepting this "founding subordination" is an act of agency in itself, and it engenders the resignification, redirection, and proliferation of discursive power. Accepting the name by which one is called engenders the possibility of repeating the name "never quite in the same terms ... [or] for another purpose, one whose future is partially open."[87] The research interviews were very much the scene of self-naming and renaming. Giving account of themselves, the participants explained, disputed, and qualified just how much or just how little they were the stylized feminine subject for whom I was looking and with just what meanings, implications, and possible misunderstandings.

Our discussions covered the women's past and current styles of dress and their dressing-up routines; how they thought they were seen by others and how they wished to be seen, if otherwise; their consumption of, and engagement with, both Nigerian and foreign media; and issues other than style and appearance of importance to them as young Lagosian women. These themes elicited talk from participants in the form of style biographies and descriptions of their present dress and beauty practices and rituals; anecdotes and recollections about themselves and others; hopes and desires, likes and dislikes; and opinions, rationalizations, and social commentary. The tone was conversational, and there was often much joking and laughter. Here it is worth noting that, socially and demographically, but not stylistically or, I would say, in terms of feminist politics, I had much in common with the participants. But while I was very much a coparticipant in the interview exchanges, and thus in the meanings that emerged, the flow of talk, of questioning especially, was far from equal. The women occasionally asked about my experiences or views, but we rarely spoke about my own practices of dressing up and appearing. These were at most fleeting topics as the women commented upon some aspect of my look, most often my hair (long dreadlocks at the time, which were fairly unusual for the social milieu) or as I referred to my own style or lack thereof to frame a question or to respond to their remarks.

Where my own perspectives and politics of course dominate is in this book. Concerned, as I have already said, with discursive subject positions and positioning, the approach I take to the interview talk is underpinned by feminist poststructuralist theoretical tenets and draws on the tools of critical discursive psychology.[88] Briefly, this approach proceeds from an understanding of discourse as thoroughly constitutive in the "macro," poststructuralist sense and as an action-oriented, intersubjective resource in everyday, localized, or "micro" practices of meaning making. Therefore, it entails a dual focus on the "macro" and "micro" of discourse: looking for the broad seams and patterns of cultural intelligibility in what people say and looking simultaneously at the detail of how things are said and how people negotiate what is always highly situated, and often ideologically dilemmatic and rhetorically sophisticated, talk. It also means paying attention to what is not said or what may seem difficult or impossible to voice, perhaps for lack of discursive resources or because certain subject positions are already "troubled" in the sense of morally or socially devalued.[89]

All this does not amount to a presumption of omnipotence on the researcher's part. It is not a matter of "'elevating' the feminist scholar above other women; [rather,] it starts from the proposition that we are *all* enmeshed in these matrices of power." In feminist poststructuralist analysis, the aim is not to proclaim truths or debunk falsehoods about our research subjects or about how they see and speak themselves. It is to situate and deconstruct what they say and seem to mean, doing so from our particular and declared analytic and political standpoints and investments. For this, Gill's notion of "critical respect" offers a useful ethical orientation.[90] Critical respect entails respecting women's subjective accounts and positions as a fundamental feminist principle but without abandoning critique, disagreement, interrogation, and analysis. Such critical stances are not tantamount to disrespect, and in any case our analyses and critiques are at the level of discourse and culture, not at the level of individual research subjects' words and accounts qua individual. If I invited women in Lagos to talk about themselves at considerable length in an apparently singular and unique sense, or in other words if I hailed them in a humanist vein, it was because this was (and remains) the only way I know to get at poststructuralist questions of how the nonsingular or unique subject constitutes herself. It was but one of the many "limits of [my] own epistemologies" as researcher.[91] Thus, while the women in this book are "actual persons," the book is not about, or a representation of, "their actuality."[92] It is about how power and culture contribute to making subjects who they think and feel and say that they are, and who, and how, they actively and desirously style themselves to be. It is about how fashion and beauty are intimately implicated in the production, communication, and transnational circulation of new ways of doing femininity and, I argue, new ways of both empowering and disempowering women.

1

CONTEXTUAL CROSSROADS

AFRICAN WOMEN
IN THE WORLD OF THINGS

Picture a tube of red lipstick traveling from one young Nigerian woman living and working in London to another in Lagos. It is a picture of styles and technologies of femininity, and certain brands of feminism, in motion. It is an image of the forging of new transnational communities, subjects, and subjectivities, by capitalist consumer culture and diasporic movements.[1] For the purposes of the present discussion, it is an instance of the central case to be made, which is that African femininities are necessarily worldly ones, made in and through connection, communication, exchange. The image comes from one of the women in this book, whom I call Bisi, pseudonymously.[2] Recounting how she had gone from wearing no makeup at all to what was at the time of the interview a staple regime of black eyeliner, white face powder, and bright-red lipstick, Bisi explained the part that her sister based in London had played: "I didn't use to wear makeup then along the way, okay. I started with black eyeliner and just clear lip gloss, and then, okay, the red lipstick craze started, and my sister is like (*puts on, mocking, a falsetto or "girly" voice*) 'Oh, let me send you one, you might like it; if you don't like it, don't use it.' (*Resumes regular voice.*) Then I used it, I'm like 'Okay, it's not *bad* . . .'"[3] The particular route that Bisi's first red lipstick had taken to reach her, from what could be glossed as center to periphery, begins to suggest the asymmetries, the structured topography, of the world in which African women live, desire, and come to self-fashion. Yet it would be too simple to conclude that what we do, or want, is *determined* by Western economic and cultural dominance. To continue to think with the lipstick, practically speaking the item did not have to come to Bisi via special delivery from London. Lipsticks of all colors are readily available for purchase in Lagos, if unlikely to have been produced locally—the Nigerian economy being centered around extraction as a matter of colonial design, legacy of structural adjustment policy, and failure of successive governments to broaden its base.[4] Bisi's lipstick also did not have to take the form of a gift, a remittance of sorts, from a relative earning a living abroad. The following chapters will show just how much more than a small makeup item is easily affordable for the women in this book. More ideologically, to take hold in Lagos, the taste for red lipstick did not have to be sparked from a fashion capital like London. Lagos is a city of style in its own right, and, like Bisi needing to see, to discern, for herself that the beauty product would suit her, not simply or automatically sold on its foreign provenance, Lagosians are not mimic women and men.

Bisi's brief remarks do not tell the origins of the said red lipstick craze in fact, or its location when she came to join it. It could have been a new Lagos trend that she had mentioned to her sister, or a new passion in London that her sister wished to share with her, or both a Lagos and a London thing, or more. I would venture that questions of the origins, locations, and routes of her kind of look would have been utterly moot for a woman such as Bisi, who, like all the others whom I interviewed, saw and positioned herself as a "global consumer citizen." African women are in the world of things, trends, ideas, and also politics; this should come as no surprise or require any defense. Yet surprise it often does, sometimes even seemingly offend. To paraphrase remarks made to me at research presentations about the appearance of the spectacularly feminine Lagos woman, when I have been showing images of the kind of subject and style about which I am talking: "Isn't it sad that she is losing her traditional dress"; "She is not a real African woman"; "Looks like a case of Western imperialism." In stubbornly predominant scholarly and popular visions, African and Africanist included, Africa and Africans continue to be "caught and imagined within a web of difference and absolute otherness." Placing us apart, whether for presumed better or worse, but one effect of this mode of thinking and seeing is to deny us "the full spectrum of meanings and implications that other places and other human experiences enjoy, provoke, and inhabit."[5] Fashion, the changing of styles of clothing, beauty, and adornment as a practice and mark of distinction, desire, and creative self-making, is among the things that some would deny African women, imaginatively and conceptually but sometimes also physically, even violently. So, too, is feminism. Our long-standing realities of these things, and our fundamental—and frankly obvious—capacities for them, are the concern of this brief contextual chapter.

AFRICAN LOOKS

Fashion and self-fashioning are African traditions. I phrase this quite con-
certedly to refuse at once notions that fashion is unique and endogenous to
Western capitalist modernity, counterposed to the "dress," or "costume," or
"garb"—implying the "exotic," "essential," "premodern"—of the non-West.[6]
Africans have very long and deliberately produced, adopted, and adapted
new ways of adorning and presenting ourselves: new looks, in short. In terms
of what is deemed traditional dress in any particular African context, on
inspection it becomes apparent that this is not changeless, timeless, or inher-
ent, but rather fluid, syncretic, and contingent. It is invented. Textiles, beads,
and other material goods from an array of external and shifting sources play
a part in the fabrication of traditional dress, and new patterns, cuts, sensibilities, and values also continuously alter it.[7] The new has been introduced
via centuries-old trade across the continent, Sahara Desert, and Indian and
Atlantic Oceans; via the spread of Islam and Christianity; via colonialism
and, these days, globalization. The cloth commonly known as "African print"
offers a well-known example of the wide-ranging roots and routes of what
I will call "African looks." It also reveals the performativity of this category
of dress and appearance, being a vivid example of the fact that things of foreign origin may become African. African prints are factory-printed textiles
developed and adapted by European companies in the nineteenth century,
from Javanese batiks, for West African markets and, importantly, tastes.[8] Ex-
emplifying the colonial capitalist "intimacies of continents," then,[9] the cloth
has gone on to be associated with Africa specifically: it has become cemented
"as a quintessential marker of West African culture, and of African-ness more
broadly."[10] Nina Sylvanus suggests that African prints became and continue
to become African because they arrive as "raw material, thus providing the
necessary space for the enactment of local logics of usage, interpretation and
meaning attribution . . . , [for] the ascription to the fabric of a series of local
significances."[11] The fabric also becomes and continues to "be" African for
being reiteratively called, seen, understood, and variously valued and devalued, as such—for *looking* African. Hence, for instance, people not of African
descent who wear African print risk accusations of cultural appropriation,
such as in the miniscandal on the "black Internet" in 2017, on websites like
"Curly Nikki," about the appearance of the prints on British designer Stella
McCartney's catwalks.

The literature on dress in Africa is replete with other cases of the invention
and authentication of Africa, and the assertion of African nationalisms, on

and through the dressed body.[12] These performative processes occur with and through the equally invented, and often readily essentialized, constructs of tradition, ethnicity, and blackness that centrally constitute that of Africa itself. It was in the name of both cultural and racial *authenticité* that Mobutu Sese Seko sought to define and impose a new Zairian dress code in the 1970s, for instance. It is because dress is a visual, material, and highly moralizable marker of identity, culture, propriety, and belonging, and an ostensible index of "civilization," that it has been and remains integral to imagining and representing Africa and Africanness—and likewise other "difference from" the "Euro-modern." Introducing modern European dress codes was central to the self-declared civilizing missions of colonialism and Christianity in Africa. Introducing modern European dress codes was central to the self-declared civilizing missions of colonialism and Christianity in Africa, such that for Africans, "returning" to putatively indigenous aesthetics, styles, and "model[s] of historicity and change" became acts of anticolonial resistance and postcolonial nation building.[13] The case of the Nigerian anticolonial activist and feminist Funmilayo Ransome-Kuti is quite instructive in this regard. In the 1940s, Ransome-Kuti famously discarded European attire for the traditional Yoruba style of *iro ati buba* (wrapper and blouse) and also began to speak only Yoruba in public. A clear symbolic rejection of colonialism and its cultural superiority complex, the more powerful coming from an elite, Christian, British-educated woman, for its recourse to tradition Ransome-Kuti's dress practice was not therefore also a rejection of "modernity," or of modernization as process.[14] Ransome-Kuti was not advocating or demonstrating that Africans belonged or were better off in a precolonial past, however imagined. Rather, she was modeling a way of being African in the present, and indeed for "progress," in non-Eurocentric African terms. She was fashioning a materially distinct African modernity by way of tradition, and in this embodied the postcolonial theoretical insight that tradition and modernity are not opposed, sequential, or teleological times and states, but mutually constitutive and simultaneous constructs and imaginaries of these, and of change—very much materially premised constructs and imaginaries, to be sure. Here again, the literature on dress in Africa provides numerous examples of Africans knowing and living out this complex theoretical position in practice.[15]

That the spectacularly feminine Lagos woman does not appear "distinctly African" is, of course, the starting point, and relative charge, of the earlier-cited comments made to me during research presentations. Here I will note that while it may not be her predominant style, this figure can and does also appear in traditional dress, such as at traditional weddings, and is equally "fabulous," immaculately put together, in this look.[16] Practically speaking, Africans dress in an array of styles, today and historically. This is ethnographically obvious and in everyday life on the continent quite unremarkable. What concerns me here therefore is to surface, so as to refute, the ontological, political, and moral underpinnings and what I will insist on calling the violence of any expectation that, to paraphrase Rey Chow, "the native ought to be faithful."[17] There is no authentic or a priori African subject to be recognized or found anywhere, no necessary or essential Africanness to which we must or even can be faithful. "African identity does not exist as a substance. It is constituted, in varying forms, through a series of practices, notably *practices of the self*. Neither the forms of this identity nor its idioms are always self-identical. Rather, these forms and idioms are mobile, reversible, and unstable."[18]

One idiom and medium of African self-making that has been a changing constant for centuries now is "Western dress." European companies were shipping not just textiles but ready-made clothing to the continent from as early as the 1600s. The since-continued inflow is an effect of persistent economic and trade imbalances, the cultural and symbolic dominance of the West that works to constitute its looks as universal and *the* modern standard, and in all this a product of colonial, imperialist, and capitalist forces. Succinctly put, it is an effect of power. In her ethnographic study of the contemporary market for secondhand Western dress in Zambia, for instance, Karen Hansen attributes the booming trade to a combination of consumerist excess in the West, the structural decline of Zambian manufacturing, and the delimited measure of the average Zambian's budget. But the trade also meets and engenders active demands and desires on the ground. "People in Zambia also want well dressed bodies," for which they purposely and skillfully browse the secondhand stalls to find, mix, and match items to create unique looks.[19] These, too, are *African* looks, by which I mean quite simply ways of looking like an African. We see this if we understand power as productive and practices of self as constitutive, that "even" Western dress can be incorporated into the making and fashioning of the African. But surely we should also be able to see it without taking a poststructuralist view? If Western dress has now been in the African wardrobe for more than four hundred years, how can it still be deemed foreign to us? At what point would we be able to take it as also our own? Should we even be calling it Western dress? I propose "global dress" as now more apt, "global" meaning and indexing the "dominant particular."[20]

To see the spectacularly feminine Lagos woman as "not a real African woman," as I have already said was put to me once, is not only inconsistent with the poststructuralist theoretical premises of this book. It is also ahistorical and in short order boils down to the racist or nativist logics (or both) that I began to reject in the previous chapter, according to which Africans are indeed fundamentally different and so should ideally remain fixed (mired, perhaps) in said difference. Even if framing the spectacularly feminine Lagos woman as a victim of Western cultural imperialism, to recall another of the readings proposed to me, these kinds of claims and visions constitute a further imperialist violence themselves. They deny Africans' agentic, self-reflexive, and desirous presence and participation in the flow of things, or what Achille Mbembe sums up as our "subjectivity as time."[21] They betray a postcolonial melancholia, a wishing for the times when the putative natives were native, thereby also presuming the paramount superiority and desirability of things Western to Africans, whereas in terms of dress my suggestion is rather that these things are commonplace and unremarkable to us and long become also our own. Inadvertently or not, visions of what proper or authentic Africanness should look like deny or minimize the fact that colonialism thrust immense and radical change upon us: political, economic, social, cultural, technological, linguistic, and therefore also deeply subjectifying change. After all this, how could we still look like some imagined African of yore, the "real" version of ourselves, even if we wanted to?

The Lagos woman who appears in spectacularly feminine style is just as African as the one in *iro ati buba*, and the other in a hijab, to cite yet another type of dress in many an African repertoire that also originated somewhere else, and also came to us via processes that included imperial conquest and religious conversion. In her weaves, towering heels, false nails, and everything else, in the same genre that we also see on women in London and New York but also Johannesburg, Mexico City, Mumbai, Rio de Janeiro, and places in between, the spectacularly feminine Lagos woman *does* look African: she looks exactly like an African keeping up with a current transnational fashion. "Marked at every turn and at every moment by the operation of power on an uneven terrain," this practice and performance of consumer coevalness is also far from new.[22] Young urban African women participated in what was likely the first feminine fashion to trend simultaneously around the world, namely the "flapper" or "modern girl" style of the 1920s and '30s.[23] Their participation was made possible by what Alys Weinbaum and colleagues call "globe-straddling multidirectional citational practices, which included the travel of iconography, commodities and ideas," or what I follow Inderpal Grewal in this book to broadly term transnational connectivities.[24] The trend for mini- and A-line skirts, bell-bottoms paired with tight shirts, platform shoes, and large Afros reached the continent in the same ways in the 1960s and '70s.[25] Recalling the time and looks in Bamako, in which he participated himself, Manthia Diawara explains that young Malians were styling themselves after pop music icons like James Brown, Jimi Hendrix, and the Rolling Stones—complete with the dances moves![26] According to the women in *Fashioning Postfeminism*, nowadays it is highly mediated and circulated figures like Beyoncé and Rihanna contributing to the transnational dissemination of the spectacularly feminine, including as a specifically *black* look.

Blackness has been and remains central to "cultural traffic" both to and from Africa.[27] From what Tanisha Ford calls the "afro look" associated with the Black Panthers in America and the Black Consciousness movement in South Africa, made iconic by figures like Angela Davis, Diana Ross, and Miriam Makeba, to the dreadlocks of Rastafarianism and reggae culture, to the marked Afrocentric symbolism in black America of Ghanaian *kente* cloth, fashion and style have long connected black populations across the Atlantic and beyond.[28] As these few examples begin to suggest, and as Paul Gilroy elaborates in *The Black Atlantic*—if not sufficiently including Africa in the discussion—black styles and sensibilities have traveled via popular music and dance cultures especially, as well as via black nationalist politics and paraphernalia. There has also long been business in the export and import of black hair and makeup products and tools. According to Lynn Thomas, what were in 1933 probably the very first makeup advertisements for black women in southern Africa were for cosmetics produced by an African American company, albeit marketed locally by a white South African businessman.[29] It was African American female beauty entrepreneurs doing the direct marketing in Africa (and elsewhere) by the mid-1940s, however, capitalizing on both their blackness and their Americanness to position themselves as "the world's premier authorities" on modern and glamorous black beauty.[30]

One of the women whom I interviewed in Lagos, Kim, invoked the kinds of histories of transnational black style culture and community that I am sketching here to contextualize and defend the weave as merely the latest black look to have "rolled around" to Nigerian shores: "There was a time when it was all about the afro when our parents were in their, in the seventies . . . and no one judged them then. They put hot combs in their hair and they straightened their hair out. And then the nineties brought relaxed [that is, chemically processed] hair. . . . And then came the noughties, where fake, like obviously fake [that is, weaves] was in, and it's all about larger than life hair and all that." That "our parents" may not have been judged for their

Afros some forty years ago is not strictly the case. Despite the hairstyle's unambiguous, indeed purposive, signification as black, it was contested in some quarters as un-African, meaning not traditional or indigenous, and therefore not appropriate for African youth. Take 1960s Bamako, where the remit of a government militia established to police citizens' behavior extended to youth fashion, and those "caught wearing mini-skirts, tight skirts, bell-bottom pants, and Afro hairdos were sent to reeducation camps. Their heads were shaved and they were forced to wear traditional clothes."[31] Or in Dar es Salaam around the same time, where the ruling party targeted a long list of trending dress styles, imported beauty products, and other cultural paraphernalia and practices: "miniskirts, soul music, wigs, cosmetics, trousers ranging from 'drain-pipe' to bell-bottom, so-called Afro hairstyles, and beauty contests, all in the name of national culture."[32]

In fact, moral panics have recurred across the continent about the appearance of new youth fashions, along with both state-sanctioned and vigilante actions to police the looks in question.[33] These reactionary agendas have tended to proceed in terms of the popular and easy binaries that I am seeking to challenge and complexify here and across the book as a whole: authentic/inauthentic, traditional/modern, African/Western, black/white, and so on. "Decency" and religious values—both Christian and Muslim in places like Nigeria—also tend to be invoked. Like all moral panics, the base concerns are with perceived threats to the dominant social order. Hence in the 1968 miniskirt ban in Tanzania, Andrew Ivaska sees anxieties about young women's increasing independence in the city, including young men's fears that they were being priced out of these women's lives by older "sugar daddy" types with whom they could not compete.[34] Sylvia Tamale reads the more recent Anti-Pornography Act passed in Uganda in 2014 as a fundamentalist backlash against decades of women's rights activism and gains in the country. Over and over again, across the continent, it is *women's* new fashions that face particular censure and women's bodies that become the paramount "battlefield for cultural-moral struggles" over appropriate dress.[35] This is of little surprise. It is, after all, women who are "constructed as the symbolic bearers of the collectivity's identity and honour"[36] but at the same time as morally weak and polluting, needing to be checked. Also unsurprising is that it is women in the working classes who bear the brunt of the moral panics. From Lagos to Kano, Kampala, and Cape Town, women moving through the city have been verbally and physically harassed, stopped, and even stripped naked and sexually assaulted for daring to appear in whatever style is in contention.[37] In

2009 a young woman was raped and killed in northern Nigeria reportedly for wearing trousers.[38]

A highly gendered trope of "indecent dressing" is quite alive in contemporary Nigerian public discourse, including to account for sexual harassment and violence against women. In 2007 a panic about young women's dress exploded in the country, invigorated by both Christian and Muslim fundamentalisms. Alleging "Western corruption" of traditional and religious values, and that women were deliberately using scantily clad bodies to tempt and manipulate men, prominent institutions such as universities and churches banned clothes that they branded too revealing, such as spaghetti-strap tops and trousers in some cases (the particular contention with trousers seems to be that they reveal the contours of a woman's crotch and buttocks). The following year a female senator sought to capitalize on the populist sentiment with a bill prohibiting "public nudity," the definition of which skewed to implicate young women's dress. The bill failed to pass, not least thanks to the concerted Nigerian feminist response.[39] In a strident critique of the ideological incoherence, practical futility, and also blatant sexism and hypocrisy of the bill, Bibi Bakare-Yusuf, a Nigerian feminist scholar and activist who was herself part of the pushback, writes that by attempting to preserve and indeed legislate "a pristine Nigerian cultural and moral universe, [the bill betrayed an] ignorance about the way in which Nigerian society is overlaid with what we can call the globalisation of signifiers. Nigeria is not immune to global cultural flows of images, vocabulary, sartorial practices, language, memes and concepts." And, Bakare-Yusuf continues, this "influx of global fashion styles and imaginaries" serves young Nigerian women to fashion new femininities, including in opposition to local restrictive rules and norms.[40]

Bakare-Yusuf's point here is neither celebratory nor resigned, but constative. Her point, mine too, is quite simply that young Nigerian women are in the world: we are exposed to, hailed by, and in our various ways come to be active partakers of new and transnational fashion and beauty cultures. This is in the context of but also despite Africa's structural impoverishment and the many other forces that bear upon our lives. In fact, the argument could be made that on a "continent trapped structurally . . . the body's image is one of the few outlets for expressing some form of agency and indulgence in pleasure."[41] Nigerian and African women also seek and strive to self-fashion, that is, "to transform [our]selves into singular beings, to make [our] lives into an oeuvre that carries with it certain stylistic criteria."[42] In this we are no different from women elsewhere, which is not to say that the particular places and locales in which we self-fashion do not matter and, indeed, shape and enter into our practices.

"EKO FOR SHOW!": LOCAL CULTURES OF FASHIONABLE SPECTACLE

Lagos is a bustling port city now home to an estimated twenty-one million people.[43] Traditionally, and in terms of its geopolitical location within Nigeria, Lagos is Yoruba terrain—the Yoruba being one of the three dominant ethnic groups in the country.[44] The Yoruba name for the city is "Eko," while "Lagos" derives from the Portuguese *lago*, for the lagoons around which the city is built, an etymology that begins to tell the city's story as a translocal and transnational crossroads and erstwhile site of imperialist occupation. From its origins as a rural settlement, Eko or Lagos grew rapidly to become an increasingly important regional center for European trade in the seventeenth century; the "largest slave exporter north of the equator" in the first half of the nineteenth century;[45] a British colony in 1861 and later capital of the colony of Nigeria; a place of return for former slaves from Brazil, Cuba, and the West African subregion in the late nineteenth century; and, after Nigeria's independence in 1960, the country's political capital until 1991, when the seat of power moved to Abuja. It remains the indisputable commercial and cultural nerve center of not just the country but the subregion. Tejumola Olaniyan notes "the distinctive character of the city in Nigerian public consciousness as the anonymous-neon-lights capital of immense opportunity and bottomless uncertainty."[46] It is a place with a "lottery economy."[47] The epicenter of Nollywood, Nigeria's massive, hyperpaced film industry, which has been called "the most visible form of cultural machine" in Africa,[48] Lagos is also at the forefront of other creative industry and expression on the continent, from music to art to fashion.

Already noted in the introduction to the book is that Lagos is a city with a particular history and culture of fashion and fashionability. Dress and appearance are very important markers of social status in Yoruba culture; Justine Cordwell goes as far as to state that "the most important form of aesthetic expression to the Yoruba is clothing and its accessories."[49] With and beyond this accent on dress is a culture of visual splendor and display, including of money spent. At necessarily expensive social gatherings like weddings or funerals, for instance, guests will offer their host the Yoruba greeting "*eku inawo*," meaning, quite literally, "greetings on the spending of money," recognition and salutation for having expended so expansively.[50] I would argue that it is the ongoing articulation of such indigenous values and sensibilities with the urbane cosmopolitanism of everyday Lagos life, and with the drive for and dreams of upward mobility that fever the city, that engender what has become a distinctive Lagosian culture of—or reputation for—dressing up, dressing to impress, or, to use a Nigerian colloquialism, to *oppress*, to almost forcibly imprint one's distinction and rank in others' minds. It is for such reasons that we can find Lagos described as a "cosmopolitan, showy, shallow, elegant and ruthless" place,[51] or as symbolizing, for Nigerians, "ambition, glamour, danger and modernity."[52] One of the women whom I interviewed there, Tobi, explained that not wanting to fall victim to the relative ruthlessness of the feminine dress culture spurred on her own spectacular practice:

> You wanna be with your girlfriends and still look *fine* [that is, beautiful]. Even if you're having a girls' hangout, I mean even if girls hang out, do you see how they oppress themselves [that is, with their dress]? (*Puts on an emphasized Nigerian accent.*) They carry their expensive designer bags, they must look—(*returns to less emphatic accent*) if you go to your friend's house and she's already dressed up now, you have an inkling into what she's already wearing, so you wanna look just as good or probably better. So you know, it's, the competition *sef* is even among girls.

As is also said in and about Lagos, somewhat vaingloriously when voiced by Lagosians themselves: *Eko for show!* "Eko for show" is a local expression that brands Lagos, or its denizens to be more exact, showy and flamboyant, given to spectacle, overinvested in appearances, competitively seeking to impress and oppress through visual and material display. Olawale Ismail attributes the rhyming phrase directly to the city's cultures of "fashion and pleasure."[53] In Nigeria (and possibly beyond), Lagos's reputation extends to a culture of lavish and decidedly consumerist merriment, of which fashionable looks are again central.[54] Okechukwu Nwafor's considered view is that there seems to be a near belief in Lagos that "every trivial occasion calls for celebration and excessive partying."[55] "Eko for show" says that one can count on Lagosians to put on a show. Or, we can read the saying as performative, as meaning, advising, perhaps even warning, that show is part of how one does Lagos and belonging there.

The reader familiar with Nigeria may have perhaps already had the thought that what I am describing as the reputation of the city of Lagos is in many ways the reputation of the country itself in Africa, and again maybe farther afield. Nigeria is the self-appellated "giant of Africa"—a "crippled giant," Eghosa Osaghae qualifies, referring to the country's failure so far to live up to its immense potential.[56] Among the top-ten exporters of crude oil globally, the country is naturally wealthy, and it is here that some of the contradictions and especially social inequalities of direct relevance to this book lie. In almost sixty years of independence from British colonial governance, the wealth has been stupendously squandered and misappropriated by successive regimes, military and civilian.[57] The wealth has been channeled to and through a rentier elite class, such that the socioeconomic landscape is marked by extreme inequality: public squalor, private wealth. Nigeria ranks very poorly in global human development indicators—for instance, it is 157th out of 189 countries in 2018 in terms of a composite of indices such as gross national product per capita, life expectancy, and maternal mortality and literacy rates.[58] But on the uppermost and minority extreme of the class spectrum are "lifestyles of overt and conspicuous consumption," of which pronounced elements include "flamboyant dress codes marked by excess [and] fleet[s] of expensive vehicles."[59] Describing the oil boom of the early 1970s, Andrew Apter writes, "Nigeria's oil bonanza was literally sensational. Lavish parties, fleets of Mercedes-Benzes . . . the dizzy excitement of new wealth and opportunity."[60] More recently, around the time that I was conducting the interviews for this book, in 2013, there were news reports in both local and foreign press that Nigeria was the second-fastest growing market in the world for champagne, that Nigerians were among the top spenders on the British high street, that Oprah Winfrey had been dethroned as the richest black woman in the world by a Nigerian oil baroness, and so on.

Thus, while there is a culture of material showiness in, of, and for Lagos in particular, it is also more generally a Nigerian phenomenon. This is the experience of the women in this book. I discuss in chapter 4 how the women perceive and respond to a social expectation to be all the more dressed up in and for Lagos and Nigeria, such as in Tobi's comments above about keeping pace with her girlfriends. The point, then, is that Lagos and Nigeria, or Lagos/Nigeria, are not places where the women simply happen to be, mere backdrop to what I have already framed as a new transnational style of appearing. Rather, these places are in the very fabric of what it is that the women are up to. However else the spectacularly feminine in *Fashioning Postfeminism* can be understood, it is also always about, and a product of Lagos/Nigeria, and in turn (re)making the city and country as particular kinds of places, and the women as particular kinds of Lagosians and Nigerians. "*Sisi Eko*" is just one of the local types that the women can be seen to be performing and embodying, although neither they nor I explicitly named them as such in the interviews. Translating literally as "Lagos lady" but more to the point as "Lagos chick" or

"Lagos babe," *Sisi Eko* is a fashionable Lagos woman who lives and circulates in popular Nigerian representations and imaginaries, from fiction to music to everyday talk. A slew of artistes have recently released songs titled "Sisi Eko"—Darey Art Alade in 2011, Subzilla in 2015, and Skuki in 2017—variously referencing and remixing E. C. Arinze's popular 1962 highlife track by the same name. A 2017 track by another artiste, Ade Bantu, is titled "Lagos Barbie" but in its first line reverts to the more familiar and local name for its hyperstylized feminine subject: "*Sisi Eko*, you're looking sexy tonight." The video for the song shows a *Sisi Eko* traveling through time, and trend, from a chair in a hair salon: back in 1967, her hair is in an indigenous style called "thread"; a decade later, it is in an immense Afro; 2017 brings a weave.

I could not find the figure of the *Sisi Eko* by this particular name in scholarly discussions of popular figurations, such as in film and fiction, of urban African femininities. She might look like a "good-time girl," a figure that has been parsed in the literature, but, if per Stephanie Newell's analysis, the latter is painted as "a hoarder and accumulator *par excellence*," and deployed to tell cautionary tales of the "beautiful young woman's misuse of her sexuality," then it is vital to distinguish the *Sisi Eko*.[61] The name *Sisi Eko* does not carry negative moral charge or imply sexual impropriety. To the contrary, it is complimentary and aspirational and a name and subject position that a woman might desire, claim, and enunciate for herself. One of the young female characters in Chika Unigwe's novel *On Black Sisters Street* provides an example of just this: she is described imagining that, through the rich older man to whom she has just lost her virginity, she will be able to invest in a new wardrobe "to make her look like a real Lagos chick, a veritable *sisi Eko*," to strut down the street "going *koi koi koi* in her new shoes, her extensions stretching her hair all the way down to her shoulders."[62] Speaking directly to the virtual synonymity of Lagos with fashion and style in Nigerian cultural imaginaries, to be called *Sisi Eko*—"Lagos lady," "Lagos chick"—is to be called fashionable. "Eko for show," indeed!

DOING AND UNDOING FEMINISM IN NIGERIA

Disciplinary, protectionist discourses of African authenticity extend to African women who claim the name and politics of "feminism." We might find ourselves accused of having lost our way, of "being blind copy-cats of Western European feminists," and therein agents of Western cultural imperialism.[63] A popular view of feminism is that it is "un-African" and instead a dangerous and destructive—antimale, antifamily, queer, generally antinormative—Western ideology that Africans should reject therefore. Once again the historical record tells otherwise. In Nigeria and other places on the continent, there are long traditions of women's autonomous movements and organizing for their own particular ends, as well as in anticolonial, national liberation, and prodemocracy struggles.[64] That these have not always occurred under the explicit banner of feminism is not only due to the disputed legitimacy of the political ideology and label. Amina Mama notes that in Africa, women were mobilizing and resisting "long before modern feminism came into being"—"modern feminism" as defined, imagined, and propertized in and by the West.[65] African women who could be called feminist in the sense of seeking "to challenge both the restriction of women's rights, and women's marginalization from centers of power and decision-making," have also long had the experiential, intersectional appreciation that gender struggles cannot be separated from others such as anti-imperialism.[66] For instance, in an article that she published in 1947 in the British newspaper the *Daily Worker*, Funmilayo Ransome-Kuti, whom many consider the first modern Nigerian feminist, argued that it was colonialism that had made women in Africa "slaves."[67]

Historians and feminist scholars of Africa widely concur that colonialism and the introduction of its Christian and Victorian gendered norms tended to erode women's traditional social standing and rights, their relative economic independence especially.[68] Finding the West African climate inhospitable, the British did not develop settler colonies there but governed through a policy of "indirect rule," which, as the name implies, entailed ruling through local intermediaries either previously vested with traditional authority or newly and illegitimately created to this end. In keeping with their gendered worldview, the colonialists recognized and worked with male intermediaries only. Thus, the policy of indirect rule further marginalized women in what was to become Nigeria by ignoring and undermining their complementary political and other institutions where existent. Among the Igbo ethnic group in the southeast of the country, for example, "women's sociopolitical organizations, age-grade societies, and other institutions that helped to foster checks and balances in the Igbo political system . . . were weakened. The colonial administrators [dealt] directly with male agencies on all local matters including those that previously belonged to the female domain."[69]

As could be reasonably expected, such changes spurred women's discontent and resistance. The most famous example from Nigeria is the 1929 "women's war" in Aba, also in the southeast of the country. Reacting to the specter of

arbitrary new colonial taxes, market women leveraged their traditional as-
sociational networks, communication channels, and symbolic repertoires
and practices to stage dramatic protests across a series of towns and vil-
lages, including physically attacking colonial edifices, singing and dancing,
and stripping off their clothes to shame their opponents.[70] Similar protests
occurred in Lagos in 1940 in response to the introduction of a new income
tax on women. Led by the Lagos Market Women's Association, women demanded their enfranchisement and political representation or else a halt to
their taxation.[71] Ransome-Kuti also led market women in similar protests
over new taxes, market fees, and other colonial administrative impositions
in 1947, in the town of Abeokuta, where she lived.[72] The Abeokuta protests
swelled into a broad "effort to force the colonial state to recognize women's
economic and social condition as well as their contribution to the state.
Moreover, it was an opportunity to make clear their expectations of the
state and redress the political marginalization they had experienced under
colonialism."[73] So effective were the women that their actions culminated in
the temporary abdication of the *alake*, the local king, whom they had come
to view as a corrupt colonial stooge.

Women continued to play active individual and collective roles in the 1940s
and 1950s as the nationalist and decolonization movements gained momen-
tum. The Nigerian Women's Union was founded in 1949, the Federation of
Nigerian Women's Societies in 1953, and the National Council of Women's
Societies in 1959. In addition to pushing for women's enfranchisement, which
was gained progressively in southern Nigeria in the 1950s and eventually introduced by military fiat in 1976 for women in the predominantly Muslim
North, the FNWS, styled as a "parliament of the women of Nigeria," aimed
to encourage the participation of women "in the political, social, cultural and
economic life of the country; to create facilities for female education; and
generally to raise the status of women and to secure equal opportunities for
women, relative to men."[74] Women joined the emergent nationalist parties,
including forming women's wings. A select few were included in the parties'
leadership structures; few also won positions during elections for local and
regional councils in the 1950s. However, heralding the direction of things to
come, only three participated in the final negotiations in 1959 for national independence. Gloria Chuku writes the following of Igbo women's participation
in national politics at the time and subsequently, but I would suggest that her
words apply across ethnic lines in southern Nigeria: "Although women were
very active as a result of their enormous involvement in political mobiliza-
tion and electoral processes in the period [of decolonization], they exercised

subdued political power due to the politics of co-optation and tokenism that have continuously characterized Nigerian political history, especially since independence."[75] The heady days of independence in 1960 soon gave way to political violence and instability across the country, resulting, in January 1966, in what was to be the first of many military coups over the next three decades.[76] The militarization of Nigerian politics further exacerbated the marginalization of women, and women's concerns, in public life, including by entrenching a "male-dominant and masculinized culture of the state that generates structural violence" against Nigerian women to this day.[77]

In 1983 an explicitly feminist national organization, Women in Nigeria, was formed, committed to intersectional gender and class-based analyses and struggle for women's advancement. Recognizing the indigenous feminisms and many women's associations and actions that preceded WIN, Bene Madunagu nonetheless characterizes the organization as the origin of "feminism in Nigeria in its present form—consistent, organised, with clear objectives and ideology."[78] The core strategies of WIN included research and documentation of Nigerian women's diverse lived realities, to inform policy formulation, advocacy, and strategic action. In 1985 there was an apparent opening in the national discursive space for such issues and approaches: the new military regime led by General Ibrahim Babangida announced an official concern with women and called for submissions on their socioeconomic and political status as part of a broader process of designing an appropriate democratic structure for the complex and fractured nation. It was soon revealed to be a hollow, populist invocation of women's rights, however, as well as militaristic in implementation, and centered on the figure of the first lady to boost her profile.[79] It was also aimed at boosting the dictatorship's international legitimacy, the international community being engaged itself in a "turn to women" in development and human rights discourse and praxis[80]—one that has remained ascendant in these fields and, as briefly discussed in the previous chapter, moved from liberal feminist to neoliberal postfeminist tenets.[81] "Women" and "gender" thus remain "obligatory references," indeed "indicators," in Nigerian government policy and discourse. Evaluating the government's neoliberal reform program after the 1999 return to democracy, Charmaine Pereira critiques the evident assumption that a single, mostly economistic, and top-down set of measures "to address women's concerns will, in and of itself, bring about empowerment. This is a far cry from challenging the ideologies that justify gender inequality, changing prevailing patterns of access to and control over resources (as opposed to providing the resources themselves), and transforming the institutions that reinforce existing power structures."[82]

The ideologies and patterns and power structures that Nigerian feminists identify as barriers to Nigerian women's substantive equality and citizenship, and that we variously seek to challenge, are manifold. In no particular order, they include violence against women; the nonrecognition of marital rape; child marriage and abuse; institutionalized cultures of sexual harassment in the workplace and on university campuses; rising religious fundamentalisms, Christian and Muslim; systematic discrimination against the girl-child and against women in the name of "customary law," a constitutional category; and contradictory and in some cases blatantly discriminatory constitutional provisions regarding women's status and rights, including inconsistent definitions of citizenship between the federal, state, and local government levels that combine to disenfranchise and silence women. The list goes on.[83] All this is in, and exacerbated by, a national context of wide and deep poverty and socioeconomic inequality; grossly inadequate legal frameworks that are, in any case, insufficiently implemented; a corrupt and demoralized police force notorious for extrajudicial action; weak democratic institutions and systems of accountability; state-sponsored ethnic and vigilante violence, and, most recently, religious fundamentalist terrorism.

Fashioning Postfeminism is not about any such issues in Nigeria. In fact, they do not come up at all. I enumerate them here to put into starkest relief the problematics and politics of the fact that, in this national context, women like those in the book might consider themselves beyond the need for feminism because they consider themselves "already empowered," that is to say, already beyond issues and problems that other Nigerian women face.

2

CHOOSING IT ALL

FROM PLEASURE TO
SELF-CONFIDENCE TO PAIN

Explaining the evolution of her dress style, how she had come to be drawn into the spectacularly feminine, Tobi reflected: "I really used to like simple and comfortable, but I started growing up and I realized that lots of girls out there were doing uncomfortable and they were looking *so fine! (laughs)*. . . . So, you know, I mix a little uncomfortable with comfortable [now]. I mean the first time you saw me I was wearing heels. Trust me they probably just, they killed me that day." I first saw and approached Tobi in an upmarket Lagos shopping mall, and as she recalls she was in heels that day. It was the heels, high and spindly, that first drew my attention, in fact, and I distinctly recall thinking that the woman in them was walking rather gingerly, not looking too comfortable or steady on her feet. Thoroughly entangled in Tobi's brief account of her dress practice above, as in all the interviews that I conducted, are lines and expressions of desire, agency, constraint, discomfort, and even physical pain. In what follows, I disentangle these considerations to show that, in fact, whether talking about pleasure or pain, the uniqueness or conformity of their style, a particular taste or distaste for one or more of its parts, the women arrived at the fundamental postfeminist value of unfettered, individualist, self-pleasing choice. What was being chosen was "postfeminist feminine beauty," for its promise of self-confidence especially. An attractive and urgent choice, then, it demanded the recuperation and repression of its less than pleasurable aspects and conditions. Much as Tobi's remarks begin to suggest, spectacularly feminine style became the "*necessary* choice."

Attentive to the affective charge of the women's talk, the chapter begins to develop the book's new conceptual view of postfeminism as cruelly promising happiness. If happiness is a positive state said and expected to follow from certain styles and technologies of being, then, as Ahmed contends, it requires the subject to find and express happiness in these things, to confirm that they are indeed happy making.[1] Part of postfeminism's promissory address to women is that, now thoroughly technologized and commodified, a matter of lining up and deploying the right tools, feminine beauty is now attainable. This beauty is proffered also as now *for* the beautiful woman, not for others, even as it comes to function as a near condition for particular forms of recognition and respect. "Cruelties" range and reside in all of this: from the injurious premises and conditions of what postfeminist beauty is said to offer to their obscuring and sublimation by their upbeat packaging and the practical costs and risks of pursuing what is an ever-intensifying set of norms and practices of appearing. Inviting women to choose, perform, and communicate a new disposition that Laura Favaro captions "confidence chic," effectively the invitation is to consent to, and shore up, the patriarchal construction of femininity as deficient and unworthy of self-confidence in the first place and to do so all while exuding good cheer.[2]

Confidence chic is a hot, neoliberal postfeminist commodity, and imperative: "lean in," "love your body," "strong is the new skinny," and so on, women are now advised and exhorted.[3] These kinds of new and proliferating injunctions encourage women to work on feeling good about themselves and asserting confidence, including if and when they do not feel that they *look* good. But what about when, as with the women in this book, they do feel beautiful? What does beauty do, when, contrary to Rebecca Coleman and Mónica Moreno Figueroa's insight about its typical elusiveness, it *is* present?[4] That beauty does anything at all is because it is a resource or form of capital—a "gendered, racialized, and contested" one, Maxine Craig rightly specifies.[5] In his book on the biopolitics of beauty in Brazil, Alvaro Jarrín expands well-established understandings of beauty as social capital—that is to say, a product, sign, and potential driver of "a body's social standing"—to further conceptualize it as "affective capital."[6] By this Jarrín means that beauty has visceral and transitive qualities that variously affix to and circulate between bodies, and in and through this variously moves them, including potentially up the socioeconomic ladder for those deemed beautiful. In this chapter I show that under postfeminist cultural conditions, for the new type of woman enjoined to be wholly independent and self-regarding, beauty, including because of its affectivity, is proffered as what we could call "psychic capital." Rather than external or circulating, its new, premier promise is internal. Beauty matters less to be seen by and therein have effects upon others than to be seen by and, with this, prop up and propel the self. Postfeminist feminine beauty is, in the words of one of the women in Lagos, a "crutch."

PASSIONATELY ATTACHED TO POWER

Hearing the women describe what, over the course of the book, will be shown to be a highly disciplined, laborious, and expensive style of dress, and sometimes physically painful, as I have already indicated, I often asked if they could say why they pursued or wanted or liked it. I endeavored to preface this kind of question with acknowledgment that it is a hard one to speak to. Ethical poststructuralist research practice demands that if we ask the culturally constituted, and therefore constitutively splintered and shifting, subject to give account of itself, we do so "without any expectation of a full or final answer."[7] Desire, in any case, is particularly hard to explicate; at some point, the subject can only conclude that she likes what she likes. As could be reasonably expected, then, many of the women could not easily articulate a response to my question beyond (re)stating their wish to look a certain way, the pleasure they felt in putting on or achieving the look, or their sheer love for a particular dress item. One woman, Amaka, was sporting off-red nails about two inches long when I interviewed her. I assumed the nails were acrylic, or "fake," and was surprised when she revealed that they were actually her own, grown purposely for about five months. To my question of why she had wanted and duly endeavored to have her nails so long, Amaka replied: "I just like them. I like, I think I prefer them long than if they were short. Like I think I prefer them long, it's just kinda, I just like to keep my nails, I think it makes you kinda, I don't know, I just like to keep them long (*both laugh*)." Amaka and I both laughed not only because of how she had struggled to express herself but also because of her blasé tone and the manner in which she styled her body as she spoke. Swaying from side to side, coolly waving one hand in the air, Amaka's tone and gestures cited the habitus or bodily dispositions of the subject that could be called "woman who does what she likes," a confident woman, then. This was a subject position that Amaka also took up explicitly at various points in the interview, saying, for example, "I have this attitude, like I won't really say 'I don't care attitude,' but I'm just me." Amaka's bodily stylistics and demeanor further positioned her as a woman who *need not* explain herself; it sufficed to know that she was the type to dress as she pleased.

Repeatedly, I heard from other research participants, particularly near the start of their interviews, that they dressed as they felt and fancied and in a manner like Amaka's that suggested little to no external consideration. In the words of Folake: "I'm just, the way I dress, it's really, everything about me depends on my mood at that time." Chika echoed this position and phrasing, saying of how she dressed: "It depends on my mood really." Kim, like many others, expressed the fun of experimenting with her look. Wearing extra-long false eyelashes made her "giggle," she said, and she loved to play with her hairstyles: "My hair is a constant source of amusement to me. . . . I will put in a short weave today, do it black tomorrow, do it in blonde, do it in red." Sharon was quite emphatic about her attachment to her style, declaring, "I love to look all glammed up. I love the glam look. I just love it." Adaeze spoke of how much she had loved to dress up since she was a child. She stressed that her dressing up was first and foremost a self-referential and self-pleasing practice because of how it made her feel about herself, "inside":

> Adaeze: I just like to, like even if I'm at home, I wanna look a certain way. It's not even about, it's not about how other people perceive me, it's for me. It's like looking good makes me feel good.
> Simi:[8] It's not about like being out and being seen?
> Adaeze: Nooo . . .

The women's talk of their moods, desires, internal drives, and states framed their dress practice as an outward expression of a "truth of their being"—a thoroughly gendered truth.[9] Sharon, for instance, spoke of having and being driven by an "inner glam puss," which she further suggested that all women did and should have. Reference to such drives can serve as a rhetorical resource to try to untrouble one's positions by mystifying and essentializing them. Diane took such recourse in relation to her extensive collection of human hair extensions, which she had tipped out of a bag on to her bedroom floor for me to see. To my summation that there was "like over N1million worth of hair on the floor," about US$7,000 worth at the time,[10] her reply was "Okay, I'm vain, but I love looking good."

Yet however much the subject might love what it loves, however deeply or internally felt, the fact is that desire and pleasure are not originary, nor simply and inexplicably personal, but rather of cultural and contextual origin. Things are proffered to the subject to love, to choose. This becomes the more evident if we consider that the style of feminine dress and appearance that the women were speaking of simply and naturally desiring was highly normative and delimited. Folake, heard above nonchalantly linking her style with her mood, proceeded to give an example: "You know, things like my nails, like I can wear them—I don't wear them short, I always wear them long—but it depends on, I can decide to have them sharp, or you know square, depending on my mood really." Sharon reported that short, medium, or long acrylic nails were equal stylistic possibilities for her. I felt quite naive for having asked what might swing her one way or another between these styles when I heard the utterly casual response: "It just depends how I feel, to be honest." However, Sharon then added a caveat, her stylistic limit: "I would *never* be caught without my nails properly done (*laughs*) . . . as long as they're clean and they're, you know, filed properly and they look nice, with a nice nail polish on it and not chipped."

In postfeminist discourse, through repertoires of "individualism and consumerism, stereotypical femininity is reinstalled as a conscious choice and prerogative of (young) women."[11] In practice, what varied with the women's moods and desires were the particular stylized and commodified choices that they might make on any particular occasion, from a delimited range of normatively and spectacularly feminine options. Mood notwithstanding, some things were already not really choices. If it was being seen with short nails for Folake, or with chipped nails for Sharon, for Ima it was leaving home without doing up her eyebrows, or for Diane and Adaeze stepping out without having made up their entire faces. Adaeze also stressed: "My hair has to be done. Has to, has to, has to, has to, has to be done. Even if I'm sick." "Done," in order of stated preference and likelihood, meant a weave, a wig, or a style fashioned with Adaeze's own hair while she was on a brief break from weaves and wigs—while she was taking "aesthetic rest," as I conceptualize it in the following chapter. The grip of power is so strong precisely because it forms, not deforms, the subject's sense and image of self, the subject's sense of what "has to, has to, has to be done" to be, remain, and appear who it is or desires to be. Power's efficaciousness lies also in its capacity to affect, to stir at a preconscious and bodily level, and in this also to surface or materialize boundaries of self and other.[12] Take Alero, who reported being so disgusted and irritated by the mere sight of what she deemed unkempt (if not "ugly") femininity that she made sure not to fall into the abjected category herself: "I cannot stand and see girls with like messy *hair*, messy *face*, messy *nails*, just yeah, it's just irritating, so I always try to like do my *hair* regularly or even if I don't do it regularly keep it *neat*." With my bushy eyebrows, less than neatly twisted dreadlocks, flea-bitten nails, I wondered if the mere sight of me was irritating Alero at that very moment!

Alero and I met for the interview in a bar that she had suggested near her home. Being afternoon, the place was empty. She explained that she had come casually dressed and barefaced as she had only been coming down the road to meet me. She would never allow herself to appear like this in more typical social situations, even if others thought she looked good—or good enough, perhaps more to the point. She explained: "If I'm with somebody and I don't have any makeup on and like [they say] 'Oh, okay let's go to somewhere else, let's go to this place,' and I'm like 'Sorry, no, I have to go home and get dressed.' 'Oh no, you look all right,' I'm like 'Sorry, I can't.' Like there is no way you're going to drag me out to certain places, yeah, if I'm not dressed up." According to Alero, no one could prize her away from her attachment to the spectacularly feminine dress and appearance standards that, at least implicitly, she recognized as somewhat constraining. If constrained by her dress practice, disciplined by how she had to look, her position was that she also actively *chose* to be. Alero's defiant tone further cast the choice, and her refusal to forego it, as empowered.

But what was the content of the choice, exactly? To choose spectacularly feminine style is, manifestly, to choose femininity and beauty. Technologies of dress such as high heels, weaves, and makeup promise to beautify by enhancing, complimenting, accentuating, concealing, transforming, and the like, and to "feminize," to make one look, feel, and become "more of a woman." Illustrating Judith Butler's brief contention that the habitus is performatively constituted, that culture and discourse become bodily disposition, the women spoke of the beautifying and feminizing effects of their kind of dress from their embodied, affective, and therefore seemingly authoritative experience.[13] Tinu explained that "pencil heels" make "your leg look more straight and more narrow, and it helps you catwalk [that is, sashay] *very* well. It helps, you know, to walk like a lady." This was buttressed by Nene, a student and freelance model, who said that pencil heels helped you walk down the runway in an "elegant" and "classy" manner, while dancing in them made you "look like a lady and stuff." Bisi reported that she did not really like high heels and tended not to wear them, but that even she had "found out" from experience that "sometimes when you wear high shoes, they give you this oomph." What another woman, Misan, did not particularly like was artificial nails. Yet she had recently affixed a set to attend a wedding, she recalled, because they made her fingers look longer and hence better to her, and perhaps also made her "feel a little more feminine." Sade, on the other hand, declared that she did not wear artificial nails because her own nails were "pretty." This element of feminine beauty was already within her grasp without an additional technology on which other women might rely.

Feminists have long critiqued dominant ideals and standards of feminine beauty as mostly unrealistic and unattainable for women, including because of dominant racialized standards.[14] In this vein, Rebecca Coleman and Mónica Moreno Figueroa conceptualize feminine beauty as a state that women tend to experience as already passed or yet to come, almost never in the here and now.[15] But not so for my research participants. The women positioned themselves as attaining and embodying feminine beauty, or at least being quite capable of doing so. Diane recalled her twenty-first birthday party when she had been wearing a long-desired, especially expensive brand of human hair weave as follows:

> Diane: I knew I was looking nice, believe me, 'cause everybody was tell-
> ing me I was looking awesome.
> Simi: (*laughs*) Because of the hair or the whole package?
> Diane: *No, the hair!* The hair just gives you a different look.

Although harking back to her attainment of spectacular beauty about four years prior to the interview, the almost magically transformative weave in question was still in Diane's possession and still in use. In fact, the weave was in the bag of hair that she proceeded to empty out for me to see. Now a matter of the right techniques and technologies, versus "nature" or "destiny," feminine beauty was a practical achievement. It could be reached, manu-factured, purchased, put on, albeit iteratively, day in and day out, and with the necessary range of resources and requisite labor—not inconsiderable considerations, as we will see.

We can hear all this in one woman's lament about an occasion when, as she saw it, she had failed to make the mark. As in the quote from Tobi with which I started the present chapter, and as in her remarks cited in the previ-ous chapter in the discussion of Lagos fashion cultures, about not wanting to find herself inadvertently "oppressed" by other women's spectacularity, Tobi explained that her choice of style was directly motivated and, again, affected by "seeing chicks with *hair, nails* . . . and they look *good*, it's not like they don't look good, they do look good, and then you're thinking, why can't I look good too?" Tobi told me about having recently turned up at a wedding to find that, unlike her, most of the other young women had had their makeup profession-ally applied. She reenacted her disappointment in herself: "Aaargh, I'm like (*mock whining*) God couldn't I, couldn't I have been looking fly? (*Resumes regular voice.*) You know this is, that's what I'm talking about, you see girls looking so good, and you're like (*whining dramatically, knocking her hands on the table*) I want to look this good!" Tobi had segued into this account to explain why she wanted to learn how to apply false lashes by herself, the link being that many of the beautiful women at the wedding had been wearing the accoutrement. Hearing her resignation to the fact that she just lacked a know-how with false lashes, of which she owned an underutilized set, I asked Tobi about the possibility of getting the lashes affixed professionally.

Happy again, remembering what I argue is a new postfeminist pledge that feminine beauty is in fact a present possibility, Tobi roundly declared:

Tobi: The next wedding I go for I *WILL* get it professionally done!
Simi: Everything? [that is, all her makeup]
Tobi: *YES!*
Simi: (*laughs*)
Tobi: Even if it kills me.

Tobi's joking suggestion of dying for feminine beauty if necessary is a good place to turn to consider why this state was so desirable to her and the other women.

THE PROMISES OF POSTFEMINIST BEAUTY

If we understand the object of desire as "a cluster of promises," we see that, of course, feminine beauty promises women things.[16] Among others, the promises are of better experiences, happier feelings about oneself, nicer treatment by others, and romantic or sexual attention. The women all rejected dominant and heteronormative assumptions that women want beauty to attract men. Tobi, heterosexual, single, and in her early thirties, reasoned that, in fact, some men were wary of the most beautified women; a man might want to date such a woman only casually, but not settle down with her. She cheerfully concluded, "But I don't care!" Regardless of men's preferences, her claim went, she desired and intended to pursue beauty. The pursuit was *for herself*. Alero, too. Alero was adamant about what Lazar terms women's "right to be beautiful"—a postfeminist right that Lazar suggests is packaged by the fashion-beauty industry as part of women's broader rights to freedom and self-determination.[17] Alero spoke of a previous heterosexual relationship that had ended in part over her insistence on exercising this right, when her then boyfriend had said that he preferred her look without makeup and weaves, so she should wear less of them. Alero recounted her attitude to this request: "(*hisses*) Like please, excuse me . . . I don't believe in changing myself for anybody, *you know*. I like wearing makeup and, you know, I like getting my hair done, and these are things that I'm very serious, I take very seriously. . . . You can't just come from nowhere and tell me, 'Oh, change, change this,' and you expect me to listen to you? I can never answer [that is, comply], ever."

Other women echoed this kind of "independent beautiful woman" repertoire, if in a more ambivalent manner that suggests its competition with other, more traditional, views of what young and unmarried Nigerian women should be prioritizing, namely, men and marriage. Diane spoke at some length early in her interview about Nigerian men's attitudes to how young Nigerian women now dress, prompting me to eventually interrupt to ask if she was suggesting that Nigerian women dress *for* men:

> Diane: *Yes!* Why would you dress up in the first place?
> Simi: Okay (*slight, awkward laugh*).
> Diane: No, or why? Okay, or why? No, I get dressed to look good because I *looove* looking good.

Here Diane found herself caught in an ideological dilemma between competing discourses and subject positions about feminine desire, aspiration, and independence in relation to heterosexual attention and relationships. In the microcontext of our interaction, and probably not unrelated to my awkward response that seemed to suggest that she had said something wrong, Diane quickly and reflexively shifted back to a postfeminist position. She did so by concluding that "every woman loves [male] attention." This invoking of an essential feminine trait served to reconcile the contradiction of Diane's positions and allow her to reclaim that of the ultimately self-pleasing, beautiful, and in this fairly uncommon woman. The bridge between her positions became that she dressed for men's appreciative gaze, like all women, but really dressed for herself, being a woman of a particular sort: agentic, knowing, empowered.

A similar slippage and rhetorical recuperation occurred as Folake and I were talking about young Nigerian men's attitudes to educated career women like herself. I started posing a question to relate what Folake was saying back to the theme of her dress. Suddenly animated in what had been an otherwise fairly sedate interview, Folake interjected the following about Nigerian men: "They're the ones that spoiled everything . . . that girls have gone crazy and everybody just wants to look, you know, human hair, nails, everything, you know, at whatever cost. . . . A lot of people out there, why people dress up and look good, look fly, is because of the men." From "girls" to "people out there," the shifting subject of Folake's remarks makes it unclear if she was including herself in the imagined community of women said to be dressing, at major expense, for male attention. I started to remind Folake that she had earlier insisted that she dressed for herself:

> Simi: But you said that for you—
> Folake: It's both ways. But, em (*pauses*), a (*longer pause*), a lot more of it has to do with me. I like to look good for myself, you know, but also

like to go out, at least if people see me and say, "Oh, you look nice,"
"Thank you."

Folake's logic, repeated by others, was that other people's appreciation of her appearance was certainly welcome and pleasant, but this was not the motivation for her choice of style or desire for feminine beauty. Feminine beauty promised something else, something more.

For my research participants, or to be more precise, for the kinds of subjects that the women were presenting and positioning themselves to be, the most valuable and desirable of beauty's promises was a sense of self-confidence and power. Beauty comprised psychic capital, operating on the inside, even if this deeply subjectifying operation went on to have or engender external and intersubjective effects. Eight of the women said directly that their dressing up in one or another item, or in its totality, made them feel or become more self-confident. A ninth, Funke, spoke of this effect in general and in relation to both her female and her male colleagues to illustrate the importance of being well dressed for work. All the others communicated similar points more implicitly. About her feeling that a weave just gave her a different look, Diane reflected, "I think when I look nice, I have this (*pauses*) a different me. I'm so confident." She later returned to this point: "Like I said, I love looking good, it gives me this confidence, it brings out another person in me, and I like that person. I think I'm already used to that person, and I wanna stay with that person, I don't to go [*sic*]—like, em, Beyoncé has Sasha Fierce." "Sasha Fierce" was Beyoncé's onetime "fierce" alter ego.[18] Saying that she felt prettier with makeup, Ima remarked at the same time, "I definitely think it makes me feel more confident." Kemi commented that high heels made her feel dressed up and imparted "a certain like confidence as well. I think it just makes you, I also think it makes you stand better sometimes and walk a bit stronger. But that's just me." While Kemi expressly individualized her sense of the potency of high heels, what she was citing and feeling is a long-standing cultural repertoire, packaged most recently within a discourse of postfeminist power femininity. Postfeminism tells us "nowadays that high-heeled shoes are emblematic of a confident, powerful femininity, a femininity that is 'out and proud.'"[19]

Suggested clearly by Kemi's comment above is that a sense of confidence enabled action and achievement in the world, in front of others. It empowered, in a word. Alero spoke about how her "dressed-up confidence" so boosted both her state of mind and her physical dispositions that it became palpable to others: "When I get dressed up, I feel very like *oooh* and I carry myself very, so people tend to respond you know, or react to me." Bisi shared Alero's feeling and experience. She stressed that her choice to dress up in spectacularly feminine style and thereby gain confidence was fully self-motivated. Constructing this self-referentiality as a new and uncommon feminine logic or sense, not known to all women, Bisi spoke of actively propagating it: "I always tell my friends: (*punctuating each word for emphasis*) Dress. Up. For. Your. *Self.* Make yourself—not even for your boyfriend, not for your husband, for your *self.* 'Cause if you wear something and you don't feel you look good, other people will automatically, they'll feel that vibe about you. . . . When I dress up, I feel like I glow and I'm happy and I'm comfortable and I'm confident. Wherever I go, nobody can put me down." If a woman was not satisfied with the dressed-up self that she saw in the mirror, Bisi's logic went, she would not feel confident even if her male partner was satisfied, and others would pick up on and possibly exploit her lack of self-assurance. Via the practice of dressing for and to please themselves, women were now to take responsibility for their self-empowerment. If so, to share this knowledge with women who did not have it, as Bisi claimed to do, was to empower them, a practice and ability that implied one's prior or already established state of empowerment.

Governmental, advising others on the conduct of their conduct, Bisi's logic was thoroughly postfeminist and neoliberal. It entailed women investing further in the heteropatriarchal scopic economy in which their worth is tied to their appearance.[20] What was new and, again, not obvious to all, the postfeminist difference, was that women were now to do so for themselves and with regard to their sense of their own value. Misan claimed to be a subscriber to this new way of thinking as well, and thus an adherent to its prescribed practices of self and of heterosexual relationality. She explained that her boyfriend preferred her to wear her weaves flowing down instead of pulled up in a bun, but that she would always say to him: "It's all about my look. If it, if my look doesn't go with down hair, I'm gonna pack it up. If it happens to go with down hair, good for you . . . but I'm not going to compromise on the way I *look* . . . 'cause it doesn't make me feel confident." In the first part of her comments above, Misan took up an assertive, self-regarding, and seemingly feminist position with her boyfriend, much like Bisi seemed to be advising her friends, or like Alero had reported in relation to the exboyfriend who had tried to change her style. The woman so positioned was one who could and would not dress to please a man; her male partner would have to count himself lucky if the look that he preferred happened to be the one she went for on any given day. Now that the postfeminist subject "is able to make her own choices, it seems as though the fearful terrain of male approval fades away." Yet postfeminism is not postpatriarchal. According to McRobbie, patriarchal authority is instead reterritorialized, and more insidious. It is now "subsumed within a regime of self-policing whose strict criteria form the benchmark against which women must endlessly and repeatedly measure themselves."[21] We hear just this from Misan, too, where she reveals the feelings of insecurity that would ensue if *she* saw that her look was somehow not right, a possibility heightened by the sheer number and detail of the elements that make up the look, as well as by the intensified self-surveillance that postfeminism incites, the even keener gazing in the mirror that Misan described.[22]

Like feminine beauty itself, the confidence that it promised the women in my research was tenuous, fleeting, and belabored, in need of constant reiteration, effort, and vigilance. More problematically, the promise of feminine beauty, and its promise of self-confidence in turn, obscured and thereby reinforced their patriarchal terms and conditions. To paraphrase Sarah Banet-Weiser, the content of the promise of postfeminist self-confidence is that women will feel self-possessed and powerful under and despite hostile cultural conditions. But to achieve this, women are called and exhorted to *better conform* to these very conditions and to thereby contribute to their perpetuation and normalization.[23] To feel self-confident under patriarchy, they are to choose patriarchy, to make the normative, or "right," choice.

CHOOSING THE "RIGHT CHOICE"

Tinu is a Nollywood actress who told me that she had fans around the world and could not go anywhere in Lagos without being recognized and hailed. I met her at a cultural event, and, to me, her appearance that evening was the most spectacularly feminine of all the women whom I was to approach in the field. Furthermore, her heels were the highest that I have ever seen anyone wearing in person. In the interview (during which Tinu was completely dressed down), I asked her if she faced or felt pressure to dress up in the manner that she had that night. Tinu mulled over the question, repeating the word *pressure* just under her breath before replying in the negative. She reckoned that *she* put pressure on other women by setting new fashion trends in her films. Tinu had spoken about having moved to Lagos about seven years earlier from her hometown elsewhere in Nigeria and having since stopped putting her hair in braids or cornrows. She now almost exclusively wore weaves, which she described as "in the spirit" of the city. It was only in telling me about this stylistic transition in and because of Lagos, Tinu reflected, that she had become fully conscious of it herself. Rendered agentic by her subjection to desiring and dressing up in weaves, by her acceding to a certain Lagos norm, Tinu suggested that she would perhaps proceed to resist by trying out a different hairstyle, "not just what is in the air."

To use Tinu's astute expression, the normative, the putatively correct and best, functions more often than not by being "just what is in the air": present and self-evident yet invisibilized; silent yet clearly communicated; expected, advisable, but rarely imposed or forced. Chika reflected that she had never been told outright how to dress and that this was an imposition that she would probably resist. She claimed that now that she was in her midtwenties, her attitude to dressing up was "However I feel is however I just turn up." The considerable time and effort that Chika reported spending on her appearance, and the normativity of her final look, belied her claim, however. And while she might not have faced outright pressure or instruction to dress as she did, what Chika reported experiencing was questioning about why she was *not* wearing something or other expected of a young woman like her and with which she typically appeared, like makeup. She had been subjected to a more insidiously normalizing gaze. June told of similar and recurring interrogation at work from both male and female colleagues if she happened not to have had time to apply her makeup before getting to the office. Whereas a feminist poststructuralist analysis would ascribe such intrusions and interventions by others to a patriarchal logic that constitutes "everyone and yet no one in particular" as agents to police women's appearance and steer them toward the norm,[24] June depoliticized and downplayed her colleagues' looks, attributing them to innocuous habit: "People are used to you in a particular way, so if you appear anything different, they would notice."

How the subject appears to others is fundamental to its founding and survival. Hailed into being, the subject exists before others and therefore depends on their ongoing recognition, naming, and address for its subjecthood. This is an inherently unstable position; "it marks a primary vulnerability to the Other in order to be."[25] It gives further lie to postfeminist claims and rhetoric of unfettered individual agency and choice, that a woman might simply do as she pleases without any external consideration or influence, as if an island. Even as my research participants voiced these affirmative positions, the full course and detail of the interviews revealed the extent to which external gazes and considerations also governed their choices. Tobi, for instance, explained that she had affixed acrylic nails for years before stopping because of the damage that the beauty technology had caused to her real nails. Yet as of the time of the interview, she was back to acrylic. A presenter on a Nigerian television station, she explained why: "One day I was on TV, and my friend says, she sends me a message that 'Babe, fix your nails, they look horrible' (*laughs*)." I noted earlier that Misan was also not a fan of acrylic nails. But she too had been guided to them as the "right choice." An entrepreneur in the local fashion, beauty, and lifestyle fields, Misan explained that her female clients complained if she did not appear in spectacularly feminine fashion. She mimicked these women's advice to her, and tone: "(*snapping her fingers impatiently*) 'You're earning some money: do your hair, do your nails . . . ' So I remember one time I said, 'Okay, you know what,' I remember this new year, I said 'my new year's resolution is I'm going to try to do my nails'—which I, anyways—'I'm going to always try to do my hair' [that is, put in a weave]."

It was quite conceivably to her already stated dislike of false nails that Misan started to go in the aside, above, that she repressed or silenced with the word *anyways*. As Misan and two others put it, part of their choice of dress was to "look the part"—which is to say, look like the kind of intersectional feminine subjects they were expected or assumed or supposed to be. It was Misan's experience and understanding that spectacularly feminine style was expected of her as a young and upwardly mobile career woman in Lagos. This was the look that went with the part. In her account, this understanding had led her to once commission both a professional photographer and a professional makeup artist to produce pictures of herself for a work forum. She had done so to produce pictures in which she would look "professional and older," she explained. Although Misan reported finding the professional makeup session fun, she made it clear that putting so much on her face and spending about an hour on it were neither her normal nor her desired practice, not least because at the end of the session she had barely recognized herself and "in a way that was scary." Also experiencing the spectacularly feminine as the new appearance standard for the young professional Lagos woman, Diane did not repress her feelings about how this restricted her choices. A corporate customer service representative, Diane explained that she had noticed that customers treated her rudely when she did not have on a weave. Allegedly they would say things like, "Look at this small girl! What do you know? Get out! Shut up!" *Small girl* is a colloquial Nigerian term for a young woman lacking status or clout. It can be used humorously or, as in Diane's narrative of how she was sometimes treated, to dismiss, to disempower. She continued angrily:

> Diane: I noticed that immediately I, I put my weave on and probably have that fake look that they all want, they, they talked to me with a

bit of respect . . . because that's, that's what life is all about, people are
very fake (*pauses*) and—

Simi: What do you mean?

Diane: Let's be real, you can't (*long pause*). These days we hardly find, we
hardly find people that go [with] the natural look . . . and say, "Oh, I'm
going to work like that, without makeup and [with] my real hair."

It is crucial to keep in mind here that the style of feminine appearance that
Diane was decrying as "fake" and as effectively demanded by both the times
and her career was the very same one that, elsewhere in the interview, she
claimed to love and embrace, and for herself. Also crucial is that it was the
style to which she reported directing and inculcating in other women, in what
can be read as an act of postfeminist "girlfriend gazing" in which women
subject each other's bodies to strategic "analysis, calculation and control."[26]
In Diane's words:

Diane: If my colleague comes to work looking scruffy, I'll tell her, I'll
ask her if there's something wrong with her.

Simi: But what does looking scruffy mean? As in what (*pause*), is that
like (*pause*) makeup?

Diane: Looking scruffy: not brushing her hair, wearing a bit of makeup.
I'm a girly-girly person, so (*long pause*) probably, I'll probably make
her up.

Despite its insistence and celebration of individual choice, postfeminism
entails policing of "any manifestations of 'off-script' femininity."[27]

Multiple and inevitably conflicting scripts interpellate the subject across
the different social and cultural fields that it inhabits, offering also multiple
and conflictual desires, choices, and styles of being.[28] Submission to any
one or set of these means the necessary loss or relinquishment of others.
Doing the "fake" style of femininity that Diane alternatively denounced and
embraced meant forgoing the "natural look." Dressing up to be appraised
by one's clients as a hot, young professional woman might mean almost
misrecognizing oneself in the mirror, as Misan had, and so on. This need
to make trade-offs between different styles of being is a foundational and
constitutively melancholic dilemma of subjecthood. Sade cast and sought
to resolve the dilemma as simply one of coming of age, which necessarily
meant leaving behind younger or now outgrown versions of oneself. Joking
that the dress culture among her girlfriends in Lagos was so fabulous that
she could not show up "looking like the maid," she ruminated in somewhat
biblical terms and not without a trace of regret:

> Sade: There's a season for everything, and at a certain stage in your life there's a season where you just have to take on that (*long pause*). You know, I don't know the word, but it's just like, yeah, okay, you just have to take on that—
> Simi: What, like identity, or persona?
> Sade: An identity of being a lady, you know. I think that would be the way to describe it.

Playing a stylized part like "lady" included not being mistaken for some other feminine type such as "the maid," unglamorous, working class, physically laboring, or, as in Diane's experience, the "small girl." In chapter 5, I elaborate on the different parts that the women spoke of playing, and also rejecting. What needs noting for now is that the preferable parts were the more powerful, glamorous, and socially valued.

Unlike the majority of the participants who claimed to have loved dressing up since they were children, Sade recounted that she had been a tomboy when she was a child and, later, an assiduous teenager and university student who had rejected what she deemed the distraction of fashion. As she told it, it was entry into her adult working life that had sparked her love for the spectacularly feminine and for dressing up. In the first place, her field of work, Nigerian television, demanded the look. Sade recalled that she had been sporting an Afro when she first started out in the field, but could not appear on air with it "because it's not exactly the standard." She gave a detailed account of the alternative hairstyles that she had tried to manage the "professional problem" of her chemically unprocessed or "natural" hair, from braids to weaves to chemical straightening. The results had not been good: she had reportedly lost some of her hairline before reaching wigs as the "solution." In what struck me right there in the interview and in my later reading and rereading of the transcript as an extraordinarily celebratory recuperation of the painful and costly subjection that Sade was describing to a racist industry norm of appearance, in Nigeria for that matter, she concluded about her ongoing use of wigs:

> Sade: So now I just have a two-second salon in my house, and I have ten wigs.
> Simi: Yeah, I was gonna say, and you have variety probably.
> Sade: (*putting on an African-American accent*) Ah girl! (*returning to her regular accent*) Like in one day I can actually have three hairdos, and I don't care (*claps her hands*) because this is, that's how I feel.

To position oneself as a postfeminist subject, to play *that* part, "it is imperative that all one's practices (however painful or harmful they may be) be presented as freely chosen—perhaps even as pampering or indulgence."[29] Above, with the help of my suggestion that she now had "variety," Sade swiftly transmuted the constraint and loss that she had described with regard to her hair into feminine consumerist and stylized choice and gain, into fashion. With this, she resolved rhetorically any ideological and possibly also psychic dilemma between what she had been almost compelled to do to her hair, the relative cruelty of it, and the upbeat subjectivity that she performed and communicated repeatedly in the interview, of the independent, self-pleasing, happy woman. Positioning herself "beyond racialized and gendered violations to a point where they no longer affect" her, Sade enacted what Ralina Joseph calls a "so what" girl power that individually shrugs off the structural and the painful.[30] This shrugging off preempts even the mere imagining of alternative, maybe even seemingly "incorrect," choices. Also disallowing even a moment of mourning for what has been lost or renounced, the girl-power shrug is itself cruel.

NECESSARY FEMININE EVILS?

Kim, who worked in Nigerian television like Sade, explained that she was "*compelled*" to be a "swan" on her lifestyle show, when in fact she was "content to just be a duck." If covering red-carpet events, for example, "I don't like to wear high heel shoes, but most of the time I find I have to wear them . . . 'cause it fits the look better, for the red carpet, at least our perceived notion of what red carpet would be." One thing Kim did love was experimenting with her hair. But even in this were certain pains and griefs: "I hate going to the salon, ironically. It's a very tiresome thing. I find I'm spending the whole day there, ah I'm spending so much money, trying to sell me some new product that will change my *life*, you know. It's so tedious—the hair, the noise, the pulling, everything. If I could go to the salon every week, maybe I would, but on average I change my hair every four weeks." Kim did not specify if she did not go to the salon more often because of her dislike of the experience or for other reasons. In suggesting that she would nonetheless like to change her hair more frequently, and in noting the irony of her position, she pointed to a contradiction that many of the women shared: that while they variously desired their hyperfeminine stylization, they disliked and, in some cases, suffered certain aspects of the processes and practicalities of embodying it. "Painful" was how Sharon characterized the length of time that she spent at the hairdressers roughly every other Saturday taking out one weave, washing and treating her own hair, and then reaffixing a new weave, with all the waiting around between each stage. I could not quash an exclamation of shock on hearing just how much time she was talking about: six to eight hours.

If the process of getting dressed up in their kind of style could be painful in the sense of tedious, laborious, and also financially costly, the final or achieved state could plain hurt. Adaeze remembered how much it had hurt to touch her eyes when she had on false lashes, while Sharon warned that wearing very long acrylic nails meant courting pain: "You don't want to get your finger caught in like a window or something, 'cause it *hurts.*" It was with regard to high heels, however, that the matter of physical discomfort and pain most arose in the interviews. Ima said that she tended not to wear heels because of her tall height. She recalled an occasion when she had ventured out in a pair but had to take them off before even arriving at her destination, because "they were just hurting . . . very uncomfortable." Sharon, by contrast, was inclined to push through the pain of heels for the sake of their promises. She framed this as both an embodied feminine skill, something that a woman learned to do with her body, and a feminine rationality and value, something that "totally" made sense for a woman: "I guess you learn to (*pause*) carry it [that is, heels] very well and walk in it. Eeeem, em, what can I say? Yeah some, of course, after some hours it starts to pay out, you feel the tension and of course you feel the, the part, you know the point of your feet hurting. But it's worth it, it's totally worth it so I don't think—beauty is *pain*, they say." Except when it came to her "Loubs" (that is, her Christian Louboutin heels), which were "*ridiculously painful,*" Alero shared Sharon's logic of "no pain, no feminine gain." In her opinion, not only did a woman have to "swallow the pain" of wearing heels, but doing so also placed her in a shared feminine community of suffering. Alero rationalized this putative reality of femininity as follows: "I am not the only one suffering with [the pain of heels]. It's a group thing so (*briefly laughs*) everyone has to just (*pauses*), it's just, I mean like they say, 'beauty is pain.' It's just, you just have to deal with it."

Lauren Berlant proposes that attachment to an object is cruel if this object threatens the subject's well-being, if it "contributes to the attrition of the very thriving that is supposed to be made possible in the work of attachment in the first place."[31] Such an attachment is therefore also cruelly optimistic because it draws the subject repeatedly back to the object, for its promises. Cruel optimism keeps the subject "in proximity to the scene of desire/attrition."[32] It keeps women like Sharon and Alero dressing up and stepping out in their painful shoes over and over again, in pursuit of feminine beauty and its confidence and other boosts. Or, more cruelly optimistic in my hearing of it, was the women's continued attachment to the technologies of hair weaves, false eyelashes, and acrylic nails. As I discuss at length and theorize in the following chapter, in the interviews the women said repeatedly that weaves, false eyelashes, and acrylic nails were not good for their own hair, eyelashes, and nails, respectively. At times speaking from personal experience, other times commenting generally, they explained to me that weaves could cause one's own hair to thin out; that in the process of removing false lashes, real ones could be pulled out too; that overuse of acrylic nails could weaken, break, stunt, and yellow one's real nails. Given that she had quit acrylic nails previously because of the damage that they had done to her own nails, but was wearing them again following the advice of a friend, I asked Tobi if she worried about the renewed risk. Her reply: "Yes I do . . . but you know what these are necessary evils, ugh! (*Putting on a "girly" voice.*) A girl has to be a girl!"

Citing the commonplace repertoire that "a girl has to be a girl," putting on a high-pitched "girly" voice for performative emphasis, Tobi's suggestion was that it was because she was a woman that she had to wear false nails: this was something a woman just had to do, as a woman, being feminine. The said necessity did not resolve the multipronged dilemma that a woman might face and feel between subscribing to the risky beauty practice and worrying about the risk. It merely explained why she persisted in the practice and in Tobi's case explained her resignation: evil though acrylic nails might be, she just had to choose them. I would argue that Tobi was making a claim about the ineluctability of femininity to not only explain her return to acrylic nails but also defend it, and herself, against charges like irrationality or irresponsibility. The concepts of cruel attachments and cruel optimism can also help in this last regard. They "allow us to encounter what is incoherent or enigmatic in our attachments, not as confirmation of our irrationality, but as an explanation for our sense of *our endurance in the object*, insofar as proximity to the object means proximity to the cluster of things that the object promises."[33] Thus, these concepts allow us to not dismiss women as "silly girls," say, or deem them simply inscrutable, for continuing with heightened or intensified practices and technologies of the self that they consider potentially harmful. Instead, we are enabled to see, and respect, that the subject is quite likely to accept certain risks and cruelties in order to continue to be or become the kind of subject that these risks and cruelties are supposed to engender, which, in the case of the women in this book, was not only "feminine beautiful" but also, therefore, "happy."

Yet, sticky or enduring though they may be, attachments are not immutable. While the notion that a girl has to be a girl appears essentialist, declaring that femininity is a must for the female subject, it actually points directly to the performativity of gender. That a girl has to be a girl means, reveals, that the subject that is called and supposed to be a girl is not already, always, or ineluctably one. Rather, this subject has to be *made* a girl as a matter of cultural compulsion, and this over and over, such as through "girling" or feminizing technologies like false nails and false lashes. Just like Butler has theorized, we can see that it is out of this practical need for reiteration, out of the fact that to be or become a girl one might have to fix one's nails repeatedly or put on a full face of makeup every morning, that the possibility of change, slippage, and resistance emerges.[34] Resistance is hard to concretize or specify from a feminist poststructuralist perspective, but for the purposes of the present discussion, I will take it to entail at least a minimal sense of contestation, oppositionality, and displacement with regard to dominant norms. Therefore, I do not deem it resistance when the women spoke of not having a taste for particular elements of spectacularly feminine style, such as when Diane derided false lashes as "tacky" or when they regretted not having the time to pursue the style in full, as in the case of June, for whom the demands of motherhood precluded time to get her nails done at the salon. I would also not cast as resistance the kind of individual strategy that Alero divulged to try to mitigate what she had claimed was the quintessential feminine problem of suffering painful heels. This strategy entailed sometimes carrying a pair of flat shoes in her bag to slip on when no one would notice: "Like if I go clubbing, when everyone is drunk I will just, you know, take [my heels] off." While Alero voiced the practice as knowingly subversive, and while we might be able to picture her stealthily enacting it, I would argue that it has the effect of solidifying the cruel feminine norms that it aims to resist, that women look best, and so should be seen, in heels.

Across the interviews as a whole, there were, in fact, very few instances in which the women questioned what was actually necessary in their kind of dress practice and why, if so. The most deliberate example and enunciation of choosing to *not* conform with dominant norms of immaculate femininity came from Chika. She said in reference to her eyebrows: "It's a weird feminist thing where I refuse to pluck or thread my eyebrows, 'cause I feel like it's just like one extra thing you have to do as a woman, like if I start threading my eyebrows, forever more I'll be under the tyranny of having to thread my eyebrows. . . . 'Cause I feel like being a woman *is* tyranny sometimes." Notably, this was the only instance in all the interviews in which the word *feminism* was uttered—by either a participant or me—if disclaimed in the same breath as a "weird" position, reflecting the postfeminist necessity and rhetoric to repudiate feminism.[35] Chika also explained that recently she had come to resist the quite normative practice of wearing foundation. She partially attributed her ability to do so to a relative coming of age that meant becoming more comfortable in one's own skin, as well as the practical discomfort of the stuff in the heat of Lagos. But most important in her account was the realization that her use of foundation had gone from "fun" to what she termed, emphatically, a "*crutch.*" Chika recalled that before she had made the conscious decision to stop wearing foundation, she had gotten to the stage where "I couldn't *not* wear it, like I got *addicted* to it kind of thing, so like if I *didn't* wear it, I felt *really (pauses)* I don't know, not—I don't want to say ugly 'cause that's pretty, too strong—but I just didn't *feel* like my *self* or something, so I, so then I just decided to stop wearing it one day and I felt weird and I felt like I looked blotchy, but I just didn't care." Her attachment to foundation had come to feel too risky and detrimental to her sense of self and worth, and so, pushing and reassuring herself through initial discomfort and feelings that she looked "weird," "blotchy," "ugly," without the makeup, Chika had severed the attachment. Rather than continuing to think that foundation was a necessity for her to cover what she saw as her physical imperfections, to thereby present what she called her "best self," Chika, citing the kind of language of authentic and optimal selfhood propagated most famously by the neoliberal self-help figure of Oprah, explained that she had come to realize: "*I* am my best self."

What Chika was reporting was her undertaking of a labor on herself that Gill and Elias term "love your body."[36] This is a different route to postfeminist confidence chic than that which I have been discussing in the chapter thus far. Love your body entails women striving hard to feel good about themselves *without* the tools of feminine beauty, in the face of the conditions that tell them, overwhelmingly, that they have ample cause not to feel good, that they do indeed have physical imperfections, and that these things need covering up and correcting. As with buying wholeheartedly into technologies of feminine beauty as a means to feminine self-confidence, the individualized and interiorized work of soldiering on without these technologies also fails to challenge or question, or even acknowledge, the cultural and structural conditions that necessitate it in the first place. It therefore does not lend itself to a more thoroughgoing or sustained resistance or critique than pushing through one's insecurities—all, some, just the one—by oneself. The fact that Chika laughed when I asked if she had other beauty crutches, as she had gone on to name what foundation had been for her, illustrates my point here, as does her reply: "I have *o*, I have *o*." "*O*" is a Yoruba word inserted into Nigerian English almost as a matter of course at the end of a phrase. As used here by Chika, it served to lend strong emphasis to her words. She *absolutely* had other beauty crutches was what she was conveying with the word *o*. She went on to reflect and conclude, "Oh my God, being a girl is so funny." This was mere minutes after she had described it as "tyranny sometimes."

Even more depoliticized, eliding even passing insight into spectacular feminine appearance standards as perhaps a kind of tyranny, was Bisi's account of how she often faced and attempted to resist concerted pressure from other women to wear high heels, which she disliked. Bisi enacted a hypothetical scene with first her mother and then friends in which she was getting ready to go out in her preferred flat shoes. A note of translation before I cite her: the word *now* as it appears twice in her comments below is not referring to time but is a Nigerian colloquialism that, in the following context, conveys a plaintive, almost whiny sentiment. The quote starts with Bisi responding to my question of why she ever agreed to wear heels at all if she disliked them so much: "That's the thing, my mum would have said (*plaintively*), 'Nooo, *this dress goes with only heels.*' We'll go back and forth. My friends too: okay, we're going out, and then [they'll notice], 'Ah, you're wearing flats? (*plaintively again*) 'No now! Please just wear heels now, *pleeease*, okay just for me, okay once you get there [you can take them off], just wear it.'" Enacting a second hypothetical scene in which a female work colleague complained that Bisi was the only woman in the team at work in flat shoes, Bisi's defensive retort was "To me it looks nice." Puzzled that other women would be so invested in, and discomfited by, Bisi's choice of shoe, I asked her why this was the case. She, too, was puzzled and could not say.

Ahmed's notion of the happiness duty, and the undutiful "killjoy" who refuses to comply, suggests some answers. In the scenes that Bisi described, she and her flat shoes were effectively killing a certain feminine joy: dampening the mood among the group of young women prepping for a night out, dashing a mother's hopes for her daughter's fullest embodiment of feminine beauty, and so on. The killjoy is the figure who refuses to find or affect happiness in the things and practices and arrangements that promise it. Happiness "involves a way of being aligned with others, of facing the right way." Being happy, or merely passing as such, thus becomes a social and intersubjective duty "to keep things in the right place."[37] Keeping things on an even keel is quite familiar to feminists as women's long-standing work, physical, emotional, and symbolic. To refuse is to give lie to it all. It is to suggest that the things that promise happiness do not, in fact, do what they say. The woman like Bisi, then, who insists on wearing flat shoes while others are in the highest of heels, disrupts and disproves the notion that heels are a necessary (if evil) technology for feminine beauty and therein feminine happiness. She lays their cruelty all the more bare.

A crucial question is whether this is a *feminist* revelation or disruption. In Ahmed's formulations, the killjoy is a feminist, which, incidentally, is also the postfeminist representation of this figure, as grumpy, humorless, spoiling women's fun.[38] Bisi positioned herself as neither killjoy nor feminist, though. In refusing to wear heels, she was not trying to be "difficult" or to make others unhappy. It was not a political move. Her stance was simply that a woman should wear "what works for [her] at the end of the day," should dress for herself, choose what she likes and wants. As Bisi saw it, this was a matter and means of a woman's self-empowerment.

3

"I'M WORKING, YOU KNOW"

THE SERIOUS BUSINESS
OF SPECTACULARITY

The women's insistence that they dressed for and to please themselves was matched and continued in claims that they also dressed, achieved their spectacular style, *by* themselves. The practicalities of how the women did so revolved around the continuous and not inexpensive acquisition, use, and management of a proliferating basket of feminine goods and services, as well as the work of putting it together. The women positioned themselves as knowing, skilled, and calculative consumers of fashion and beauty, hence able to make themselves in their desired image. Kim offered an exemplary declaration: "I feel like if God had made me with longer lashes, I would have a prettier face. God *didn't* make me with longer lashes, so I put false lashes in." Strikingly agentic, claiming a power to consume and to thereby better (re)create herself, implicitly Kim's comment also located her power and can-do in knowledge: in her knowing how, and when, and why, to marshal the technologies of spectacular femininity. However, understanding knowledge not as a route to power but a vehicle for it, as power/knowledge, allows us to see that the women's celebratory framings of their knowing how to self-fashion worked to not merely rationalize but also valorize the forms and sites of power to which they were being subjected, and thus continue to preempt critical resistance or questioning, to celebrate conforming. The rationalities of power in the women's accounts, that is, the implicit knowledges that "make any particular form of power seem reasonable or inevitable," were decidedly entrepreneurial.[1] As in Kim's remarks above, the common sense was to take not only a market-based but also a business-minded approach to one's "beauty problems."

Kim's particular comment was pervaded also by a sense of entitlement. It is a fundamental logic of the market that the subject has a right to that which she can afford of its (legal) offerings. Postfeminism adds to and amplifies this. Along with its new and intensified cultures of feminine consumption, postfeminism promotes new rationalities, practices, and also temporalities of feminine consumer entitlement. Not the least of these is the message to women that they are now "entitled to be pampered and pleasured, and to unapologetically embrace feminine practices and stereotypes, and invited to become 'girls' once more."[2] The women in Lagos closely and enthusiastically recited this message. They further anchored their right to consume spectacularly in claims that they paid for it independently. Despite critical recognition that consumption is at the crux of postfeminist culture and subjectivity, there is gaping inattention in the literature to how exactly women afford it. The question is never posed, and moreover the apparent answer, that women earn independent wages now, is barely stated or discussed. It is taken as obvious.[3] The financing of young *African* women's consumption is called into question repeatedly in both scholarly research and everyday life, however, haunted by a trope, and analytic, of "transactional heterosex."[4] Thus, while the assertions of financial independence by the women in this book may sound "obviously postfeminist," I contend they should not be heard too readily or singularly as such. Oriented to local suspicions about how it is that young women come to get their hands on consumer goods and enjoy consumer experiences, expensive ones especially, the women's assertions of financial independence were first and foremost assertions of sexual respectability.

This finding becomes all the more important to the extent that women's sexual agency and display, even "shamelessness," are central to how Western feminists have characterized and typologized postfeminism.[5] It speaks to a necessary analytic and methodological note of caution that an understanding of postfeminism as transnational culture should not engender inattention to the other currents of meaning and practice that traverse and make up the particular locales with which we may be concerned. In her ethnography of new subjects and affects of neoliberalism in Barbados, Carla Freeman, citing Michel-Rolph Trouillot, warns against an analytic of "déjà vu" in the globalized present that would lead us to miss that which is still particular in that which may seem now or evidently general and "everywhere."[6] In terms of postfeminism, nuanced attention to the local and particular can serve to illustrate and thereby enrich our understandings of the culture's "resilience, adaptability and generativity within a variety of different social [and cultural] conditions."[7] In so doing, it can also serve to provincialize the so-called center, to show, remind, that, as is a core presupposition of this book, postfeminism in the West—in the many locales that constitute the West—is also always local, a vernacular, and not the prototypical or necessary form that the culture takes in itself or in its travels.

EXECUTING THE LOOK

From shopping for the various elements and technologies of their elaborate style to coordinating and managing the use of these things, the women positioned themselves as "oriented towards optimizing [their] resources through incessant calculation, personal initiative and innovation."[8] Shopping, to start here, entails highly normative considerations such as knowing what one "needs," knowing how to appraise and value the goods and services on offer, and knowing how to manage and ideally maximize one's budget. The women presented themselves as skilled in all these regards. Kim recounted her history of trying to beautify what she described as the "short stumpy mess" that were her eyelashes. It was a history of coming to know the commodity options available and best suited for her putative needs: "I tried every kind of mascara under the sun. I bought every product in my teen years, you know, lash mascaras, I went for lash perming, nothing worked. So at some point I just realized I just have to start putting in false lashes." Naturalizing false lashes as the inevitable end point and resolution for her, Kim was reciting the interpellative address and assurances of the beauty product itself, and therein revealing and lending further force to her subjection to and subjectification by the product as the kind of woman who *needed* false lashes, and the kind who therefore took to the market to procure the necessary solutions for herself. Equally market-centered processes and logics of agentic subjectification surfaced in the women's talk of hair extensions. Echoing the branding and marketing of this technology as a way out from a state of "bad" or "not good enough" hair, the women positioned and presented themselves as therefore self-empowering, indeed self-investing, for buying and wearing it.

The women tended to buy *human* hair, that is, hair extensions said to originate from the heads of real people in places like Brazil, India, Vietnam, Peru, and Russia.[9] Human hair is typically labeled according to its supposed national origins. Suggesting that this labeling is meant to index something of the hair's type and quality, Folake expressed an active disinterest in attaching to or acquiring different types of hair on this basis. She claimed to have developed an alternative, tacit bodily method and skill to know and recognize quality by herself: "I just buy hair, to be honest, as far as I like the texture. I don't—when people say 'Brazilian, Peruvian, blah blah,' no, I'm not, I just want good hair. And when I feel it and I see it, I can tell if it's good hair or not. And that's just how I buy my hair." Sharon was one of the kinds of consumers Folake was describing, who appraised and differentiated human hair extensions by nationality as it were. However, Sharon too framed her approach as informed and skilled, quasi-scientific, in fact. To my hearing, it was underpinned by essentialist racial imaginaries:

> Sharon: I've worn *Brazilian*, I've worn *European*, I've worn, err, *Vietnamese* recently. . . . I've also worn *Peruvian*. Er, Indian not really 'cause it's a bit weighty. The difference is with Indian you can feel the weight, it's a bit, the other hair textures are a bit lighter than the Indian one. The Indian is a bit, you sweat a lot when it's hot, you can, yeah, you can tell the difference.
> Simi: I wonder why that is?
> Sharon: 'Cause it's a bit *thicker* than the normal, than the other hair.

Human hair is very expensive: the lowest sum that any participant reported spending was US$400, while the highest was more than US$1,500. Bisi attempted to convince me that for the spectacularly feminine woman, human hair is a more rational choice than synthetic hair because it is more cost-effective. Reasoning as an exemplary entrepreneurial subject "according to a calculus of utility, benefit, or satisfaction against a micro-economic grid of scarcity, supply and demand, and moral value-neutrality," Bisi's argument comprised a series of mathematical calculations to prove that it would quickly become more expensive to spend lesser sums of money repeatedly on synthetic hair, which can be used only once, versus a larger one-off amount on human hair, which can be reused many times.[10] An additional market value Bisi proffered in favor of human hair was that "it also has to do with investing as well." Other women also suggested this, that human hair was a good place for a woman to park her money. I queried Bisi, who happened to be a banker, on this suggestion that human hair was an economistic investment. This sparked a relatively technical exchange:

> Simi: When you say investing, I mean does it, doesn't it, er, depreciate? Presumably? I don't know.
> Bisi: The hair?
> Simi: Well, yeah, in the sense that you reuse it and reuse it, but it's not like you can—the value doesn't appreciate.

Bisi: If you treat it [well] it remains the same; it doesn't depreciate. I've
had this hair [that is, what she was wearing] for three years, and I've
used it . . .
Simi: Over and over.
Bisi: And used it and used it and used it again, over and over.

Strategic investment or not, that expending as much as the women did on
human hair constituted a specifically *feminine* rationality was indicated by
Misan, who said that her boyfriend was very keen on her wearing hair extensions: "But he's not going to give me the money for it, like 'I ain't spending
[N]100 or 80K or 70K on hair.' Like to him it's not practical, you know, and
I've met so many men like that, that will be like, okay, yes, they *appreciate
it* but they don't get it." Men appreciated or liked the hair on women, but
they did not "get" the sense in spending so much on it. Folake also did not
deem it a good sense to spend too much on human hair. She imagined that
if tempted to "*really* go crazy" and shell out a sum like N250,000, were she
to stop to consider how much this was worth in a more stable currency like
pounds sterling, namely £1,000, she would realize the true opportunity cost
and forgo the purchase: "£1,000!! I can buy a bag with that. Why would I
want to buy hair with that?" Indicating that her fashion and beauty budget
was not boundless, Folake revealed its nonetheless very considerable extent:
she was in the privileged class of women—globally privileged, I would insist—who could spend £1,000 on a handbag.

Myriad other forms of calculating, planning, imagining, and weighing up
were reportedly needed for the women to execute their look. Sharon spoke of
the need to plan to beat the crowd to the hairdressers on a Saturday morning, to try to reduce the already long hours (six to eight) that she would be
spending there. She called this "the race to getting your hair done." Misan
shared how much she would think through and try to plan in her mind's
eye the details of her intended look in advance of special occasions. For example, "If I'm going somewhere and I'm getting dressed for it, I'll actually
sit down to think what hair will go with this dress." Reflecting on this kind
and degree of thinking, which sometimes led her to the salon to change her
hairdo to complement her intended outfit, Misan wondered, "Maybe I'm too
fussy . . . like who the hell thinks about the hair they're going to wear for a
dress?" Having analyzed Misan's practice of matching her hair and outfits in
the previous chapter in terms of intensifying postfeminist appearance and
self-surveillance standards, we can understand what she decried as "fussy"
as a practical disposition that women must adopt to even attempt to meet

the standards. Any such attempt also called for sheer effort, practice, and time. Alero described herself as now thoroughly adept at doing her makeup by herself, after considerable practice. This included doing her eyebrows in accordance with a process that she had learned from makeup video tutorials on YouTube, "tutorials in hegemonic femininity" Banet-Weiser terms them, transnational in both origination and consumption, I would add.[11] I will quote Alero's description of her eyebrow process in full to convey its technical, laborious, and hypercommodified scope. The ellipses in the quote are where I interjected a clarifying question or word:

> I fill it [that is, my eyebrows] in . . . with a pencil *and* eye shadow . . . and then I make it look sharp around the edges with concealer, which I blend in, so that's why it looks very defined and then I use (*pauses*)—it's a long process— concealer, when I finish I use concealer around my eyes which highlights, it's meant to highlight your eyes 'cause it makes it brighter. I use a color below my actual [skin] color so it's light . . . and then I put foundation over that and then powder, blot powder because my skin is very oily, and then this mineralized powder just to give it a bit of a glow—all from MAC.[12]

Admitting that she put on "quite a bit of makeup" in the forty to sixty minutes that she spent on it every morning, Alero noted that her skill extended to making it look "natural": "It's not like caked on or piled up. Even though there is a lot of stuff on my face, you can't like tell."

A similar rationalizing link between long practice, established skill, and final naturalized effect was made, and positively spun, by a number of women explaining not merely physical ease but physical prowess with the highest of heels. I cited Tinu in the previous chapter stating from embodied experience that high heels improved a woman's carriage. She specified a condition: "if you master it. Like me, it's been part of my life for a very long time. Yeah, I can run with it [that is, in heels], and I can outrun you on flats." The following discussion ensued:

> Simi: How do you master it? Do you practice at home—not now, but back then [that is, when she was younger]?
> Tinu: Let me just say this thing is part of me, 'cause I've never really come out and I say, "I'm rehearsing how to walk on these shoes." I started wearing it like quite early in life.

It was in wearing heels over and over again, from "quite early in life," that they had become part of her, incorporated. Or, as Butler might put it, it was in doing femininity over and over again, reiteratively taking up the cultural injunction to be a woman, that Tinu had become one. In Tinu's own account, this had not been a conscious process: she had not been "rehearsing" as if for a role. To go again to Butler, gender is not a performance in the sense of theater or acting. This is not to say that it is enacted without any consciousness or agency, like rote. If gender is a performative style of living, the gendered subject is agentic in its *self*-stylizing.[13] In Tinu's case, this included actively choosing, buying, and wearing high heels over the years. I, on the other hand, had not; hearing that I found high heels painful, Tinu's diagnosis was "You didn't start on time; you didn't get used to it."

Problematizing the implicit voluntarism of Foucauldian notions of the self-stylizing subject variously choosing from the technologies and practices of self available to it, and, as Tinu suggested, getting used or habituated to its choices, Lois McNay points out that there are "limits of reflexivity." Deeply inscribed and normatively compelled aspects of the self, like gender, cannot be adopted or discarded at will. McNay also notes that there is an inevitable "recalcitrance of embodied existence to self-fashioning."[14] Regardless of what a subject reiteratively rendering herself a woman like Tinu might desire or choose, there would be a practical physical limit to how high she could go with her heels. The laws of gravity would at some point become determinant. Misan had experienced physical or bodily limits to her desires to self-stylize. We both laughed as she recalled an occasion when she had "really wanted to have a full head of weave," and so put on more bundles of extensions than she had found she could carry comfortably. Holding her neck out taut, Misan reenacted how wearing so much hair had been "the most uncomfortable experience. . . . It was really heavy. I remember coming out of the salon, I'm like 'Oh, my goodness, what did I do to myself?'" Misan and the other women spoke of the risks and occasional experiences of "going too far" in their pursuit and execution of spectacular femininity. The risks included that one could be misrecognized as the wrong kind of subject. I return to this moral consideration later in the discussion, and again in the next chapter. For now, the concern is with the physical and psychic risks of which the women also spoke.

RISK MANAGING THE LOOK

During the interviews, I often heard the women talk about letting one or more parts of their bodies "breathe" or "rest"—their hair, their nails, their lashes, their faces, their skin. The women were referring to a practice of taking off for a period the technologies of spectacular postfeminist feminine beauty that they deemed potentially detrimental or already experienced as such, theorized as cruel in the previous chapter. These periods of rest, breathers, were to enable both their bodies and their minds to "recover" before and in some cases for the purposes of the redeployment of the very same technologies. For instance, having said that she had taken out her false lashes shortly before the interview, Folake explained why: "'Cause I wanted my natural lashes to breathe, and you know the longer you do them [that is, false lashes], the more you do them, it weakens your natural lashes, and when you take them out, you look like you don't have lashes at all. So I just, I was just like let me take a break." I propose to call this kind of on-off dress and beauty practice "aesthetic vigilance" and to understand it as a new and specialized form of aesthetic labor incited by the certain cruelties of new postfeminist standards, technologies, and practices of feminine beauty. As heard from the women in Lagos, aesthetic vigilance entails keeping a watchful, reflexive eye on one's attachment to, and employment of, cruel feminine beauty technologies and scheduling and taking "aesthetic rest." The aim of both the vigilance and the rest was to preempt the bodily and psychic loss that the cruel technologies could engender and to encourage a subsequent return to the technologies. Thus, cruelly optimistic, aesthetic vigilance and rest were rationalized and responsibilized practices of *risk managing* one's spectacularly feminine appearance.

Detailing how she wore makeup every working day for her television show and then most weekends when she had "somewhere to go," Tobi welcomed the odd day that her face could have off: "Sometimes I don't go out on Saturday. I *loooove* the fact that on days like that my face can *rest*. I'm not wearing *any* makeup. 'Cause I mean I feel, I feel that once I give my face that rest, once I put it on again, I'll be looking too *fine!*" According to Berlant, the "return to the scene where the [cruel] object hovers in its potentialities" may not always "*feel* optimistic."[15] The surrender to one's cruel attachments may be tinged with dread or ambivalence, for example. But a happily optimistic affect is clearly palpable in Tobi's remarks above. This followed from her view, perhaps experience too, that for having had brief respite from makeup she would look even better with it subsequently. I asked Tobi if one day was "rest enough" for her face:

> Tobi: It's not, but what can I do?
> Simi: Eh, how much rest would you need ideally, to now be back to—
> Tobi: 'Cause I've been putting on—like maybe if I can do, if I can do two days without makeup, I will be happy. I will be happy.

Tobi returned to a logic of "necessary feminine evil" to account for her resignation to the fact that although one makeup-free day did not really suffice
as aesthetic rest, it was all she tended to have. The necessary evil here was the
requirement to wear makeup in both her professional and her social lives, a
norm that she left completely unquestioned. If, again, the logic and language
of necessity work to forestall resistance, to rationalize power and the normative, in Tobi's comments above they had the additionally depoliticizing effect
of construing, rationalizing, and even celebrating aesthetic vigilance as the
also necessary response. Tobi's account distilled to the following: because she
had to wear makeup virtually every day, what she therefore also had to do
was find time and space to give her face a break. In this way, aesthetic rest
became a form of "me time," which can be understood as effectively a brief,
individualized postfeminist and neoliberal retreat from the very pressures
that postfeminism and neoliberalism put women under![16] "Me time" shores
up the structures and logics that exert pressure on women, while being proffered to women as an act of empowerment. Tobi depicted her me time as
also further empowering because it was further beautifying. Not only was
it good and beneficial practice for the present, it also was an investment in
her future feminine beautiful self.

Other women equally represented their practices of aesthetic vigilance
and rest as empowered and empowering by proffering them as the informed,
responsible, and strategic thing to do so as to continue to pursue and achieve
their desired look. In this the women once again positioned themselves as
knowing and agentic feminine consumer subjects, women who knew how
to do their dress, how to make it work. Diane positioned me as also knowing when, describing her typical routine for getting dressed in the morning,
she made an aside about her use of an exfoliating face scrub: "[I] use my
scrub 'cause I use makeup every day to work—like we all know makeup is
not good for the skin, your skin has to breathe, and with the kind of job I
do, I see people every day, so I know I have to look nice every day." Here
face scrub was constructed as a tool for Diane to risk manage the potentially
adverse effects on her skin of her daily need for makeup. Yet it transpired
that she also had to risk manage her use of the scrub! Having said that she
used the scrub several times a week, Diane later made a casual error about
this frequency and corrected herself with another aside: "I use my scrub
every morning—not every morning 'cause it's not good . . ." Hearing from
and performatively reenacting my own feminine consumer subjectivity and
know-how, I took it that Diane meant that too frequent use of an exfoliating
face scrub could be harsh on one's skin. I concurred: "Yeah, a few times a

week." In this example, the commodified solution (makeup) to the putative core and baseline feminine problem of inadequate beauty could engender a new problem (bad skin) for which there was another commodity solution (exfoliating scrub), which could engender yet other beauty problems, and so on. For this kind of iterative and arguably exhausting aesthetic dilemma, vigilance became the solution. The possibility of saying no to it all, such as foregoing makeup altogether, was not so much as mooted.

Weaves constituted another potential iterative aesthetic dilemma. While their promise was to solve hair problems, in practice weaves called for their own vigilance because, such as discussed in reference to Sade in chapter 2, they could engender a new and possibly worse beauty problem in the form of hair loss—traction alopecia. But as in Sade's experience, and as Adaeze also explained, if this new problem arose, wigs offered a further solution. Adaeze brought up this example of wigs solving weave-induced beauty problems after hearing me say that many of the other women whom I had interviewed had spoken in terms of the on-off dress practice that I have been discussing here. Seeking to explain why a woman might return to a feminine product or practice that she recognized as risky, Adaeze said, "You know, it's addictive, though, like the weave, for instance. I started wearing wigs because the weave does actually damage your hair, so just, you have to change things up. But you get so used to how you look that when you don't have a weave, you don't think you don't look good [sic]. If you don't have [false] eyelashes, if it's something you're used to, you don't feel you look good." Adaeze's theory, and implied experience, of the addictiveness of the spectacularly feminine look speaks to Chika's difficulty in severing her attachment to foundation as well as to Tinu's feelings about her false eyelashes. Tinu explained that she had recently come to notice that she did not quite feel good about herself, indeed did not quite feel herself, without the lashes that she habitually wore. She described vividly how she would find herself feeling when she did not have the lashes on: "I feel something is wrong with my face. I look at the mirror. I'll say, 'Oh God, what is wrong, why am I looking so pale, so ugly and I'm looking sick?'" Concerned that she was becoming almost psychically dependent on false eyelashes, to the point of self-misrecognition and self-alienation, Tinu explained that she now "deliberately weaned" herself off them. But she always put them back on, she explained, when she had to appear publicly as a Nollywood celebrity. This was not a cruelly optimistic move but a strategic entrepreneurial one, a boosting of her "brand."

Theorizing the rationalities and sensibilities that govern the neoliberal subject in the realm of consumption versus production, Sam Binkley cautions against simply assuming that these, too, must be entrepreneurial. "Like the entrepreneur, the freedom of the consumer is the freedom to transform the self by stepping back in thought, but the medium of such thinking is not that of instrumental planning but of something quite different—it is one of fantasy, play, distraction and imaginary escape." My research subjects' accounts of and manifest and latent attitudes toward their fashion and dress consumption contradict Binkley's proposition, however. While not therefore devoid of fantasy, play, pleasure, eroticism, and so on, in its organization, coordination, and execution, in the making it happen, the women's fashion and beauty consumption *was* characterized and underpinned by "calculative dispositions."[17] That feminine beauty is a form and site and process of work or labor at the same time that it might constitute and be felt as play and pleasure is a feminist insight.[18] Arguing that the concept of aesthetic labor, the labor of looking good, has applicability and thus should be extended beyond the workplace, Ana Elias, Rosalind Gill, and Christina Scharff go further yet to contend that neoliberalism and postfeminism demand of women not only aesthetic labor but also what they call "aesthetic entrepreneurship."[19] Aesthetic entrepreneurship can be defined as a disposition toward and execution of aesthetic labor characterized by concerted and responsibilized planning, calculating, investing, maximizing, risk managing, and so on. It is a heightened work on and of both body and mind incited by postfeminist cultural conditions that not only position women under a luminous glare but also posit feminine beauty as feminine power. It means and entails governance by a new rationality that, with all that it entails and all that it says it will do, feminine beauty is now a most serious business and so must be pursued accordingly.

FINANCING THE LOOK

The women claimed to pay for the whole business of their dress by themselves, or, in the case of the three who were still students, said that they would or expected to do so once they were no longer financially dependent on their parents. While these claims were certainly continuous with, and bolstered, the women's self-representation as the kinds who did or handled it all, it would be a mistake to gloss the claims themselves as postfeminist. Although interrupted to some degree by colonialism and Christianization, in much of West Africa the norm, long predating second-wave feminism in the West, is for women to pursue independent incomes, in demarcated spheres such as farming and trade traditionally. In her book about the making of "modern"

Lagos women across class lines in the late nineteenth and early twentieth centuries, Abosede George writes that in "traditional Yoruba communities in Lagos and the broader region, women of various faiths worked outside of their homes as farmers, traders, and artisans, and they grounded their respectability as women in their roles of providers." What was new and imported (and elite) at the time, Kristin Mann corroborates, was for married women to be financially dependent on their husbands.[20] Indeed, that wives were not ordinarily dependent in this way and that "spouses generally did not pool their incomes" were among the justifications that the British colonialists gave for not paying Nigerian male laborers wages that could support entire families.[21] Women's roles as traders had and still have enabling implications for their fashion and beauty practice. Esi Dogbe notes, for instance, that Ghanaian women's "history of controlling the distribution and retail of cloth has enabled them to forge avenues of economic self-reliance, in addition to setting new fashion trends," while Nina Sylvanus discusses similar patterns elsewhere along the West African coast.[22]

The foregoing is not to paint a rosy picture of African women's ability to consume independently, or indeed at all. It is to make and briefly situate the claim that, as with the women in this book who did not present themselves as doing anything special in this regard, the mere fact that a Nigerian woman would pursue, expect, and manage some income of her own is neither new nor noteworthy. It is a long-standing social and cultural expectation. Saying along these lines that she was expected to "hold [her] own," Folake, for instance, explained that her family's attitude toward her professional life was that "you're not sent to school, they didn't spend all this money on your education for you to be, you know, just another person on the road. You have to stand out, you have to stand out, you have to work out to get to where it is you want to get to." Other than the students all the women worked outside the home, and all the students voiced future career ambitions. June, a corporate professional, explained that she had hardly dressed up when she had been a student, back when she had been reliant on her parents. It was only after graduating from university, she recalled, that she had started to ask herself: "Okay, what can I buy?" She was talking about an increasing lure and subjectification by feminine consumer culture, as she had acquired also increasing and, importantly, independent means to engage. According to June, the invitation to "up" her feminine consumption was ongoing. Asked how much she spent on hair extensions, June explained that before "the advent" of human hair, "we were using the synthetics, which were much cheaper. . . . So my budget has actually grown. This [that is, the weave she had on] cost me I think 150 thousand [approximately US$1,000] but before, you know, a lot cheaper, cheaper, cheaper." She reflected, "As you get older and probably if you move on in your career . . . your income gets bigger, so you can afford what you couldn't afford before." Casually and indirectly conveying that her expensive style of dress was materially enabled by her career, June rendered this "obvious" and unremarkable.

Where the women were concerted and assertive in seeking to make plain that they exercised relative financial independence was only if and when the theme of transactional heterosex came up, as in the interview with Funke, another corporate professional. Hearing Funke enumerate a range of things that were important to her as a thirtysomething single woman in Lagos, which included career, "leadership qualities," and finding happiness and contentment, including outside of marriage, I ventured financial independence for her consideration. She replied affirmatively and swiftly:

> Funke: Very important too, you know. *Very*, very important. You need to identify opportunities, decide on, em, an alternative source of income [that is, beyond one's salary], and, em, being able to, em (*long pause*), maintain a standard of living without having to resort to what some, a lot of women, let's just say some, lots of women are *doing now*, where they just feel that they should be supported by men.
> Simi: A man.
> Funke: Yeah, they feel they should be supported—morally right, morally wrong—they just, em, some people's extra source of income is *a man.*

Funke did not state explicitly the morally questionable thing that she was alleging "lots of women" were doing nowadays to supplement their incomes, but as a young Lagos woman myself, I got it: I recognized what I have already called a trope, a stereotyped and primed pattern of meaning, implication, explanation. Minutes after Funke's remarks, I named the trope openly when I recounted to her my experience in the field, of encountering and resisting the view of some of my friends and family that the spectacularly feminine Lagos woman whom I was researching was necessarily a "runs girl"—runs girl, again, is a local slang name for young women said to be engaged in transactional romantic or sexual nonmarital relationships, typically with older men. Laughing, Funke asked whether it was only this type of woman who dressed in the style I was researching; *she* was participating in the research, after all. She next sidestepped any association or conflation with the morally troubled feminine type by describing an alternate way in which her fashion and beauty expenditure had been judged: "Someone asked me that what's the most expensive hair I have, and I said, 'Em, it was N140,000' [approximately US$900] . . . and she [screamed] '*Eeeeh!*' And I said, 'Why, is it expensive?' and she said, 'Yeah, it's very expensive.' I said, 'Well, I could pay three times you know [that is, in installments], and besides I can afford to buy. I'm working, you know.'" It was not the source of Funke's funds for fashion and beauty but her financial priorities that had been called into question. In the short narrative that she offered, being judged as irresponsible with money, unpleasant as it may have been, worked to confirm that the money in question was properly her own, placing its provenance beyond doubt or reproach. As such, that Funke had reportedly pointed out to the person judging her that she funded her fashion and beauty consumption by herself ("I'm working, you know") was not a necessary or literal rendering of how she did what she did but a rhetorical one. It was to remind of, and ground, her *moral* right to do what she liked with her money, to expend as spectacularly as she wished.

Speaking to hypothetical onlookers who might disapprove of her mode of dress, Amaka reasoned in a similar way, "If you're not paying my bills, nothing like that, I'm sorry: I'm paying, I'm dressing for myself. So if you like it, fine. If you do not like it, that's your problem, but you know I dress for me at the end of the day, so if someone wants to stare, if they appreciate it, fine; if they don't appreciate it, I really don't care." That she paid for her dress on her own became further proof and ammunition for Amaka's repeated assertive self-positioning in the interview as a self-pleasing and self-regarding postfeminist subject. She dressed by herself, for herself, was the long and short of her position. And she neither expected nor sought to be funded by a man someday, Amaka explained, because she imagined that this would compromise her independence. Bisi also shared this last view. She stated that she did not want to be married to a man before she had attained meaningful earning power, to ensure that she would have standing in her marital home. She also linked her intent to retain independent financial capacity in marriage to her intent to continue what she admitted was a "high maintenance" dress practice. Her reasoning: "'Cause it makes me happy, I won't wait for anybody to do that for me." I asked Bisi what she meant by high maintenance, to which she explained that it was a term men used to describe women who dressed and appeared like her: "Oh, that's what Lagos guys say, 'high-maintenance girls,' when you have to buy them [human] *hair*, or when they, or when you see a girl and she already has Brazilian hair and [then Lagos guys think] 'Ah, this girl, what can I, what can I say to her?'"

At odds with Bisi's claim that the prospect of spending on spectacular feminine consumption scared away "Lagos guys" was the view of Chika, Alero, and two others that it was actually men who instigated transactional modes of heterosexual relating, purposely seeking to attract women with lavish gifts. Chika mused, "It's crazy, it's crazy, being a woman in Lagos, it's crazy, and how, you know, how *common* it is for [men] to just tell you they want to whisk you somewhere"—to romantic destinations like Paris, she meant. Alero opined that Nigerian men enjoyed propositioning women as a masculinist performance. She described it as "a Nigerian thing. . . . Nigerian guys just like to be known for taking care of girls." In her experience, this meant navigating not only unwanted male propositions but also other people's assumptions and judgments that one had accepted and benefited from such propositions. Alero mentioned a man she was casually dating who, she claimed, had offered her gifts like international flight tickets and expensive items of dress. Avowing that she was not "into the whole living off people," she expressed a strict stance toward these kinds of offers from this man:

> Alero: He tries to buy me shoes, and I was like "Em, I'm okay, I just bought it myself." So he likes the whole, *he* likes the whole taking care of you thing, doing this and doing that, yeah.
> Simi: But you're not really into that?
> Alero: No, I'm not that, I'm not into it *o*. . . . I know I have age mates [that is, peers] who, you know, are known for following guys with money, and you know, and I don't really like, that's like the *worst thing* I think that I could be known for.

Alero's strong concern was to not be misapprehended as the type of woman motivated in her relationships with men by material gain, a "gold digger" in everyday sexist parlance. Her concern included misrecognition by me in the interview. Not only did she stress that "*he*," the man she was talking about, was the one into such practices, where she said, "No, I'm not that, I'm not into it *o*," I hear the reiteration in the second phrase plus the appending of the Yoruba word "*o*" for added emphasis as directed squarely at me to make clear an unequivocal position, had *I* any doubt. Self-positioning in talk is very much fueled by a micro-interactionist orientation and moralized accounting.[23] But if it is clear that Alero was orienting here to the interview exchange, the exchange itself cannot be understood fully outside the local discursive and moral context in which it was situated and to which it was also geared. Alleged and hinted at in Funke's, Chika's, and Alero's foregoing comments, the context is one of heightened imagination, talk, suspicion, even moral panic, that transactional heterosexual relationships are a systematic occurrence in Lagos; that "it's crazy, it's crazy . . . how *common* it is," to recite Chika; that "following guys with money," as Alero's put it, is in actuality what many a young Lagos woman is doing and is wont to do.

Very briefly, extensive research—mostly in the field of public health and concerned with the implications for the spread of HIV—suggests that in diverse African contexts, there are common and marked cultural expectations and practices of gift giving in exchange for romance or sex (or both), from men to women.[24] Suzanne Leclerc-Madlala argues that the young women in her study, in a Durban township, see transactional sex as "normal," while also in reference to South Africa Marc Hunter proposes and historicizes the notion of a masculine "provider love" as distinct from, if enmeshed increasingly with, "romantic love." In her research on experiences and perceptions of female students at the University of Ibadan, an institution less than two hours away from Lagos, Abiola Odejide finds "recurring references to the existence of transactional sex and the alleged preference of some of the female students for "*aristos*" [for "aristocrats"], sugar daddies" and the like. The said prevalence of transactional sex in Africa has been attributed to gendered inequality of access to material resources, to broader cultures of (mostly male) patronage, and to contextually meaningful "notions of gender, love and exchange." The express concern of scholars like Leclerc-Madlala and Tsitsi Masvawure is to show that, for young urban women, the practice is motivated less by subsistence and survival than desires to consume, to have "flashy" things. However, noting that the not inconsiderable degree of attention to the materiality of love and sex in Africa can be pathologizing, and racist, Tamara Shefer, Lindsay Clowes, and Tania Vergnani remind that the "exchange of sex for material goods or other gains is universal and embedded in normative heterosexual relationships, especially in a consumerist, materialist global context."[25] This makes it impossible to definitively isolate or set apart a category of "transactional sex" and foregrounds that transactional sex is, of course, a matter of construction—allegation, rumor, moral consternation, and so on, as well.

Although it takes at least two to heterosexually transact and exchange, in Lagos as elsewhere on the continent, public discourses and imaginaries about the phenomenon are predominantly about, and panicked by, the female side of the equation. The men are at most spectral figures in the discussion.[26] Onookome Okome, discussing the iterative presence of the transacting "good-time girl" in Nollywood film, states that this figure has sedimented into "social fact" across Africa. The details and media of her figuration may change, but she has been and remains a "fixture in the landscape of the city." This figuration, this fixing of a type—a type of femme fatale, Okome suggests—can be traced back and attributed to the times and vast social, cultural, and economic dislocations of colonial urbanization when, moving to, finding work in, and embracing modern lifestyles in the city, young women were moving outside traditional bounds, which is also to say male control.[27] The consolidation and sedimentation of "transactional sex" into an explanatory repertoire to account for the appearance and possibility of urban consuming women are also an effect of the subsequent and continued failings and frustrations of the postcolony. It is a scapegoating of women for larger structural problems, such as in the closely interrelated panics over "indecent dressing." Thus, as I have already suggested and begun to show in the foregoing discussion, operating as a relative local common sense, a ready-made way of already knowing and recognizing what lies behind young women's consumerist lifestyles, transactional sex was a suspicion, a specter, that hung over the spectacularly consuming women of my research, from which they therefore had to dissociate.

Chika brought up the issue by effectively refusing to bring it up. She did so in the context of telling me that since she had moved back to Nigeria after many years studying abroad, she had developed a taste for designer handbags and started to acquire them. She justified this as "a treat" for herself. Still by way of justification, Chika started to add that it was not as if "someone" was buying her the bags. In other words, the further justification for her luxurious consumption was that she was funding it by herself. But having invoked the possibility that there could be a shadowy "someone" enabling her expensive dress taste, Chika stopped herself from pursuing what both her pause and her subsequent aside suggested was a troublesome line of discussion about a common and well-known issue in Nigeria: "I'm like treating myself, it's not like (*pauses*) someone, you know it's not like—I don't want to talk about Nigeria and what happens—but anyway it's a treat for myself so (*pauses*) . . ." Once again, from my local positionality and local discursive resourcing, it was unambiguously clear to me what Chika was referencing, as I believe that she knew it would be. Like in the exchanges with Funke and Alero cited earlier, the trope of transactional sex constituted the "taken for granted discursive back-cloth" that rendered this slice of the conversation, indeed what was effectively a silence, intelligible.[28]

Given that Chika had made it clear to me that she did not want to talk about "what happens" in Nigeria, after an awkward pause I changed the topic completely and asked how she tended to style her hair. However, the theme of transactional sex came up again later in the interview, when Chika was describing

Lagos as a particularly materialistic and showy place. This, she suggested, might explain "the phenomenon of all these like (*drops voice slightly*) sugar daddies." Continuing to express hesitation to broach the topic, Chika nonetheless went on to allege that it was "very, very, very common," not "like a folklore thing," for young Lagos women to have sugar daddies. This included women within her already privileged social circles who were thereby enabled to do fashion and beauty and "jet-setting" all the more extravagantly, she claimed. I asked Chika, whose shoes and handbag were monogrammed with the Chanel logo, if all this impacted how she presented herself, given that onlookers might see her manifestly expensive style of dress through such a locally dominant lens. Otherwise put, my question was if and how she had to negotiate a label like "runs girl" in light of what she was purporting as its real and close prevalence. Before sharing an experience of having once been suspected to be this kind of feminine subject, Chika, like Alero, made sure to communicate plainly to me that she was *not*: "You know, it's a funny thing that—I mean I *do not* do it." The "funny thing" that she went on to recount was a conversation in which a female friend had asked who exactly had paid for some of Chika's new dress purchases, doubting that Chika could have afforded these things by herself. Chika said that she shrugged off such skeptical views and, in terms of her dress, continued to proceed in her own terms: "'Cause I know what I know. . . . I just carry on like I would normally carry on."

Sade, however, considered that these kinds of question marks around how a young Lagos woman came to appear were too potent, and potentially too detrimental, to be dismissed or resignified with a self-referential shrug. The social and moral risks of being misrecognized as "the wrong type" meant that one could not always simply dress up and step out as one pleased. To illustrate her point, Sade referred back to when she had been a university student, reasoning that had she appeared in her present, expensive style back then, she would have been seen as "a spoon-fed kid or a hooker." She contrasted this with her easy and obvious capacity to now afford the look by herself and thus not attract suspicion: "As an adult, grown earning power, yeah, nobody is gonna flinch if you roll up with some article of (*pauses*) grandeur." Her spectacular feminine consumption was not only a result of her empowered adult femininity, but, for anyone who might be looking and wondering, also a signal of it. But here I want to draw out the fine yet crucial distinction that I have already proposed earlier in the discussion, to argue that, for the women whom I interviewed in Lagos, the imperative to afford one's own dress did not arise from the new mode of feminine empowerment and independence that the women were otherwise quick and keen to claim. Rather, it had to do with very old values of feminine sexual propriety and respectability.

The one exception, which, I would argue gestures toward what I am pro-
posing was the more typical rule among the women, came from Funke. Of
the purported type of Nigerian woman who took men as an "extra source
of income," from whom she dissociated, Funke said, "I think, em, women
should have moved beyond that stage by now. . . . Nigerian women should
have gone beyond that stage by now and, em, and started thinking progressively. . . . I seriously think women need to be, em, they need to empower
themselves some more and stop being dependent. Yeah. I think we've gone,
we need to move beyond that stage." This was yet another instance of the
kind of self-positioning as "already empowered" versus "still disempowered"
others that I am arguing in this book is central to how postfeminism can take
root and make sense in a place like Lagos without reference to feminism or
feminist history per se. But compare Funke's thinking about new versus old
or outdated Nigerian feminine attitudes toward male financial patronage to
Bisi's morally loaded viewpoint and language. Like Chika, Bisi happened to
be toting a handbag branded Chanel in her interview, which she said had
been a gift from a relative. Sighing twice, deeply, when I brought up talk of
transactional sex in Lagos, Bisi explained that the bag was the first and only
designer bag that she owned and that she could not fathom why a woman
would sleep with a man to get her hands on such a transient and material
thing: "[Why] degrade yourself 'cause of a designer bag that will probably
go out of season and you degrade yourself again to get the new one? So how
long will you do that for is the question I always ask . . . ? Why bother when
you might carry a plain, simple, nice bag that you can afford yourself and
still look as good?" In a place where transactional heterosex was imagined
and said to be "very, very, very common," not "like a folklore thing," to again
recall Chika's emphatic wording, it became imperative to dress within the
bounds of what one could afford and morally account for or what could be
audited satisfactorily. Within these bounds, where all the women located
themselves implicitly or explicitly, their attitude to spectacularly consuming
fashion and beauty could be summed up by Kim's enthusiastic remark: "Go
ahead and do it!"

GOING FOR THE LOOK
("YOU KNOW WHAT, SCREW IT")

Kim expressed the words just above while telling me that the cheapest human
hair extensions that she had ever bought had cost about US$400, whereas
she was now buying and wearing hair in the range of $1,000 to $1,500. Paint-
ing excessive and entitled consumption as an essentially feminine practice,

she continued, "There's absolutely nothing wrong with just having two or three bundles of hair that you can, you know, keep reusing. But because we're women and we tend to buy things that we like, and you want as much variety as possible, you would have, for some people, twenty, thirty different [bundles]." Other women confirmed that they owned a lot of fashion and beauty stuff. Referring to her makeup kit, Folake said, "I have all the brushes, I have all the MAC brushes for blending. . . . You know, we just buy them, but I don't really know how to use it." With regard to her shoe collection, she explained, similarly, that some of her purchases were motivated more by their affective and aesthetic than use value: "I wear flats a lot, but I also buy a lot of heels because, em, you know sometimes they're just nice to have, nice to look at. I have shoes I haven't worn." Diane offered to show me just how much she consumed with the words: "If you wanna see, I have like a thousand perfumes in my wardrobe (*both laugh*). I just got three more [today]." Explaining why she had such an extensive and expanding wardrobe, Diane cited a "retail-therapy repertoire," declaring, "I love shopping. It makes me happy. When I'm unhappy, I shop."[29]

In addition to notions that consuming makes one happy, part of what postfeminism sells women is "guilt-free consumerism" via suggestions that they have earned it—in multiple senses of the term.[30] Sade very much subscribed to this promise. She embraced the postfeminist subject position that Lazar calls "entitled femininity," attributing her doing so again to the fact that she was now a career woman paying her own way. In her interview as a whole, Sade offered a highly "'storied narrative' of the self," giving me right from the outset of our conversation a carefully plotted and temporalized account of just how and why, and when and where, she had come to desire and dress in her current spectacularly feminine style.[31] Her narrative had a distinct "past versus present" structure. For example, she recalled that while she had been at university abroad, going to a professional salon had been out of the question because it was "too damn expensive," such that she had had to "DIY it, you know"—DIY meaning "do it yourself." But in the present, as a career woman and also back in Lagos where she found professional beauty labor inexpensive, it was with a casually entitled air that Sade spoke about going to have her false eyelashes professionally applied on an occasion when a relative who usually put in the lashes for her had been unavailable: "She wasn't around, and I just was like, you know what, screw it, and I went and got it done."

Lazar argues that "there is a certain 'knowingness' that underlies [postfeminist consumerist] entitlement which allows for the construction of a narcissistic, confident and fun female subjectivity."[32] Sade expressed as much when she reasoned:

> I think because of age or because of growth, age-wise and career-wise, you know the compartments are beginning to fall into place where you know now I can, I can actually aff—I can, I can be a girl! You know, I can, I can just sit back, and you know, you know I can go to the market and look at fabric and buy fabric (*claps her hands*) and that kind of stuff and get things sewn, and you know now I can, I can indulge in fashion, 'cause like, 'cause I think it's an indulgence. It's luxury, you indulge it.

I presume that where Sade said "I can actually aff—I can, I can be a girl!" the word that she did not complete was *afford*. Whether my presumption is correct or not, the notion of finally affording to be a girl as an adult woman was communicated in Sade's comments at this and other parts of her interview, and it stuck with me from the time we spoke. In one later reading of the interview transcript, I scribbled with reference to Sade's incomplete remark: "Infantilizing of adult femininity!" Yet I later shifted somewhat from this analytic take, not least because of the example that Sade had given, of being able to go to the market, buy fabrics that she liked, commission and manage a tailor to sew her outfits, and so on. This is one common route through which adult Nigerian women, across class, acquire new and uniquely designed clothes and is certainly not infantile.[33]

Rather than reading Sade as citing and performing an infantilizing logic, my later analysis, to which her own language directly points, is that she was talking about a postfeminist girling of adult femininity. I want to propose that this is closely related to but not quite or necessarily the same thing as an infantilizing. Here I differ from Lazar, who sees postfeminist girling as inciting a "juvenile" and "cutesy" femininity, and McRobbie, who figures the postfeminist masquerade as "silly," with her nervous giggling and so on.[34] Such representations of adult femininity abound in popular postfeminist media, too.[35] Yet for the most part, girliness was not constructed or performed in such ways by the women in the interviews, and where it was it was with utmost knowing, as play. My contention is that, for the women, girliness meant playing at a hyperstylized, hyperconsumerist, hyperfeminine identity, not a childish one. It meant dolling oneself up, not, say, playing with dolls. Moreover, this mode of girliness was very much predicated upon, and in turn signifying, an adult feminine subjectivity and positionality. To play at girliness required distance from being a girl in the sense of a child or minor. First, it required an adult position from which to reflexively and knowingly self-stylize. It also required adulthood practically and materially, to afford what was in practice an expensive style of self.

I earlier quoted Chika describing her consumption of designer bags as a treat for herself. She brought this up with what I heard as a slightly embarrassed laugh. Jokingly disclaiming the bags as a "terrible habit," Chika, who would not specify her age in the interview beyond saying that she was in her midtwenties, added, "But I also think I, it's age appropriate for me, 'cause I'm at that age where like I can afford to buy them for myself, so I feel like it's like a treat, like it's like, er, you know, like how far I've come kinda thing." For Sharon, routinely visiting a spa was also a reflection and result of how far her career had progressed. She explained that as a celebrity with several media platforms and a wide audience, her spa trips were often complimentary gifts from the service providers, the expectation being that she would publicize them. Thus, although she did not pay for the luxury out of pocket, she had paid her dues, professionally. As she represented it, for a busy and successful professional woman like her, the biggest obstacle to having a "spa day" was simply time. Time was also a constraining factor in Adaeze's pursuit of the full extent of the luxurious feminine consumption that she desired, in her case because she was a mother to young children. She did not reference any question of cost when explaining that, time permitting, she would love to "do like a body polish like every week." By contrast, Kim stated that the £200 to £300 that she spent at the spa was undeniably a factor in her ability to go only about once a month.

In these kinds of remarks, and across the body of interviews as a whole, the women almost never commented or reflected upon just how expensive, just how privileged, their spectacular dress practice was, in itself and all the more in the relative context of Lagos and Nigeria. At a most fundamental and implicit level, prior to and deeper than new postfeminist consumer sensibilities and promises, their sense of entitlement was rooted in their immense class privilege. Kemi was the only one to express pause over the cost of the whole exercise, but only briefly. A postgraduate student funded by her parents, she noted that the limit that she would spend presently on human hair was N100,000 (approximately US$600), but "even when I think of spending 100,000 on hair, I think it's a bit ridiculous." She described an occasion when, in the absence of her mother, who typically gave her the money for the hair, she had approached her father. She depicted him as forthcoming until he fully grasped the magnitude of the sum involved: "He's like 'You can't, I can't give you that much money for hair, I can't, you have to ask your mummy.' . . . He's like 'That's someone's salary, like what do you mean, you want to use it to buy hair?"' To put the local value of N100,000 in greater context, as of the time of the interviews in 2013, albeit considered by many to be a poverty wage, the national monthly minimum wage was N18,000 (and still is as of the time of this writing, almost five years later). Kemi concluded of the typical cost of her hair extensions: "So yes, it sounds ridiculous I guess, sometimes when you think about it specifically."

But having thought specifically, and in this critically, about the considerable expense of her style in the context of the interview, Kemi did not suggest that she would renounce it or that she had been asked or expected to by her father. That her father had reportedly redirected her request for money to her mother speaks to my contention earlier that if and when spending vast sums on intensifying and extensifying postfeminist fashion and beauty technologies made sense, it was as women's sense. But appearing in spectacular style also made a particular, local classed sense, representing and communicating an elite positionality—which might well be why Kemi's father redirected and therein sanctioned the continuance of his daughter's spectacular expenditure.

4

GLOBALLY BLACK, "NAIJA," AND FABULOUS

ASSERTING AUTHENTIC SELVES

In a 2013 publicity interview for her then new novel, *Americanah*, of which a central theme is black women's often fraught relationships with their hair, the internationally renowned Nigerian feminist author Chimamanda Ngozi Adichie declared: "I am a bit of a fundamentalist when it comes to black women's hair. Hair is hair—yet also about larger questions: self-acceptance, insecurity and what the world tells you is beautiful. For many black women, the idea of wearing their hair naturally is unbearable."[1] At the time Adichie made these remarks, I happened to be in Lagos conducting interviews for this book, which is to say speaking to black women for whom weaves, and to a lesser extent wigs, were standard, daily fare. The women's point of view, voiced in direct and defensive response to Adichie's comments in one case, was that their weaves and wigs were "just" weaves and wigs: just fashion, just choice, not a psychological or political matter, not even about race as such. Diametrically opposed are the kinds of views that Adichie called "fundamentalist." Here, the broad contention is that black people, women and men, should wear our hair in its given state as a matter of black pride, nationalism, and antiracism and that failing to do so, appearing with hair other than "nature" intended, constitutes and reveals a racial inferiority complex, maybe even self-hatred, being an orientation to a "white aesthetic."

These fundamentalist views of black hair practice are at the ready, from black and other feminist scholarship to popular talk, in Africa and the diaspora. Women appearing in wigs in 1960s West Cameroon were accused of "being race-traitors and 'un-African'" by disapproving male commentators. "Our women don't look beautiful in these wigs," declared one of these men, writing in to a local newspaper. "So let wigs give way to simple Cameroonian hairdo."[2] Looking at a magazine cover image of Diana Ross posed naked but for an extralong black weave running down her back, what bell hooks sees is not that Ross does not look good, but, rather, "the longing that is most visible in this cover is that of the black woman to embody and be encircled by whiteness, personified by the possession of long straight hair."[3] Cheryl Thompson hears a range of perspectives from the black Canadian women whom she interviews on why they chemically straighten their hair or wear weaves, including that the look of their hair impacts their employability. Nonetheless, like hooks's, her conclusions psychologize and moralize and also place responsibility for the issue squarely upon black women: "Until Black women (including 'mixed race' women, who may not necessarily process or weave their natural hair) collectively agree that hair alternation stunts any potential to overcome the legacy of slavery and a multi-generational pathology of self-hatred, hair will always be a contentious (and debated) issue."[4] According to participants on a South African television debate on the topic "Natural vs. Weave," the problem is that black women in the latter camp "mimic the standards of beauty set by whites, standards which [push] them to seek to distance themselves from their natural black African hair, seen and treated as inferior."[5]

I am in full alignment with Shirley Tate's crucial black feminist intervention to debunk the "myth," as she calls it, that "still circulates in feminist writings on beauty . . . [namely,] that all 'Black women want to be white,' because white beauty is iconic."[6] Cited and recited in the literature with little critical interrogation or empirical demonstration, a scholarly performative, this myth fails to appreciate that black beauty is a complex construct in its own right and among other things one that cannot be reduced to an either-or centered on whiteness: that is to say, reduced to either strict and stark opposition to or putative imitation of white beauty—an Afro versus a weave, say. It also misunderstands the very nature of racialized beauty—indeed beauty of whatever form. Ably shown by Tate across her proliferating body of work on the theme is that racialized beauty is performative.[7] It is a matter of doing, styling, incorporating, naming, and claiming, and in all this "race-ing." It racializes the body to which it is attached and is recursively racialized by this multiply racialized body. For these reasons and more, black beauty is multiple and fluid. Indeed, "the multiplicity of race-ing stylization possibilities which exist for Black women and which have been built up over centuries and embedded in our habitus means that what is iconic [for Black women] is *Black* beauty."[8] This is certainly what I gleaned from the women in Lagos on the question of whom they looked to as style icons: The answers were almost exclusively black. And, reflecting that "relationships between different Black communities are structured no less by dynamics of power and hegemony,"[9] the answers were almost exclusively American: Beyoncé, Halle Berry, Solange, NeNe Leakes, and the like. Specifying that she followed "African-American, not just American, African-American" celebrity gossip blogs like *Necole Bitchie* and *The Young, Black and Fabulous*, Amaka explained that they profiled stars like Halle Berry instead of, for instance, Nicole Kidman. About the latter, she had the following to say: "Can't be arsed." Her primary interest and investment were in *black* celebrities, *black* styles, *black* feminine beauty.

"Black girly choice" was, in sum, how the women constructed and legitimated their weaves and wigs, continuing—and racializing—the kinds of celebratory and apolitical postfeminist logics that we have heard in the previous two chapters. They also aligned themselves with the many black women around the world who made the same choice. Their reasoning recited long-standing devaluations of black hair, however, including as not girly enough. Thus, once again, their happy claims overlaid a structured unhappiness. Thinking with this unhappiness, with the fundamental roots of black hair alteration practices in white supremacist structures and violences, I propose a new and crucial conceptual understanding of weaves and wigs as not only cruelly optimistic technologies of spectacular femininity, as I have already argued, but, for black women specifically, constitutively "unhappy" too—"unhappy technologies," I call them. Conceptualizing these hairstyles as such allows us much. In the first place, understanding weaves and wigs as technologies of blackness allows us to admit them into the doing of black feminine beauty and so to actually hear and respect black women in the styles when they say that it is *this* that they are up to, not mimicking or desiring whiteness. We admit the hairstyles critically, though, melancholically even, without forgetting or seeking to wish away the painful histories and conditions that render them so desirable for many black women. This dual move allows us to keep white supremacy and antiblack racism firmly in view, but without reducing black psyches and practices to these adverse forces, as if white supremacy means that black people do not still desire, have, and do our own things.

Certainly it is a "Naija thing"—"Naija" is youth slang for both "Nigeria" and "Nigerian"—to get all dressed and done up. The women's spectacularly feminine style articulated with the local culture and sensibility of classed display and performance briefly introduced in chapter 1, such that they felt a greater need for the style, and a greater place in it, at home than abroad. In Nigeria for your presence to be even registered, much less respected, "you just have to look like you have stepped out of the page of a magazine," Sade explained. "That's just how it is here." Cognizant that the women's "here" was the very much privileged sides and circles of Lagos, I map its contours, and argue that the women imagined and navigated the city as comprising multiple spatiotemporalities, with accompanying sensibilities, that were more or less postfeminist and cosmopolitan. While locating themselves in the "progressive" and transnational present of postfeminism, the women asserted a simultaneous grounding in the equally present, alternative temporal and cultural order of "tradition." They were and were not like other young postfeminist women in other places, then; they were "complexly coeval," which is to say living, negotiating, and reconciling multiple different frames of time and mind at the same time.[10]

WEAVES AND WIGS AS SELF-TRANSCENDENCE

Sharon told me that she had gone through a phase "for so long" during which she had worn weaves of about thirty-two inches in length that reached down to her bottom. I asked her what it was like having hair this long, to which she first joked that it was a little impractical: "There's hair everywhere (*briefly laughs*). Apart from that, it's fabulous, it's sleek, it's gorgeous. You walk down the road, and it transforms [you]." In chapter 2 I named weaves as one of the elements of the women's dress that they constructed and experienced as beautifying, feminizing, and (therefore) empowering. Six of the women commented that their weaves enhanced and beautified by affording them a fuller or thicker head of hair than they had otherwise. Ima, for instance, categorized her own hair as "quite long," almost as long as the shoulder-length weave that she had on in the interview, "but it doesn't have the same like, it's not full, you know, a little bit limp." For three others, a central attraction of weaves was the extra length that they could confer. Beyond length and volume, the stylistic options that the women reported experimenting or playing with were texture, cut, and color. Sharon enumerated some of the looks that she had tried: "long locks, curly, waves, straight, bangs. I've done it all." Alero explained that she was easily bored with the look of her hair, hence constantly changing it: "I try to be very creative with my hair. Like now my hair [that is, weave] is blonde, last month it was black, and the month before that it was red—well, not *bright* red but deep red—so I'm usually, 'cause I get bored with my hair really easily, so I'm always changing it." As far as Adaeze was concerned, black women wearing weaves or wigs were simply engaging in the kind of playful, consumerist self-transcendence and self-expression being voiced by Alero and Sharon above. And they were entitled to.

Adaeze staked these positions in response to my question of what she thought about the "politics of, like, black women and weaves." Her adamant view was that "I don't think anybody dis-*likes their natural selves*, I think they're just having fun. . . . If you have your natural hair you *can't* do *fun stuff*, let's be honest. You can't do—like today I wanna have it straight or I want it to be red and I wanna have a bang and whatever. You can't do that. There's nothing wrong with that, but there's some people that *want* to, so why shouldn't they be allowed to?" Adaeze's impassioned argument speaks directly to Tate's theoretical, epistemological, and also methodological proposition that we need not always already see a black woman in a weave as "wanting to be white," as seeking, self-evidently, to disavow her racialized embodiment and identity. Instead, we can see her as experimenting with, and expanding, the stylistic possibilities and technologies of *blackness* and in this actually demonstrating that the styles in question are not inherently or exclusively white in the first place. We can read in this vein Ima's enumeration of the different kinds of weaves that she had worn: "I've been blonde, I've been a redhead." Taking on subject categories and names ordinarily linked to, even propertized by, whiteness, Ima was not therefore claiming to have embodied or approximated whiteness, nor expressing a desire or wish to do so. Quite the contrary, she was bringing these categories, names, and looks into black femininity and doing so with an utterly casual air. The more so when they come in commodity form, technologies of the self are inherently fluid and performative. It is precisely this that makes it possible for the subject racialized and called black "to *do* Blackness through hair irrespective of whether it comes in a bag or it's straight, natty or loosely curled, black, brown or blonde."[11]

Allowing for new and creative ways of being, looking, and self-naming and -positioning, it followed for the women that their weaves and wigs were "just fashion." Chika uttered these words to argue that a black woman's weave could and should not be read as a sign of her racial psyche. To make the point, she invoked the fact that she had recently had her hair in an old pattern or style of cornrows known as "Ghana weaving." In response to my question of what she thought about commonplace notions of the weave "being like some kind of racial thing," Chika argued that just as her Ghana weaving style would be understood as fashion, not as a sign that she was a traditionalist African subject, a woman harking to the past, so her weave should not be read literally, or racially psychologized: "Having a weave for me doesn't mean, you know, I'm trying to be a, a European woman or an Asian woman, or I'm not happy with my (*pauses*) ethnicity. It's just a fashion thing, just like I can have Ghana weaving does not mean (*pauses*) I've reverted back to the olden days and I'm thinking like my ancestors. It's just fashion, it's not that serious, it's hair on your head. I wish people would stop making like a political thing, you know, it's a personal thing." Tinu considered the weave more than "a personal thing" to the extent that she saw it as very much a Lagos fashion norm. Tinu described her own hair as "good," "healthy," "conditioned" (that is, chemically processed), and "long," reaching some way down her back. In a highly problematic move that I found myself making preconsciously in several interviews, a move that cited the historical and cultural "common sense" that the weave serves black women as a necessary compensatory technology for our own hair, on hearing Tinu's description of her hair I blurted out, "So why do you wear weave on . . . you have the hair already?" Tinu laughed and stated that she did not know, before adding in a provisional tone: "It's just because it's what is obtainable." Part of the weave's attraction was just that it was a current stylistic possibility.

To demonstrate to me concretely that the weave was a style that Lagos women were avidly pursuing and obtaining at the moment, Tinu directed my attention out of the window next to which we were sitting during the interview, pointing out women passing by on the street: "Here in Lagos, if you look, out of ten—okay, you can see that girl (*pointing to a young woman passing by in a weave*), okay you will see another one, another one (*pointing to another*)—ten, let's say seven out of ten girls that pass, what they're having on their hair is this foreigner's hair."[12] Later pointing to the red weave of another young woman walking by, Tinu remarked, "That's Rihanna's influence. You know Nigeria, Rihanna and Beyoncé influence Nigerian youth style." As this last remark suggests, the weave is also a trend far beyond Lagos, involving black women "all over the world," as two other participants put it. Pointing this out was simultaneously a claim of global consumer citizenship and of racial belonging. It was pointing to an imagined global black feminine community of stylized practice to point to one's place within it and to thereby surface and authenticate one's own blackness. Diane was one of the women to make this series of complex rhetorical maneuvers. Before I had turned on my Dictaphone at the start of the interview, Diane had started to tell me that the way young Nigerian women dress was changing. I asked how, to which she replied by first announcing the moral subject position from which she was speaking, saying, "I'm a proper Naija woman." Diane went on to allege that other Nigerian women—"improper" ones, the suggestion went—were now aspiring to look like "the white woman." Hearing this explicitly racialized remark, I assumed that Diane was referring to the popularity of weaves among young Nigerian women. But it transpired that she was not—in fact, Diane was in a weave herself. She went on to give the example of Nigerian women now appearing in "hot pants and bum shorts." Her allegation was about an increasing sexualization of women's dress in Nigeria, which she attributed to transnationalized media representations of white postfeminist femininity.

After we discussed the issue of sexualized dress, to which I will return shortly, I related Diane's charge about the emulating of white women to weaves, saying, "Some people feel that black women wearing weave is like, has a similar kind of thing." Diane flatly disagreed: "No. Black women all over the world, I think we're obsessed with weaves, not just Naija women. Black women everywhere, you don't touch their weaves (*briefly laughs*). Their weaves are like their precious gold." The claim that an almost militant obsession with the weave transcended Nigeria to include black women "everywhere" was proffered here to untrouble and resolve the style's racial meanings. Its logic was that the weave was a black thing, a black feminine style, again almost aggressively so, meaning that Nigerian women in weaves were not trying to be something that they were not. Diane next pivoted to an individualized position to end her defense of the weave, now insisting that, for black women, it was "not at all" about whiteness but "basically how you feel, basically it's just how you feel about yourself."

It is obvious, though, that weaves and wigs are about much more than an individual feeling or taste. I illustrate below how the women's choice of and deeply held and affective draw to these hairstyles were predicated upon a historically entrenched sense that their own hair was inadequate for feminine beauty and for postfeminist "girliness." Their feelings about their hair, and thus about the "solutions" for it, constituted a *structure of feeling*. Contrary to Diane and other women's reasoning, which, among other things, contained the postfeminist impulse to depoliticize and deproblematize by reducing to personal choice, it is actually in recognizing the structuration and historicity of their hair practices and preferences that we can get past common tendencies to psychopathologize black women for them, which is what the women were gunning for ultimately. Taking history and structure into account enables us to see that weaves and wigs are indeed black styles, or technologies of blackness, because they have been long reiterated, embodied, and carried as such. As with the related practice of hair straightening, these styles derive from a set of sedimented logics and practices of black beauty, femininity, and stylization that have become normative *within* blackness. Rather than continuing to see black stylization as an either-or, either "authentic" if it looks nonwhite or "inauthentic" if it does not, we can see instead that it has two historicized, overarching sets of logics: "one emphasizing 'natural' looks, the other involving [various forms to alteration] to emphasize 'artifice.'"[13]

Only a handful of black cultural scholars have made these kinds of arguments: Shirley Tate, Kobena Mercer, Maxine Craig, Deborah Grayson, Samantha Pinho.[14] With them I want to insist that it is crucial, and far past time, for feminist scholarship—black feminist especially—to move beyond what are reductive, ultimately violent, and also largely ethnographically unsubstantiated modes of always already seeing—and, more troubling, teaching—that when it comes to beauty, black women are racially damaged subjects, dupes. We do not reduce white women's beauty practice in this way, concluding that they are damaged by patriarchy, denuding them of agency, self-reflexivity, and pleasure, refusing to deeply consider or respect what they might have to say about it. But having taken history and power into account to understand and allow that an aesthetic of artifice has sedimented into black beauty and stylization, we must not then lose sight of these forces; we must not forget or seek to wish away the fact that this black aesthetic is indeed constituted by and continues to reinscribe root violences: the violence of race itself and that of antiblack racism.

THE UNHAPPY ROOTS OF WEAVES AND WIGS

In black hair discourse and practice, historically and ordinarily the category of "natural" designates hair of chemically unaltered or unprocessed texture, such as worked into styles like Afros or dreadlocks. But in terms of how the women in my research invoked it, and as Thompson also finds in her study of black women's contemporary hairstyling, weaves and wigs appear to be redefining and expanding the meanings of natural to refer to the hair that grows from one's scalp, regardless of what is done to it.[15] In other words, against the new standard of "artificial" that is the weave or wig, natural covers everything else, one's own hair. What Folake called her natural hair, in the quote below, was chemically straightened. She ruefully compared its properties with the weaves she almost always wore. Deeming weaves better and more beautifying than her own hair, Folake's ruefulness was also about what felt to her like the consequent near impossibility of appearing with her own hair, or in other words without weaves: "I wish—if I had longer hair, maybe I'd stopping doing all of this [that is, wearing weaves a lot], 'cause I've got really thin hair, I've got thin but long hair, but what I really like, what I would *really* want is a really, I would like my hair to be fuller. Fuller and longer. And then maybe I'd carry [that is, wear] my natural hair more often."

Tate argues that "mourning for what could be and a feeling of loss" haunts black women's beauty practice because of racism, because they are excluded from dominant visions and representations of beauty.[16] In previous chapters, I have also conceptualized my research participants' dress and beauty practice as melancholic, in their case because it foreclosed other options, more carefree ones especially. This argument was not about race. Tate is clear that she is writing about black diasporic women, women who live in white dominant societies, making it important to distinguish a context like Nigeria, the largest and arguably most politically and symbolically powerful black nation on the planet, where black is dominant and normative and *beautiful*. Yet the fact is that in Nigeria, the hegemonic image of this beauty is not of unaltered black hair. Not only in Nigeria but across Africa is it almost a matter of course that adult urban women will alter or camouflage their hair in on one way or another: "curl, dye, straighten, lengthen with extensions, and supplement with wigs."[17] Therefore, I want to suggest that when it came to their hair specifically, my research participants' melancholy *was* specifically racialized, if not quite for the same reasons as Tate finds. As Nigerian women in Nigeria, the women's problem was not that they were excluded from normative representations of beauty, but that their unaltered hair was.

The line of discussion with Chika that had led to her insistence that wearing weaves was nothing more than fashion, hence not to be attributed racial significance, had begun with her talking about her own hair. Chika recalled that she had "tried going natural," that is, tried to revert from chemically processed hair back to its unaltered texture. But "I couldn't handle it. I have very *thick African* hair. . . . I tried it but it was too (*pauses*) painful for me." I asked Chika if she meant "literally painful." She restated this phrasing in her affirmative reply: "Literally painful, yes. Like I, even getting a comb through it, even going to the hairdressers. . . . So I just think it's [that is, wearing a weave] not that serious for me really. If, if, if I had finer hair, you know hair that was like finer in texture, maybe I would go natural." In these remarks, we hear a similar recognition as with Folake, earlier, that one's hair situation could be different, if now in relation to the "problem" of "too thick hair," the very opposite of the "too fine" that bedeviled Folake. That these women referred to exactly opposing "hair problems" is quite telling, I would say: it speaks to my contention that, at base, the problem was "black hair" itself. Unlike Folake though, Chika refused herself even a moment of melancholy. In the quote above, she promptly transmuted and defused the fact that her own hair felt unwearable—or unbearable, to recall Chimamanda Ngozi Adichie's psychically loaded word—into the "not that serious" alternative choice of a weave. I theorized this kind of refusal to mourn the loss occasioned by beauty norms in chapter 2 as a cruel postfeminist shrugging away of feminine pain, as if one is too powerful and happy to feel wounded.

Sade also spoke about the physical pain of having her chemically unprocessed hair styled at salons in Lagos. Recalling when she had had an Afro, she said, "Of course nobody really understood what to do with my hair. I'd go to the hairdresser, I'd be crying, like you don't understand what a grown woman (*pauses*) was doing crying at the hair shop because they just were pulling it. . . . So eventually I was like okay, fine, I'll just do the weaves." Alleging that hairdressers in Lagos were less adept at caring for an Afro than at affixing weaves, Sade presented this as an unsurprising ("of course") and apolitical if personally inconvenient state of affairs. Alero both opined and agreed with my own expressed view, based upon my personal experience of wearing dreadlocks for years in Nigeria, that local hairdressers lacked sufficient know-how with chemically unprocessed hair.[18] Likewise, a total of five participants said that they or their friends did not know how to manage or nicely style their hair in this state. The women and I were speaking of an "erosion of cultural memory" with regard to the styling of black hair.[19] This is utterly political. It is especially so, and the more problematic, and frankly striking, in what is the largest black city in the world—a place with probably the greatest concentration of black hair salons in the world!

On the one hand, we can understand the loss of cultural and bodily memory and know-how that the women and I were describing as a historical effect of what Nkiru Nzegwu conceptualizes as "colonial racism" in West Africa. According to Nzegwu, this form of racism constituted the systematic colonial degradation and delegitimization of indigenous cultures and knowledges. Nzegwu distinguishes this from the "body racism" that black diasporic populations face(d), in which the black body itself was the target of vilification and violence. Yet the loss of a relative memory, feel, and also taste for unaltered black hair in Nigeria must also be understood as an effect of the latter form of racism, insofar as the loss is also a compounded effect of "the racializing forces of neocolonization and globalization."[20] The importation of new hair styles and tastes from the black diaspora into Nigeria invariably means, if with indeterminate effect, the importation of the racialized and variously (anti)racist logics, values, and sensibilities that constitute and attend these styles and tastes in the first place. While black may be normative and beautiful in Nigeria, this does not mean that Nigerian women are therefore happily insulated from antiblack racism, past or ongoing. They are not—they cannot be because they are postcolonial and transnational subjects.[21]

Sade's further comments continue to illustrate my contentions here about the transnational roots and routes of the meaning, look, and feel of black feminine beauty in a place like Nigeria. I discussed in chapter 2 Sade's recounting of the fact that her use of weaves had caused damage to her own hairline such that, aesthetically vigilant, she had moved on to wigs. Explaining that she now wore wigs on top of her unprocessed natural hair, Sade described this as "the balance" that she had found: "where I don't have to go sit with some person [that is, a hairdresser] who doesn't know how to care for my hair and the texture, em, and sit there, and then they ruin my hair because I'm trying to look a part or at least, you know, trying to feel girly." Totally naturalized and unmarked in these comments, a *sens pratique*, was that "trying to feel girly" *required* altering one's own hair, that unprocessed black hair just did not feel this way. Black feminists have noted and problematized as much in relation to the black diaspora, that the predominant construction of chemically unprocessed black hair is as "unfeminine," and that black women come to feel this way.[22] Zimitri Erasmus reflects upon the same from South Africa and asserts that such black "hair-stories" are not local or regional but "global."[23] Whereas Thompson casts such feelings among the women in her research in terms of "self-hatred," again I eschew this kind of analysis.[24] I do not deem it productive, or fair, particularly from and for black feminist positions because it is blaming and pathologizing black women for cultural and historical conditions, and structures of feeling, that are not of our doing or first choosing.

Other participants were like Sade in making utterly implicit representations of their weaves or wigs as simply and self-evidently best and in so doing revealed the passionate, rigid, and often inarticulable hold that the beauty technologies had over them, demonstrating that power "take[s] hold—take[s] hold of the body, take[s] hold of desire . . . rigidly colonizing the flesh."[25] I have noted that many of the women valued their weaves or wigs for endowing them with a longer or fuller head of hair than what they had "naturally." If we can agree that length and volume are objective measures, bracketing critical questions of what they may mean for black women, the same cannot be said of constructions of weaves or wigs as "just" more beautiful, more professional, more manageable, tidier, or more girly fun than both chemically unprocessed and processed black hair. Tobi explained what her own hair had been like before she had started wearing weaves:

> Tobi: I used to have like really long hair, and it was kinda full. But—
> Simi: You mean your own hair?
> Tobi:—my own hair. But since I started fixing [weaves] regularly, you know 'cause of work you have to look fly and human hair is harder to manage, your own hair is harder to manage, 'cause our hair is frizzy and everything.

To "look fly" for her television show, it was a given that a weave was needed in place of "our" hair. I would draw the reader's attention to the additional cruelty in Tobi's suggestion that the prior length and fullness of her own hair had suffered decline due to her very wearing of weaves ("I used to have like really long hair, and it was kinda full. . . . But since I started fixing [weaves] regularly . . ."). Natural hair would pose a professional challenge from Sharon's standpoint, too. Positioning herself as a busy career woman, she explained:

> Sharon: I admire people who wear natural, but it's so hard to maintain. And for me I'm always on the go (*clicking her fingers*) so—
> Simi: Don't have time.
> Sharon: I can't have my hair crunchy today or difficult to style tomorrow, so the weaves are very convenient for me because I can just brush it out, just get it blow-dried, tong it, and I'm good to go.

Kim described wearing her natural hair (chemically unprocessed) as "too tedious," asking, "What can you do with it other than pack it [up]?" Kemi shared the view that it was at once more work and less fun to wear her natural hair (chemically processed) versus a weave: "With my natural hair I think it takes way more effort. Because when I have [my] hair out, there's only two things I can do with it: tie it in a bun and leave it down." It should be noted, however, that she had earlier said that she tended to alternate between these exact two styles when wearing a weave. Ima stated that she felt "more dressed up" with a weave and so when she was not wearing one made up for it with other feminine technologies and accoutrements: "Like I would wear more earrings. . . . I don't know if that's to like *distract* or to give me something *else*?" Folake, likewise, explained that she made sure to put on false eyelashes when appearing with her own hair. This was to ensure that she would not look babyish, "look like a schoolgirl." Misan asserted that she was "comfortable" with her own hair (chemically processed). She struggled to articulate why she nonetheless preferred her appearance with a weave and consequently felt more self-confident in the style: "I don't know, I really don't know why. I just feel it—or maybe I do—I feel that it makes, it just makes my look, it completes my look." Nene, by contrast, declared that she was not comfortable with her own hair (chemically processed). She also could not articulate why:

> Nene: I don't (*briefly laughs*) carry my own hair. It's long, though, it's very long, but I'm not comfortable with it.
> Simi: Okay. Why?
> Nene: I don't know why. I don't just like carrying my hair. So, em, okay (*pauses*). I don't like my hair.

While the weave is a relatively new technology for black women (and others), the structure of feeling that rendered it necessarily best and most beautifying, and comfortable, for the women in my research is very old, as I have begun to say. The weave is merely the latest style in long-standing black feminine orientations away from unprocessed natural hair, orientations that are founded in white supremacy and antiblack "body racism."[26] Yet to this old orientation, the weave adds new sentiments, logics, and also risks and cruelties. Kemi, who was twenty-two when I interviewed her, explained that she had been allowed by her parents to wear weaves only after she had turned sixteen. She said that in the few years since, she had come to "just prefer" the way she looked with weaves over braids or her chemically processed hair and noted that when wearing her own hair, she now tended to put on a "headband." She shared her reason for doing so, but also her mother's differing take:

> Kemi: I think otherwise [my own hair] just looks too *flat*. But my mum thinks the reason I think my hair looks so flat is because I'm used to having my hair so big [that is, with a weave] so that I don't—
> Simi: When you have your hair out?
> Kemi: It just looks so *strange* to me.

The weave set new and heightened standards for doing black feminine beauty and girliness. The women positioned themselves as happily doing: in and by wearing weaves, and wigs to the lesser extent that they did, they were agentic, choosing, playing, experimenting, and so on, and all the while being racially authentic and cosmopolitan. In and through weaves and wigs, they were doing black postfeminism, being fabulously black like fabulous black women the world over.

Yet as with other elements of their dress practice, the women's celebratory talk and positions were undercut by fundamental ambivalence and contradiction. The new and heightened feminine beauty standards of the weave especially reconstituted and heightened old insecurities about, and feelings of alienation from, their own hair. Next to the fetishized appearance of a long and full head of a weave or wig, a now expanded category of "natural" became even more inadequate. Ahmed defines unhappy objects as those that "embody the persistence of histories that cannot be wished away by happiness."[27] This definition encapsulates weaves and wigs for black women: my research participants' happy postfeminist claims and affects, for instance, could not resolve or even mask the melancholy and painful histories of their hair choices and stories. Yet what I am arguing here is that the constitutive, historicized unhappiness of weaves and wigs for black women do not render them any less *technologies* of black femininity. Rather, we can see that unhappiness, as well as happy-making moves to sublimate or "get over it," exactly enter into the technologies' black feminine performativity and promise.

SHOW FOR EKO

To turn now from race to that other imagined community that is the nation, let us start with Misan's declaration that Nigerians are not really a stylish people, an opinion whose mere assertion was part of her self-distinction in the interview as an exception to the rule. In her words: "I always say that I don't think Nigerians are stylish. People find that really, really harsh. . . . I think we are appearance-obsessed and we make an effort, and I think that's where we lose it, 'cause we make too much of an effort." Misan illustrated her claim by explaining that if she happened to remark about a Nigerian woman generally considered stylish—and here she "put on fone," as we call it in Nigeria, to say—"oh, she's not stylish," her friends would tease her for being too sophisticated for her own good and for the local environment. "To put on fone" ("fone" derived from "phonetics") is to put on a foreign accent, successfully or not; when successful or convincing, as in Misan's case, it can be understood as a practice of class-privileged and cosmopolitan Nigerian code switching. Later Misan alleged that if a woman was wearing a simple yet stylish dress, for its simplicity a "normal" Nigerian would not perceive that it was actually stylish. Here she put on an emphasized Nigerian accent to mimic how this kind of undiscerning subject would wonder: "What is dis woman wearing, dis simple dress?" "Dis" is a very common, and again classed, Nigerian (mis)pronunciation of "this"—Innocent Chiluwa considers it a mark of "uneducated Nigerian English."[28] Including via her putting on of differential Nigerian accents, Misan was distinguishing between differentially classed and cosmopolitan Nigerian style sensibilities and positioning herself on the most sophisticated and exposed end of the spectrum, as not a "normal" or average Nigerian.[29]

Other women did not judge the quality or stylishness of what, in concurrence with Misan, they deemed a Nigerian cultural obsession with appearance and dress. I introduced the popular rhyming expression "Eko for show" in chapter 1 as referencing and also inviting a certain material showiness in and for Lagos, indeed as a way of being Lagosian. Noting that both ceremonial and everyday traditional Nigerian dress tend to be ornate and elaborate—for instance, "you tie *gele* [a headscarf, in Yoruba] and you have *beads* and you have *gold* and you have *lace*"—Chika reflected as follows on the dress culture, including as it might be an unconscious influence on her own practice:

> Chika: It's a culture that is enamored with (*long pause*). Er, what's the word I'm looking for? Ostentatiousness, if that's the word.
> Simi: Yeah.
> Chika: Yeah.
> Simi: And appearance.
> Chika: And app—exactly. And your *finery* and show. Like my friend has this saying, "Eko for show," which I find hilarious, but it's true. "*Eko for show!*" Like you know in Nigeria—maybe that's why I'm even into all these designer bags, you know, Prada sunglasses—everybody knows, everybody knows every designer.

In Chika's view and experience, appearing in one or another "ostentatious" fashion was in the nature of Lagosian/Nigerian life, and cosmopolitanism, "a sophisticated appreciation for international mixing and appropriation of cultural styles and symbols from multiple, geographically dispersed sites," was part and parcel of this.[30] Being Lagosian/Nigerian and cosmopolitan were mutually constitutive positions. That this looked like Prada sunglasses and designer handbags in Chika's mind's eye is, of course, indicative of the particular and bounded kinds of Lagos/Nigeria within which she and the other women resided.

Ima also spoke directly to the "Eko for show" repertoire by claiming that, in comparison to elsewhere in Nigeria, when young women dressed for a night out in Lagos, "they proper bring it all the time, you know what I mean. So sometimes, you know, if I go out with certain people that maybe are more

Lagos girls, so to speak, they're like 'Oh, now, like wear a dress.' I'm like 'No, it's not my birthday.'" If not the most Lagosian of girls, the kind to always bedeck herself like it was a special occasion, Ima suggested elsewhere in the interview, much like Chika, that she was steeped nonetheless in a heightened local practice and expectation of dressing up. She did so by comparing the attentiveness and spectacularity of her style with the casualness of that of her sisters who lived abroad, remarking, "I'm definitely more Nigerian than them, so maybe it's just the culture here, doing your hair and having longer hair, and stuff like that. They don't understand it." Ima recalled an occasion when one of her sisters had been visiting Nigeria and the family had been heading to the domestic airport to catch a flight: "We both came downstairs at the same time. She's like 'Where are you going?' I'm like 'Where are *you* going?' 'Cause she was wearing like trackies, a T-shirt, and a cap, and I'm like, I'm wearing like nice *jeans* and a nice *blouse* and *hoops*, and we looked like we were going to different places." Ima recounted that her mother had intervened, berating her sister as inappropriately dressed and instructing her to "go change!" While her sister had reportedly protested that she had dressed to be comfortable on the flight, Ima described the contrary impulse that had informed her own choice of outfit: "Do you know how many people you see at the airport?" She had not been dressing for a journey, but dressing up to appear, a rationality, an instantiation of the "Eko for show" mind-set, that, according to Ima, her mother also shared and sought to have the family perform.

The question "Where are you going?" is an accusatory interpellation. It hails the subject as out of place.[31] As with Ima's sister, it may be that the subject is seen to be performing inappropriately for where it is or should be emplaced or for the kind of subject that it is supposed to be or look like. Or it may be that the subject's performance is productive of what is deemed the wrong kind of place. Back in Lagos after having studied and then worked for some years in America, Adaeze characterized her former professional colleagues abroad as people who "just roll out of bed," who would raise their eyebrows, therefore, when she came to work in her immaculate and hyperfeminine style: "In my dress, and my nails are done, and my hair, and they're like, you know, 'Where are you going?' So anyway, moving back here really enabled me to sort of like *enjoy* getting dressed up, 'cause everyone dresses up." What had been deemed excessive and inappropriate abroad was standard, commonplace, in Lagos. The spectacularity of the spectacularly feminine fitted in with a local norm and rationality. As a result, Adaeze's belonging was not questioned. She claimed, in fact, that if ever hailed in Lagos for her appearance, it was positively: "Nobody ever says (*in a mock judgmental tone and mimicking an American accent*) 'Where are *you* going?' (*resumes regular accent*) because everybody dresses up. I mean [here] they'll compliment you."

That the women had such "multiply-located senses of self . . . emerging through both geographical mobility and multiple forms of ongoing emplacement" heightened their ability to see the generative place of Nigeria in their dress.[32] More simply put, they could better see how Nigeria influenced their dress practice for being or having been sometimes at a distance from the place. Kemi remembered that when she had been a student abroad, she had dressed up much less than she did now, back in Lagos: "I would wear makeup, but it wouldn't be that much. I would do my hair, but I wouldn't do it every three weeks." She characterized as "worse" the lengths to which she would go when she was coming home for summer holidays: "I would go shopping, buy *loads* of clothes, loads of shoes, loads of new everything, *just because* I'm coming to Nigeria for the summer, I have to look good *every day.*" In and for Nigeria, she felt a heightened and continuous imperative to appear. Cultural, but again also thoroughly classed, this felt imperative contributed to rendering Nigeria a particular kind of place for her and likewise to constituting her differential senses and practices of self there, abroad, and in between.

Class is thoroughly central to the particulars of the subject's emplacement within and mobility across social fields, transnational and otherwise.[33] Considerable material privilege is implicit in Kemi's recollections of how much dress shopping ("*loads*") she would do before going to Nigeria on holiday, a preparing to appear that was itself premised on many other privileges, from being abroad for further education in the first place to being able to travel home regularly. Sade was quite clear that her spectacularly feminine dress practice was partially incited by her elite positionality in Nigeria and in turn constituted a performance and signification of it. On the one hand, as with the other women I have been discussing above, her transnational subjectivity helped her to see this. She talked about how, moving back to Nigeria to begin her career after having studied and worked briefly in America, she had soon relearned that Nigerians "wanna size you up based on how you appear" or the "articles of status" that you display, such as designer handbags. This was in contrast to what she depicted as the more meritocratic and professional "American mentality" with which she had returned, in which what mattered for your job was "the value of what's in your head." Sade was also particularly reflexive about the classed logics and spaces of her spectacularly feminine dress in Lagos because her job as a journalist took her across the city's widely disparate fields, from its poorest to wealthiest neighborhoods. On an average working day, she explained, she was more likely to be "grungy" than "carrying no lambskin bag." However, if she knew that the workday would take her to the "kind of environment" where an unspectacular appearance would be appraised negatively, back to elite Lagos we could call it, Sade reasoned that she might dress to show her social level or status by throwing on some expensive accessories. Her reasoning was that even if she still looked "grungy and bummy" overall, people would be able to see, would espy in the detail of her dress, that she actually had "spending power," and would therefore give her due respect.

Saying that she did not have any "hang-ups" about how far a typical day on the job took her from her own social milieu, and from her preferred style of dress, Sade reflected: "Sometimes I have to remind myself, like wait a minute, like, yeah, you know you actually like enjoy being all fancy and stuff. I have to just kind of like—it's like you're living in two worlds." This comment about the multiple worlds of Lagos brings me to the final point that I want to make here about how the very fabric of the city entered into the women's dress practice—or how what I have framed from the outset of this book as a transnational style of dress and self-fashioning was also very much grounded in, and about, the local too. Other than in Sade's few words above, the Lagos where the overwhelming majority of Lagosians reside is hard to find in the interview transcripts. It was not the subject of discussion, and it is not the place that the women inhabit or really know—nor I. But this is not to say that it was not in the interviews at all, gestured toward, implicit, taken for granted. For instance, explaining that she wore high heels a lot, Alero appended the note: "Especially in Nigeria here, where it is not like I have to walk anywhere long." In Nigeria a woman of Alero's socioeconomic demographic does not walk on the street or take public transport as she would in London, say—as Alero herself said that she did. She rides in private cars. Incidentally, this last point was made acutely apparent to me while I was out and about looking for research participants as, from the vantage of my own private car, I often saw spectacular-looking young women in cars alongside mine. Wanting to access such women, wondering where I could find them, it struck me how much they and I experience and navigate the city in and through privatized and securitized space.

Alero also indicated how her privileged class position at home encouraged not only the ease of her spectacular self-stylization but also its constant reiteration. She did so by first noting that she could afford to use beauty services much more in Nigeria than in England, "where it is expensive." To my subsequent question of how often she visited the salon in Nigeria versus when she had been an undergraduate in England, Alero explained:

Alero: Here it's a lot cheaper. I can do my hair, depending on my mood,
I can do my hair every two weeks, or sometimes I have hairstyles—
Simi: So is that like change it completely?
Alero: Yeah, change it completely because it's cheaper here. So some-
times I change it completely every two weeks. I know sometimes I'll
have my hair for a week and change it again.

In Lagos Alero was able to completely change her hair, meaning her weaves, as often as every one or two weeks, as she felt inclined. By contrast, she reported that she would typically change her weaves in London "monthly. So let's say four (pauses) to five weeks, four to five weeks ideally, because that—it can be six weeks." Whereas she reported spending about forty-five pounds per visit to the hairdressers in London, in Lagos the cost was about a quarter of this sum.

Chika stated that she went to the hairdressers "a lot." She meant "like four times a week." As with when Sharon told me that she spent about six to eight hours per fortnightly visit to the hairdressers changing her weaves, this was one of a few moments in the interviews in which I could not suppress an expression of shock at the extent of aesthetic labor in which the women engaged:

Simi: Four times a week! Wow!
Chika: Yeah. That's a lot, right?
Simi: But to do what, like what sort of thing do you get done?
Chika: Em, I don't really get anything major done. Sometimes they just
kind of blow-dry my hair [that is, her human hair weave]; sometimes
I have like treatments applied to my hair. Sometimes, I'm ashamed to
admit, I just go there so they can comb out my hair (both laugh). Yes,
it's true.

I would presume that Chika's "shame" to admit to her practice was due to her recognition that it could be perceived as excessive and indulgent, as my initial exclamatory response had perhaps suggested.

Mohanty notes that the subject position of "citizen-consumer depends to a large degree on the definition and disciplining of producers/workers on whose backs the citizen-consumer gains legitimacy," and sheer material and practical possibility I would add. This leads her to pose the question, "Who are the workers that make the citizen-consumer possible?"[34] I cannot answer this question: the workers were largely invisibilized in the women's talk, but in any case the question is beyond the scope of this book, and what

I asked the women in the interviews, and demands critical inquiry in its own right. What I can say here, however, is that from the women's perspective, Lagos and Nigeria were all the more places of their spectacularly feminine and spectacularly classed dress practice because of the ready availability of feminized labor that they found cheap.

KEEPING UP WITH THE TRANSNATIONAL

Clear from the foregoing discussion is that my research participants enjoyed international mobility. They traveled often out of Nigeria for work and for leisure, and nine of the eighteen had pursued further education, and in some cases subsequently worked for some years, in the United Kingdom, the United States, France, or South Africa. Cosmopolitanism is not only performed or possible via physical travel, though. The cosmopolitan subject can be at home, participating from there in "various discourses of the global, national and international that [move] across transnational connectivities and [thereby enable] subjects to cross borders or claim to transcend them."[35] In terms of their media consumption, for instance, the women presented themselves as very much "plugged in" to the transnational from Lagos. They reported watching mostly American television channels like E!: Entertainment Television and TLC and content like *Keeping Up with the Kardashians, Fashion Police, Modern Family, Scandal, The Real Housewives of Atlanta, Jersey Shore, The O.C., The Good Wife*, and *Gossip Girl*. They were "on board" with the latest social media, as Kim put it when she spoke of her use of platforms such as "Twitter, Instagram, Keek, Facebook." Chika laughed about the fact that she and her friends were "all obsessed with Instagram—it's crazy," where they followed the images of both Nigerian and foreign "fashionistas." She also spoke of using new media technologies to continue the media habits that she had developed abroad: "I just follow the stuff I used to read when I lived in the UK, so I read, I still read the same magazines I used to, I just read them on my iPad now."

The magazines that the women reported reading included *Cosmopolitan, Grazia, Glamour, Elle, Red*, and *Vogue*. As of the time of this writing, only the last two of these titles do not have an official South African edition. This needs noting because South Africa is the key regional source and exporter of "glossy" media content in Africa, including of satellite television.[36] Thus, where the women spoke of reading *Elle* in Lagos, they may well have meant *Elle South Africa*, and where, like Kim, they glossed what they perused as "international magazines," this may have included original South African titles like *True Love*, a black women's magazine that sells in Lagos—and, it is crucial to note, also franchised and published an edition for West Africa out of Lagos between 2005 and 2010. Such transnationalized South African content is itself influenced by broader transnational trends and repertoires.[37] According to Sonja Laden, new (in the sense of postapartheid) black consumer magazines "give black South Africans access to a vast 'marketplace' of global and local commodities, routines, linguistic practices, and aspirations."[38] Reading a number geared at upwardly mobile black South African women, Tom Odhiambo sees them as "a space where allusions to female empowerment, gender equality and women's emancipation are retailed alongside a most blatant call to consumerism."[39] Or, in the terms of this book, they are spaces and vehicles for postfeminism as transnational culture.

Where I am going here is to make the point that my research participants were exposed to, and embraced, postfeminist culture and representations from multiple sources, directions, and routes, including local ones. On the one hand, this was a function of Nigeria's position in global and regional political and cultural economies, and the consolidation of global media empires that intensifies "the creation of transnational markets and transnational distribution systems."[40] It was also an effect of their privileged class position in Nigeria and in transnationality, including the cosmopolitan sophistication and know-how that they repeatedly claimed, as well as the material access that they enjoyed to technologies like cable television, iPads, and costly imported magazines, luxuries for the average Nigerian. But as well demonstrated in cultural and media studies research on the globalization of consumer culture, as well as in audience studies, the women kept up with the transnational with reflexive distance.[41] They did not just soak up whatever postfeminist content came their way. Take Kemi's stated views of the popular reality television show *Keeping Up with the Kardashians*, a show that Maria Pramaggiore and Diane Negra have argued exemplifies postfeminist notions that "gender equality is synonymous with 'girl power' and can be enacted through luxury consumption and the cultivation of a fashionable self-image," or in other words the very notions that the women in this book espoused.[42] Kemi said that she watched the *Kardashians* via satellite in Lagos, and while she "might like what someone is wearing in it or [think] that her hair looks nice," the whole thing had gotten "ridiculously fake." Her strongest critique was reserved for the show's celebratory representation of sexualized femininities: "The mere fact [Kim Kardashian] got famous from a sex tape should be enough evidence that she should not be anybody's role model. . . . [T]hat's what she's famous for, and that's what she continues to (*pause*) do is all sex appeal, and all sex,

sex, sex, sex, sex. I don't think you should emulate someone like that. All she does is sell magazines in bikinis."

Almost all the women expressed even greater critical distance from local media—in fact, borderline disdain in some cases. Comparing Nigerian televisual offerings with the American women's programming that she tried to stream online, like *Good Morning America*, Adaeze noted that on the American shows, "Every day there's like some beauty tip. . . . There's tons of beauty *experts* and different things. . . . Obviously they don't have that here [in Nigeria], or what they do have here, I'm like seriously? . . . I'll give *you* some tips." The local content was not instructive for a woman like her; she was already past it, too skilled and sophisticated for what was being touted locally as such. Kemi also indicated that quality was the problem when, referring to one of the leading Nigerian women's glossy fashion and lifestyle magazines, *Genevieve*, she said, "I don't really find it that (*pauses*) great to be honest. . . . If I see it somewhere I pick it up, but I wouldn't buy it, no." Amaka said that she would "flick through" *Genevieve* and other Nigerian women's publications if she happened upon them, but "actually go out and go and buy a magazine by (*pause*), you know to follow, see, what Nigerian celebrities are doing? No." After an awkward pause in response to my question of if she consumed any Nigerian media, Folake explained why the short answer was no: "The Nigerian celebrities are trying, they look at, they get it from *E!*" As she saw it, Nigerian celebrities were simply mimicking the foreign ones who they saw on cable television, and this was neither appealing nor edifying to a woman like her.

Diane's earlier mentioned claim that some young Nigerian women were trying to be white was also a direct charge of mimicry. I went back to it right at the end of her interview, to ask Diane to further explain what she had meant. Having first made the comment in reference to the alleged new appearance of sexualized styles of dress, Diane now gave a second example: "Yes, you see a lot of, em, em, black girls, or Nigerian girls, trying to copy the Western world all because I've [that is, they've] traveled overseas, and I come back to Nigeria and so I have to wear leather pants . . . or boots, 'cause Kim Kardashian was wearing boots (*laughs*)." To Diane, dress items like leather pants and boots were laughably inappropriate for the local environment, in this case because of the tropical heat. Young Nigerian women returning from abroad with such items, or acquiring them because they had seen Western women wearing them, were therefore revealing themselves to be cultural dupes, not cultured sophisticates. The problem was not keeping up with the latest feminine trends. It does not need saying at this point in the book that the research participants were utterly abreast with and embodying "the latest" themselves. The question was how one went about it. The "wrong way" was to lose one's discernment, and in fact one's very self, in the quest to follow the new and foreign. This was not cosmopolitanism. Attuned and oriented to the wider world, the cosmopolitan subject was one who was also rooted at home, who did not lose her grounding or her sense of what was appropriate or not. It was in terms of postfeminist attitudes to "sex, sex, sex, sex, sex," to recall Kemi's impassioned criticism of Kim Kardashian, that the women most asserted their orientation to, and respect for, what they painted as the diverging sensibilities of their local environment and culture.

STAYING GROUNDED IN THE LOCAL

I asked Misan if sexuality and "sexiness" were considerations in terms of how she presented herself, explaining, when she did not quite understand the question, that I meant in terms of her sense of what might be deemed acceptable to wear or not. Her reply: "There are certain things I would generally wear during the daytime in London or when I'm abroad that I wouldn't wear here." Invoking and claiming a transnational *sens pratique*, a "practical sense of local culture" in and across different cultural and national contexts[43]—yet another mark of privilege and distinction—Misan represented herself as less sexually conservative than the norm at home, yet tending to comply with it. But she was also reflexive about the fact that "here," Lagos/Nigeria, was not just one place: "If I'm going to a café, a nice café [here], I'll wear whatever I want because I guess I know that most people in the café are in a certain way. I wouldn't wear that to the market or to some public open place. But if I know I'm going to a sort of like controlled environment, where I know sort of the type of people who come there, I would wear certain things." Just as in the global North, in Lagos "a nice café" is by definition a class-privileged space. It is a bubble of sorts: access is "controlled," to use Misan's word, structured, and filtered to include and exclude not only different types of people but also, as Misan also suggested, different kinds of mind-sets. What Misan was drawing as a classed map of Lagos could be rendered in temporal terms, too: the "certain way" in which Nigerians in nice cafés were likely to be was "progressive," "ahead" of the wider public, for which reason a young cosmopolitan woman like herself could dress freely in their presence.

Other women explicitly temporalized more or less conservative Nigerian attitudes to what I will call "sexy dress" by suggesting that they were also generational. Early in her interview, Kim enumerated the range of styles in which she might appear: "I could do tomboy, I could be very ladylike, I could be very sexy, very dressed down, casual, dressed up." Of "sexy," I asked:

Simi: So what does that look like?
Kim: It just means you're showing more tits or more legs.
Simi: More flesh?
Kim: More flesh, basically. In a more provocative way.

I asked Kim if she felt she could express such style, explaining that some of the women whom I had interviewed had spoken of feeling and experiencing some degree of constraint around the perceived sexiness or suggestiveness of their dress, including some active policing by older family members. Kim could easily understand what these other women were talking about: "Yeah, I mean, of course we also come from a traditional background at the end of the day. I mean, no mum from our, from their generation, will just see her daughter leaving the house with hot pants [and not intervene]." Even if the young woman was in hot pants because she was beach bound, a typical Nigerian mother, Kim suggested, might ask her to drape a scarf over herself until she got to her destination. Kim went on to conclude, similar to Misan, that how much sexy dress a young woman could do in Lagos depended on the kinds of people by whom she was surrounded. It "wouldn't really matter that much," if one was around people who were "like-minded" or, as she hesitantly characterized it, "enlightened."

Chika was one of the participants who talked about how certain outfits of hers were policed by an older family member, her grandmother, to be exact. If going to a nightclub, for example, "I might wear something like a mini-dress, which is not anything out of the ordinary for someone my age going clubbing, but she just, she would just be like 'You can't go out like that, like what is that, that's not a dress.'" According to Chika, her grandmother would sometimes instruct her to change into something less revealing. I sought to clarify if Chika was obliged to respond by changing her outfit or if she could ignore or resist her grandmother. Swiftly, in an emphasized Nigerian accent, appending the Yoruba word *o* to express ardency, Chika made her options very clear: "*I would respond o.*" Returning to a less emphatic accent, she continued: "No, I would change. If she said change, I would change. 'Cause you know it's a respect thing, and you know like Nigerian culture is really, it's, one of the cornerstones I would say of Nigerian culture is really respect for your elders." Ordinarily choosing her dress for and by herself, including short and tight-fitting styles that were "not anything out of the ordinary" for a young woman like herself, Chika also took up the position, emphatically, as one who understood, respected, and dutifully performed contrary cultural imperatives and sensibilities as and when and where required. She was a young postfeminist, cosmopolitan woman like others elsewhere, but also a young Nigerian who understood "tradition" and "culture." Dramatized by her changing accents as she represented the different subject positions that she occupied and navigated, the suggestion and tone from Chika were that the multiplicity of these positions was not especially dilemmatic. As with her accents, she knew how to code switch.

Amaka, on the other hand, reported actively clashing with her mother about her dress. Twice in her interview, she described herself as "not the most conservative person," and a third time said that others would know this about her: "obviously from the way I dress sometimes." She explained that her mother thought that she was "a little rebel" because of her "fashion sense." With an intake of breath, she reenacted the kind of moralized shock that her mother was likely to express if she saw a magazine image of a woman in an outfit that partially exposed her breasts. Amaka contrasted her own attitude to such an outfit: "It's the human body, it's flesh, it's no big deal." Twenty-six years old, Amaka lived with her parents. I posed a similar question to her as to Chika about whether her mother could insist that she change out of a particular outfit if she deemed it too sexy or suggestive. Amaka's strident reply: "No, she can't, no, she can't say something like that. Am I a kid?" Yet although Amaka portrayed herself as able to resist her mother specifically, and although representing herself across the interview as defiant and self-regarding, she conceded that she did not always dress quite as she wanted in Nigeria because of the relative conservatism of the general environment. She could flout it, she said, but did not always have the energy to: "You just feel like at times you need to kind of conform, not because you really care but maybe you just, you're, you're not up for, you don't care for the stares, you know, you don't feel like someone just staring you down, you're not in that mood."

The (hetero)sexualization of culture, that is, the proliferation of discourses, representations, and technologies of (hetero)sexuality, is a core concern in the literature on postfeminism, again having been identified as a core element and feature of postfeminism itself. The "mainstreaming of sexual explicitness for women" is perhaps the most visible and central feature of this cultural shift.[44] Gill contends that "for young women today in postfeminist cultures [in the West], the display of a certain kind of sexual knowledge, sexual practice and sexual agency has become normative—indeed, a 'technology of sexiness' has replaced 'innocence' or 'virtue' as the commodity that young women are required to offer in the heterosexual marketplace."[45] The case of the reality television show *Girls Gone Wild*, which Amy Dobson explores, would seem to exemplify Gill's contention; in it young women are called to flash their breasts, kiss each other, masturbate, and so on, as enactments of their (heterosexual) empowerment, choosing, and knowing.[46] Media and consumer culture offer women a range of other images, interpellations, technologies, and also spaces to "do postfeminist sexy," from the rebranding of sex toys and shops as fashionable and safe, not "seedy,"[47] to the staging of pole and other erotic dancing as exercise, classes now available at the neighborhood gym, to the myriad sex tips offered in women's magazines, self-help, and other such texts. With regard to women's dress, postfeminist sexy looks like bodies on greater public display, or "more tits or more legs" to borrow Kim's concise summation.

But according to what we have been hearing from Kim and the other women above, this look is not so much in fashion, certainly neither imperative nor normative, in Lagos/Nigeria. Gill's suggestion that we may need to understand "*compulsory (sexual) agency* as a required feature of contemporary postfeminist, neoliberal subjectivity" would seem to not apply.[48] These findings could lead us back to the kinds of a priori and Eurocentric views that this book seeks to counter, in which postfeminism outside the West is understood as a watered-down version of "the real thing," or inauthentic, not really belonging. It could also take us back to related presumptions, such as voiced by Diane, that if and where Nigerian women are doing postfeminist sexy, they are parroting Western women, trying to be what they are not, and therein losing their true, or truer, selves and cultures. Yet the literature on postfeminism is attentive to the fact that, in the West, and especially in the flesh, women's engagement in new sexually explicit practices, self-representations, and cultures is not unqualified and is not free from, beyond, contestation and consternation. In the first place, the "pornification" of culture, as it is also called in some quarters, engenders a degree of moral panic, particularly as it does or could implicate teenage and younger girls—hints of panic can be found in critical feminist work also, it must for noted.[49] And for the woman doing and flaunting postfeminist sexy, risks remain of moral and social censure and shaming. Labels like "slut" are still bandied about. If this holds even for the most idealized and sanctioned subject of postfeminism in the West—namely, the young, white, middle-class, heterosexual, able-bodied, and normatively attractive woman—how much more so for others? Imogen Tyler has written of how, in the British context, it is the presumed sexual agency and activeness of the young, white, working-class woman figured, derogatorily, as the "chav" that become central grounds for her harsh vilification.[50] The "can-do girl" that is postfeminism's poster child has an "at risk" counterpart, typically an ethnic minoritized and working-class subject, for whom a perceived core risk is "premature" sexual activity resulting in serial single motherhood.[51]

Rather than understanding assertive and explicit heterosexual agency and sexiness as virtually compulsory for postfeminist subjectification and embodiment, I would modify Gill's suggestion to propose that we must understand these dispositions and practices of self as central to postfeminism's simultaneously promissory and disciplinary *address* to young women. If so, the analytic task becomes to take a rigorously intersectional eye to questions of which kinds of women exactly can respond to and read themselves in the address, how much so, when, and where, and negotiating what kinds of considerations, risks, and relations. In Africa, however much generational figures like grandmothers or mothers may disapprove, despite public discourses and even state and vigilante actions against so-called indecent dressing, the fact is that both invitations and acceptances to do postfeminist sexy are with us, too. Indeed, the proof is in the panics and pushbacks. A case in point is that "most contemporary African music performance is marked by skimpy fashion and explicit representations of female sexuality, from the lyrics of songs to the wriggling female bodies in bikinis, underwear and hot pants."[52] While Evelyn Lutwama-Rukundo situates this within "global raunch culture," she also briefly notes its continuities with traditional forms of cultural performance where women would be, and in some cases still are, minimally clothed, bare chested, say.[53]

Such tradition notwithstanding, there is across black Africa a deep well of conservatism and moralism about what Ayo Coly terms "the un/clothed African female body."[54] But as Bakare-Yusuf notes about recent panicked discourses that young African women are unclothing themselves anew because of a now transnational raunch culture, even as they are couched and legitimized in visions of African authenticity, tradition, and "Culture" (with a capital *C*), what they bring to the fore "is a repressed indigeneity."[55] They repress precolonial histories and practices of minimal clothing, which the twinned missions of colonialism and Christianization also sought to repress in the sense of cover-up—"civilize," they called it.[56] Thus, a position like Diane's, far from uniquely her own, that says African women should cover up their bodies in the name of not only gendered propriety but also "authentic Africanness," and that sees their refusal to do so as evidence of inauthentic and corrupt Westernization, is itself caught in the logics and values of coloniality that it ostensibly aims to reject.[57] The position is premised upon a prior incorporation of colonial norms of gendered dress in Africa. Indeed, it seeks a return to this prior accession to norms that were once new and foreign to us. The claim of authentic Africanness is premised upon the very changeability or nonfixity of Africanness that it declares fixed and, rather paradoxically, revealing the utter fictiveness of the whole thing, that it moves to fix. In all the above, whiteness and white supremacy are reconsolidated because, in fact, cultural authenticity is the burden of the racially or ethnically marked subject.[58] The white subject can travel, can change, can explore, can invent and reinvent itself through time, space, and difference, be Victorian today, postfeminist tomorrow. It is the rest of us who are to stay in our said place and state and, in terms of the particular concerns of this book, fashion or be charged with mimicry, accused of wanting to be like "the white woman," as Diane put it. Just as in practice, in daily life, African women (and men) refuse this "containment," this straitjacketing of our lives, so we must, too, in our theory and scholarship.[59]

5

"NOT THAT KINDA GIRL"

RESIGNIFYING HYPERFEMININITY
FOR POSTFEMINIST TIMES

Having playfully described her style, tastes, and sensibilities as "fully girly," one of the women, Sade, rejected a line of stereotyped association with this kind of subject positioning and naming that I introduced for her consideration, namely, domesticity. Cooking and cleaning indexed a different kind of girliness, she joked, and "*no*," she was "not that kinda girl, no, sorry." The woman who, in her dress and comportment, performs and flaunts an exaggerated femininity is almost certain to be adjudged and prefigured in a host of ways. Much as I reported from my experiences of looking for interview participants in Lagos, sexist stereotypes abound: she is shallow and superficial, silly, coquettish, and so on, or, as in Joan Riviere's original Freudian theory of the masquerade, playing up such traits to manipulate and mislead, playing at femininity to mask her true masculinist ability and ambition.[1] While other feminist theorists such as Luce Irigaray and Mary Ann Doane have drawn out the notion of the womanly mask to unambiguously agentic conclusions,[2] such as seeing it as a means to "convert a form of subordination into an affirmation and thus begin to subvert it,"[3] in her consideration of this figure's postfeminist reappearance, McRobbie is decidedly more pessimistic. Post-second-wave feminism, the masquerade, according to McRobbie, is a feminine figure now anxious to not appear "too empowered," or as an even more dreaded "feminist."[4] Therefore, she hyperbolizes her femininity for the same old purpose of reassuring the world that she is "just a girl," still.

Acutely aware of how their appearances were or might be (mis)read, there were, for the women, tensions and deviations between what others might make of them and how they saw and felt about themselves. Encapsulated by the aphorism that beauty is only skin deep, the tensions concerned hegemonic gendered ontologies and epistemologies of body versus mind and surface versus depth. The women were keen to establish that behind their beauty, and exceeding it in fact, lay character, intelligence, and professionalism. Yet because they were very invested in their appearances and the empowerment that postfeminist feminine beauty promised, and because this manifest investment invited potential negative judgment or appraisal, they walked a fine line between "overdoing" and "underdoing" their self-spectacularization, particularly in the world of work. On the domestic front, meanwhile, just like Sade the women rejected and distanced norms of traditional (hyper) femininity, in particular any notion that a woman's place was in the kitchen or that when in the kitchen a woman's lot was drudgery, "sweating and slaving," as one called it. Or, to put the point otherwise, they sought to bring choice, knowingness, and "glam" to this realm of their lives too. However, continuing the line of critique that has run through the book, as in the broader literature on postfeminism, that, however new it may be or look or feel like, postfeminism constitutes an insidious retraditionalization and restabilization of gender norms,[5] I argue that the women were not as free or far from the old, and the stubbornly patriarchal, as they seemed to imagine, indeed fantasize. They were trapped between the happy vistas of postfeminism, in which a woman could "have it all," stylishly, for that matter, and the cruel continuities of the worlds in which women actually live.

GIRLY-GIRLS AND GIRLY-GIRLS

After having heard participants talk at length about their extensive fashion and beauty practices, investments, and consumption, to start to move the interviews on from this central focus, I typically asked how important they would say their appearance was to them overall or in summary. Tinu replied with a question:

Tinu: Should I rate it in percentage? (*pauses*) 101 percent (*briefly laughs*)
Simi: Oh, really?
Tinu: Yeah, it's very important *to me* because that's just what gets recorded. Your state of mind appears, shows in your appearance. Your appearance shows your state of mind. And that's what appears to other people. That's what they, the impression they take home.

For Nene, appearance was "really, really, really, really, really" important for similar reasons. It was "like the first thing before your personality. Yeah.

Like for me, I look at your dressing first, the way you dress, if you don't really dress nice, I won't like to really associate with you, that's before knowing your personality." Alero also expressed the view that one's appearance shaped how one was appraised and treated by others: "I think appearance is very important 'cause people respond to you (*pauses*) different, I think, when you, you know, you have put in some more effort." Or, as she and two others put it, "how you're dressed is how you're addressed," a neat formulation that echoes the Yoruba proverb "*irinisi ni ihuwa sinni,*" "self-presentation dictates others' apprehension [of you]."

The reader might spot an apparent contradiction here. Whereas I argued earlier in the book that the women claimed, ardently, that the greatest value of feminine beauty was its production of a positive and powerful interior sense of self, in the forgoing quotes they constructed their appearance as most important for external purposes, for how they were seen. Often when I present the research I am asked which it is, in the final analysis: Did the women "*really*" dress to see and please themselves, or were their elaborate looks "*really*" for others' appreciation, men's especially? The binary premise of the question is flawed. Appearing, a dual condition of, on the one hand, making oneself seen, to be looked at, and, on the other hand, being seen or looked at, must be understood as entering into the very making and fiber of modern feminine subjectivity and agency.[6] As such, it does not represent the loss or abdication of selfhood in the form of (self-)objectification. Part of how a woman becomes a subject and imagines and feels herself as such is by imagining and experiencing being an object of the gaze. Postfeminism renders this complex positionality the more counterintuitive, if not impossible, by offering women a stark "for yourself/for others' logic," mapped on to an equally false binary of empowerment/disempowerment, which, as we have already seen, led the women whom I interviewed to insistently position themselves as "choosers" and "doers," not in any way put upon. But as the present discussion will cover, the fact is that how women look continues to very much matter to others, and in turn this very much matters to women. Thus, to put it quite simply, postfeminism fails and misleads them once again.

In the interviews, after hearing the women's summative views on the importance of their appearance, I would typically ask what else was important or mattered to them as young Lagos women. Tinu did not miss a beat: "Intellect. I respect intellect a lot. That's why I answered your call, yeah. I respect, apart from your appearance, when you talk, it should be something graceful, you know, seasoned, to show that this girl or this lady is not just empty, yeah, she's got the stuff." Tinu conjured up and disavowed common stereotypes of hyperfemininity as shallow or depthless to communicate that, although for her dress she might look like this type of woman, she was not.[7] Even the rhetorical structure of her claim was performative of its substance: demonstrating that she knew the "empty" feminine type and knew that she could be misrecognized for it became demonstrative of the fact that she was indeed not it. Other women echoed this performative contention that appearance was just surface, and in the end superficial, such that it had to be backed by substance or depth. Explaining how she would like to be perceived by others, Folake said, "When people see you at first, before they're drawn to you, they, it's the outside that draws them. And then when they now have a conversation with you, then, you know, they either conclude 'Okay, this one has brains or not.' And em (*pauses*) I'm, I'd like people to see me as, I'm not just, it's not just about looking, you know, beautiful." Adaeze emphasized that her concerns and competencies far exceeded her appearance, saying that she wanted "to contribute something to the society, I want to be known for something good." She continued, "I've never felt that it's all about the way you look. You have to back it up: be it education, be it your job, be it whatever."

June claimed not only that her "outer beauty" was backed by "inner beauty," but that the latter surpassed the former in scope, meaning, and authenticity. Hearing her recollect how much she had liked to wear false nails when she was younger, I asked if she had felt that she had needed to have long nails, to which she responded, "Oh, no, not at all, not at all. . . . You know, the thing is, people, the, the real you is not how pretty you can make yourself up to look, the real you is who you really are, you know. So beauty is much more than, em, what you can see outside." What June was saying, in short, is that "beauty comes from within." None of the other women cited this adage. Having heard much of it in her research on black feminine beauty, Tate understands it is a melancholic claim to beauty that black (diasporic) women make from their mainstream racist positioning outside the appearance of beauty.[8] I have argued, though, that my research participants very much saw their final or achieved appearance as beautiful and that black is beautiful in Nigeria. "Over here, we have no problem with the concept of an African woman's body as beautiful," Abena Busia writes, referring to black Africa as a whole, and contrasting this with black struggles in the diaspora to make "black women's bodies both visible and legible in contexts of beauty, desirability, and dignity."[9] The women in Lagos did not need to claim that their beauty was beneath the surface, then, as a response to racist visions of blackness as ugly. I want to suggest, though, that we must also hear the marked absence in the interview data of so common a notion as "inner beauty" as a postfeminist effect. The adage that beauty comes from within seeks to value and elevate traditional feminine virtues such as caring, goodness, and kindness over physical appearance. By contrast, as in the foregoing quotes and others to be discussed shortly, what the research participants insisted lay beneath the surface of their appearance were brains and power. Notions and rhetoric of inner beauty also caution women not to "fall prey to the conceit of artifice."[10] They advise women not to pay too much attention to the exterior when it is the interior that matters most. But as I have already argued in preceding parts of the book, in the postfeminist terms of my research participants' spectacular self-stylization, beauty was a serious affair with serious interior effects, being a route to (further) empowerment. It was already more than mere vanity or mindless artifice.

Ima alleged that all this was not necessarily the case for other young Nigerian women who dressed and appeared like her. Characterizing herself as "the most *non*-girly girl you'll ever meet," she elaborated what she meant: "Like I do my nails and I do my hair, but I don't talk about it. Like I'm not like (*puts on a mock girly voice*) 'Oh my God, it's your nails!' Like I'm not an airhead, but (*laughing*) I'm definitely into like my, my looks." As in Tinu's self-description as a lady who was not "just empty," Ima was drawing on commonplace stereotypes of exaggerated femininity as a frivolous and intellectually vacant subject position to clarify who and what she was not. This included her performance of what was to be understood in the context of her remarks as the "silly" voice of the sort of woman to get excited over something ("silly") like "*your nails!*" Although Ima named herself as a "*non*-girly girl," from her subsequent comments and line of reasoning I would suggest that what she meant was that she was a "*non*-girly girly-girl." She was not excluding herself from the subject position of girly-girl altogether but broadening and redefining it to include and set apart her particular version. She was the kind of girly-girl "definitely" invested in her looks, but not the kind whose interests and character were therein circumscribed. This was the "airhead" girly-girl, which she further described as "froufrou."

Being in a community of stylized practice with the kinds of girly-girls that she was deriding, Ima admitted that she might "bump into them in the salon and, you know, have a little chitchat." Yet she maintained that she was less likely to have substantive friendships with such women than with their *boyfriends*: "Like I can have a beer, and I can talk about politics. . . . I wouldn't have a conversation about Kim Kardashian." Funke also distinguished herself from and against stereotypical girly-girls by aligning herself with men and with masculinized norms of character and substance. She recalled that her male friends would remark, "'You can talk to Funke for five hours and not be bored.' I'm like 'What do you mean?' They said, 'No girly talk; we can't do it. You know, we find it really boring. I mean, girls just talk about a certain thing. . . . Girls talk about boys, girls talk about nails, girls talk about, and that's girly talk,' and I'm like 'Okay, it's a problem.'" By concurring that "girly talk" was a "problem," and by validating men's reported boredom by it, Funke represented herself as intellectually broader and deeper than the types of women who engaged in it. In her account, her exclusion from and critique of girly talk worked to place her on a more equal footing with men and to garner their recognition and respect as such. Elsewhere in the interview, Funke characterized the girly as "soft," "princessy," "dolls and fairies," and repudiated any possible association with such styles and signifiers. She did so acknowledging, again like others, that on the basis of how she looked she could be potentially misapprehended for this kind of subject: "I don't do princesses, oh no. I do like (pauses) edgy, you know like adventurous. . . . I wouldn't sit down and talk about, em, (pauses) shopping with you. . . . [M]y conversations are more, you know, what you hear me talk about is probably different from what you think I'd talk about."

"Distancing oneself from stereotypical femininity . . . is a claiming of power" via a rejection of the culturally constructed disempowerment and disparagement that attend the position. Carrie Paechter lists three subject positions from which women's rejection of girliness typically occurs: the feminist, the tomboy, and the butch lesbian.[11] She does not include the heterosexual woman who dresses, looks, girly. This would look like an oxymoron. Embodying this very position, my research participants resolved any contradiction in it via a postfeminist reworking of the logics and meanings of girliness, as I have been showing. From their point of view, there were girly-girls and girly-girls, old and new, we could say. Their girly, the new mode, was reflexive and agentically chosen and was a recursively empowered and empowering style of self. Their girly was "girl power." It neither reflected nor engendered a silly or superficial feminine subjectivity; this was the other kind of girly, the old and more common mode.

Misan and Sade were notable among the women for explicitly embracing stereotypes of the latter kind of girly, which, for the purposes of the present exposition, I will call the "silly-girly." I discuss Misan's example further below. Sade, as has been noted, provided a highly linear narrative account of her entry into spectacularly feminine style that included a present moral and material entitlement to it as an adult and self-financed career woman. It was also for occupying this position that she framed a certain silly girliness as a deliberate and justifiable performance or play. Enacting the silly-girly was, for her, a leisurely reclamation of femininity. It was postfeminist reprieve from the fact that "my daily life is so driven by masculinity." Sade was referring here to the demands of her job as a journalist. The work was stressful, she explained, and navigating Lagos for it was masculinizing. She would often have to "fight with area boys," she claimed, that is to say young, able-bodied, underemployed men who hang around an area or locale to, in Sade's words, "hustle" a living.[12] Her reasoning was that if a woman was "lady-like and timid . . . prim and proper" when face-to-face with Lagos-area boys, they would walk all over her. In view of her "tough" professional beat, it followed for Sade that when she was off-duty: "I just wanna relax, I wanna be pampered, I wanna be, (*puts on a girly voice*) *I just wanna be in a Cinderella world.*" Or, because for her work she had to keep up with "hard news," such as about Boko Haram, the terrorist group in northern Nigeria, when she was at home and at ease:

> Sade: I'm watching *E!*, *TLC*, you know, I wanna—
> Simi: So like those—softer stuff?
> Sade: I wanna watch *The Wedding Show*, something *soft*, you know, something like, yeah, you know, like I wanna know what the color of the month is, that kinda stuff, you know (*laughs*).

Sade was talking about negotiating a postfeminist dilemma between being a "serious" career woman in a masculine field, in an especially muscular city at that, and still being a girly-girl. McRobbie sees the postfeminist masquerade as one response proffered to young women to resolve this dilemma, the resolution being to take one's hyperfemininity to work.[13] Yet this was not fully possible or advisable in Sade's experience, as I come back to shortly. Her solution, therefore, was to perform powerful and serious femininity at work and self-indulgent, silly girliness at play. The solution was a shifting, highly self-aware feminine subjectivity and habitus across the different fields that she occupied. As she put it to me, beginning to enact and differentiate through her words the multiplicity of her subjectivity of which she was speaking: "When I find space and time for myself—*me* time—I am *the girliest girl* (*pauses*) you would ever find. Like we're two different people: Sade on Sade time is different from Sade on work time, totally different." Below I discuss the contradictory imperatives and implications for the women's styles of dressing up and appearing "on work time." The contradictions turned on the question of whether it is truly the case that "beauty is only skin deep," as that other beauty adage goes.

TAKING THE SPECTACULAR TO WORK

"For many women in contemporary [working] life, negotiating and performing a 'professional' identity is a process requiring much time, energy,
and self-surveillance."[14] This is especially the case with regard to dress and
appearance, to look "appropriate" for work, the practical and moral difficulty
of which concerns us here.[15] When I asked Sharon how important she would
say her appearance was to her overall, she replied in terms of her career as
a celebrity: "Eighty out of, 90 out of 100, 90 I think, 'cause my image is everything, my brand is everything in my profession, so I'd say 99 percent."
Tinu, the Nollywood actress, also saw herself as a brand and that its value
centered upon her embodied appearance: "If I don't represent, if I don't, em,
package or look good . . . people won't want to identify with what I do." Part
of her "packaging," as she also termed it, was to always wear false eyelashes
when appearing as a celebrity, although, behind the scenes, Tinu was trying
to wean herself off the beauty technology. Having heard Tinu explain her
aesthetic vigilance with her false eyelashes in terms of her wish to no longer
feel a sense of self-alienation and even ugliness without them, I asked how
she felt with them, to which she replied: "It just gives me that diva look, I
just feel like a diva, you know." I recall feeling almost excited to hear the
subject position of diva being named and claimed and being keen to unpack
its meanings. Keenly, then, and perhaps a little too "academically," I asked,
"What's a diva?" Tinu's definition went as follows: "A diva is someone that is
publicly (*sighs*)—let me say a diva, *to me*, anybody in entertainment that is
really, really hardworking and working on yourself too, your look. You don't
have to like look overweight, unkempt, ungroomed, because you're a public
figure, a lot of people are looking at you."

A woman whose paid work it was to appear, a diva was an exemplary aesthetic entrepreneur: a subject committed to a continuous and hyperindustri-
ous practice of surveilling, normalizing, and working on her appearance.[16] In
this a diva was not only investing in herself as human capital, appreciating
the worth of her stock, as Michel Feher might put it.[17] She was also meeting
a responsibility to her public. Within what I will borrow and extend from
Banet-Weiser to call a moralized neoliberal and postfeminist economy of
feminine visibility, it was a diva's *duty* to look good.[18] Tinu's definition of
diva did not include common negative associations that I had expected to
hear, such as that she is a woman with a bad attitude or delusions of grandeur.[19] Sade, however, understood the label as derogatory. Speaking about the
constraints of her dressing for work, Sade explained about a short wig that

she called her "work hair": "The industry has certain hang-ups. You don't wanna look too glamorous 'cause then, you know, they call you a diva or they ascribe shallowness to you. Em, you wanna look a certain seriousness, like you wanna look like you can, if you were in the, in the cut, you could hold your own, you know, so that's why I have the short hair." While Sade was in the Nigerian media industry like Tinu and Sharon, the feminized risks that she was describing here of appearing "too glamorous," too beautified, too invested in one's appearance to also appear professional, applied off-screen, when one was producing, not presenting, indeed embodying, content. On-screen, on the visible side of the industry, where Sade had been previously stationed herself, and where the norms of appearing had first interpellated her into spectacular femininity, what was risky, and not strategic, was not appearing beautiful enough, perhaps looking "overweight, unkempt, un-groomed" to draw from Tinu's list of what was prohibited for the diva.

Finding the balance between looking good and "too much" was even trickier in the corporate world, according to a number of the women's ac-counts. Looking at the sector from the outside, Sharon explained that she had stopped wearing a particular brand and style of human hair extensions because women in banking seemed to favor it: "I realized that a lot of, em, bankers and a lot of people in the corporate world wear that with their suits. It matches that look." June gave an overview of what she called her "corporate, very corporate at work" look as follows: "I always wear long hair. I always wear heels. I love heels. I have a lot of shoes. I have almost all the colors, I think." Bisi noted that her female banker colleagues tended to wear "sky-high heels" in the office, which is certainly how I would characterize the shoes that Funke, also a banker, had on when I interviewed her at her own place of work. Funke explained that she always wore high heels at work, reserving her flat shoes for "when I really need to walk really fast. After work. I don't wear them during work hours at all." She considered looking good at work good for productivity, for the bottom line, and presented herself in the in-terview as someone who stepped in repeatedly to discipline and "upgrade" her female colleagues' appearance. Among her motivations was that "there's nothing as demoralizing as someone who isn't looking nice and knows. . . . [I]t *doesn't* help [their] work really, if you have somebody like that who's just feeling pity for herself." As she later put it, "From a happy employee you can get a lot of benefits."

Funke gave a striking example of this rationality in action. The example was of a woman in her office who was considered to generally lack self-confidence, who happened to have been selected to represent their company at a public event. Funke recounted that as the woman was leaving the office, nervously, for the event, she, Funke, had waved her over with a tube of red lipstick: "I take this really red, RED lipstick . . . and [my colleague] was like 'No, I don't use red lipstick.' I said, 'No, sit down, just trust me on this one, let me just do this very,' and then I put the lipstick, and she's like (*drops voice, sounding unsure*) 'Ah, how do I look? I don't know, I'm so scared.'" Like high heels, red lipstick has been rebranded emblematic of feminine power.[20] Implying that this had been her intent and expectation for her colleague, Funke recounted that the lipstick had had a remarkably transformative effect on the woman. It had been reported back to the office that, at the company event, this woman had been "the center of attention—she's happy, she's smiling." Furthermore, according to Funke, this colleague had been subjectivated promptly as a woman who, like Funke herself, knew how to *self*-empower and intended to do so: "The very next day she came back herself and said, 'Please, can I have your lipstick.' . . . [S]he took it *herself*, applied it *herself* . . . and she says 'Funke, I don't care how much that lipstick cost, I have to buy it,' and I said, 'Yes, I will get, I will get a lipstick for you.'"

Even in the corporate arena, postfeminist feminine beauty was not only skin deep. It did things. Giving a woman an internal boost, it could then boost her career, as well as business bottom lines. If thirty or so years ago, the advice to women in male-dominated professional arenas was to "dress for success" by muting or shrouding their femininity, the converse was now the case. Spectacularly feminine style was the new "power dressing."[21] Bisi was very much of this view. In the following exchange, I was probing the extent of the opinion that she had shared earlier in the interview, that a beautiful and fashionable feminine appearance granted a woman self-confidence and self-empowerment:

> Simi: What about at work? Does dressing up also like give you confidence at work?
> Bisi: Oh, *yeaaah!* When we have this meeting and I walk into a room, they're like (*in a girly voice*) "Oh, Bisi, nice dress." I'm like (*in the girly voice again*) "*Thank you.*"

In the course of elaborating this enthusiastic position, however, Bisi recognized indirectly that regardless of what a woman might feel in, about, and thanks to her dress, she could not control its meanings or readings, and if she looked overdressed to others, she could easily be seen as less than professionally competent. Bisi gave the hypothetical example of making a presentation at work and talked through two possible scenarios in which her look differed:

Let's say at work I have this presentation, me and my group we have to do, and I'm not looking, I'm looking scruffy and (*inaudible*). I feel like they [that is, my colleagues] won't even hear what I'm saying, they'll just look at: "See her *hair*. Why is she dressed like this on a Monday? See how (*inaudible*) her suit is." It's taking them away. But when I'm looking good but I'm not *distracting* them, I'm wearing a nice simple dress or I'm wearing—all they know is I'm looking good, I don't have *too* many pieces. . . . They just know I look good, and they listen to what I'm saying.

Not looking good enough would distract her colleagues from the substance of what she was presenting to them. Instead of listening to her, they would be looking critically at how she looked. But at the same time, looking too good or too much, such as wearing "*too* many pieces," would also be "distracting" to her colleagues, "taking them away" from the substance of the presentation. Looking just right, finding the happy midpoint, meanwhile, would draw attention not to how she looked but to what she was saying. Bisi depicted what I would argue were a set of near-impossible feminine considerations as nondilemmatic. Rendered responsible for her location within a gendered economy of visibility in which her appearance not only mattered for her and for others but also always exceeded her intent and self-apprehension, the spectacularly feminine professional woman had to manage or handle things by getting her look perfect. The onus was on her to ensure that she got it right. Bisi concluded the hypothetical scenarios by suggesting that *she* knew how to achieve the almost magical balance: "That's how I do at work, I don't wear too much."

Funke took further the suggestion that the spectacularized corporate career woman could work her appearance to her advantage. Unlike Bisi, though, Funke implied that this woman was squarely in control of the meanings of her appearance. Hence, for instance, the degree of competence, care, and attention to detail that her appearance visibly demanded would translate into others seeing her as also competent, careful, and attentive in professional matters. Clients who saw her would imagine: "She looks like she pays attention to herself, she'll probably pay attention to me too. . . . Someone who (*pauses*) would handle her *dress* like this, and take time out to coordinate everything, she [will] probably coordinate me." Having effectively suggested that the spectacular professional woman was beyond sexist reading and reduction, Funke went on to note that she still had to back up the feminine beauty that had gained clients' favor with brains and competence: "Charm and good looks, [you] can get by on them for like ten, fifteen minutes; after that you'd better have something to say." Alero went further yet to position the spectacularly feminine professional woman beyond power, suggesting that, with male clients, it was this woman who held all the cards. Recounting an experience in which a male client had tried to get her personal contact details ostensibly to discuss business further, before one of her senior colleagues had intervened to stop him, Alero concluded, "Depending on how you want it to go, especially like with male clients or like male business partners, yeah, I think you consciously, especially in countries like Nigeria, [I] think the better dressed you are, the more the chance you have."

In Alero's assured scenario, the spectacular career woman was so thoroughly individualized and agentic, so thoroughly the postfeminist and neoliberal ideal, that she could trade on her appearance with confidence because she was able to predetermine and control how she would "want it to go." Utterly evacuated from this proposition are considerations of male power, sexism, sexual harassment, and other violence and injustice against women in the workplace. It is a striking example of how postfeminism and its celebration of individual feminine capacities and outlooks may denude women of not only a critical view and language on persistent gendered inequality and discrimination against women, but even the mere expectation that they might encounter these forces. Folake expressed surprise—to my surprise—to have run into sexism in her predominantly male workplace. She described her job as requiring "more than just looking beautiful. It also requires some sense. A lot of sense! And you know you need to, you need to know what you're doing; you need to be smart about it." She recounted how she had recently scored an important breakthrough with a notoriously difficult male client. She had therefore "found it a bit offensive," she explained, that on hearing of her achievement, her male manager had remarked, "Oh, they like her, she's a beautiful lady." He had overlooked her professional capacity and skill by suggesting that the client had rolled over because he found Folake attractive, giving her pause about how exactly her colleagues viewed and rated her: "Like wait, do you actually think it's because I'm beautiful?" She concluded of the episode, "So I don't just want people to see me as a pretty face." The problem, though, was that appearing with a pretty face, the spectacular (but not too spectacular) professional woman could always be reduced to it, despite whatever intelligence, professionalism, and sense of empowerment she might possess or feel and despite the postfeminist suggestion that the gendered professional playing field is level, or that women can individually make it so. For the serious and substantive career woman, the kind of feminine subject with which the research participants strongly identified, beauty, which they also claimed and desired, was a trap. Beauty empowered and disempowered.

STYLING DOMESTICITY

Oluwakemi Balogun compares and contrasts two national beauty pageants in Nigeria that construct and vaunt markedly different styles of Nigerian femininity. Whereas one pageant, Queen Nigeria, emphasizes so-called traditional values and culture, the other, the Most Beautiful Girl in Nigeria, is oriented toward the content and standards of global beauty pageants such as Miss World, for which it produces the country's annual representatives. Contestants in MBGN are ranked and adjudged for such criteria as their appearance in bikinis, as they will be at Miss World. Competitions in Queen Nigeria revolve around domestic tasks such as cooking and serving local dishes, keeping the kitchen clean, and demonstrating prudence in stretching and managing a limited household budget. Queen Nigeria cites and seeks to promote the dominant local sensibility that "conventional markers of domesticity such as cooking Nigerian meals, childrearing, or housekeeping are standard elements of [moral and Nigerian] femininity."[22] Given the kinds of positions and logics that I have been showing that the women in this book asserted, it should come as no surprise that they disidentified with Queen Nigeria's idealized kind of femininity. Misan laughed as she said, "It's *soo* funny how people think being a girl or being a woman is cooking, like sweating and slaving yourself in the kitchen." She explained that her mother was a career woman who had always worked outside the home, but was also "very traditional" on the domestic front. She described resisting her mother's view that she, Misan, must learn how to cook so as to be able to meet her duties to a future husband. Her contrary attitude was that she should learn to cook because "it's something good to have *for me, for myself.*"

More than once at prior points in the interview, Misan had named herself as a girly-girl. But as we spoke about domesticity, she qualified this, saying, "Yeah, I'm girly to an extent." If cooking was girly, she continued, "Then I guess I'm not, like I guess I don't fit the bill. But when it comes to like—like I always say I'm a girly-girl but maybe with a twist." The notion of being "a girly-girl with a twist" speaks directly to my contention that the women sought to put a spin or twist on normative or common constructions, practices, and meanings of the hyperfeminine, to distinguish what it was that they were doing. The twist was postfeminism; postfeminism is a twist on normative femininity. And hence it was that choice and knowing were central to being able to perform the twist. Diane, for instance, also explicitly named herself as a girly-girl and, when I asked, confirmed that this could include cooking. But, as to whether domestic work was a normative or compulsory duty for a woman like her: "*No, of course not!*" She did it as, when, and to the extent that she chose. Diane went on to point out that she hired someone to do the work, as is very much the norm for middle-class and more privileged Nigerians. Sade expressed pleasure and relief that she could pay someone to work in her home: "I have a housekeeper who does all that, laundry, cleaning up, everything that's, yeah. And I just think it's wonderful that you can, that you can have that. 'Cause if I didn't have it, if I didn't have the, you know, if I wasn't able to have someone doing it for me, I would be crazy." She noted that she knew how to cook well and had cooked for herself when she lived in the United States, as is the norm there. Any cooking that she did now, in Lagos, was by choice and for leisure, she explained, for special occasions such as dinner parties. Describing herself in the kitchen, Sade painted a scene of "sensuousness and craft . . . [that] idealize and eroticize [domestic] femininity."[23]

> Sade: When I do cook, it's a whole drama. I have my pink *apron*.
> Simi: Oh my gosh.
> Sade: I wear *stilettos*. I wear *shorts*.

This was another twist on the traditional. It consisted of playing at domesticity in a bounded, hyperstylized, sexualized, and again very much knowing and ironic way, all of which then rendered the domestic scene and subject far from traditional, including for overturning stereotypical associations of the kitchen with feminine drudgery. Calling it "fun" and "role-playing," Sade proffered her girly-girl domesticity as a further example of how she carved out feminized respite and recovery from "all the *seriousness*" in her professional life. We could also call it fantasy in that it entailed playing with a feminine subject position and set of practices "without having to experience their actual consequences."[24] The fantasy, playing "domestic goddess," was materially enabled and rendered meaningful by the fact that Sade did not have to cook and clean for herself day in and day out.[25] For that she hired another woman: "I work hard to pay somebody to do all that," she explained, laughing. Premised, then, on Sade's status as a "serious career woman," her domestic fantasy was also further performative of, and pointing back toward, this feminine position. Her experience of being in a postfeminist time and state was, among others, premised on the labor, but also differential temporalized state, of another woman.[26]

As in the image of the woman in the kitchen in stilettos, Folake and Tinu insisted that their spectacularly feminine style of dress did not practically impede their doing of housework. I asked Folake she if was able to "do stuff" around the house with what we estimated were the two-inch acrylic nails that she was wearing in the interview. Her reply was affirmative: "I can do everything with my nails; I'm used to them. . . . When I was in England, when I was in uni [university] I had no one, I had no maid or anything. I cooked myself, I cleaned myself, you know, I'm just used to them." Tinu also claimed to be so habituated to her long nails that she could function easily with them. I proffered different examples of everyday tasks for her consideration:

> Simi: What about your house, domestic work?
> Tinu: Yeah, that too.
> Simi: You can cook and clean with the nails?
> Tinu: Yeah, I can, it doesn't stop anything. I, I will be surprised to hear that any *lady* in this our *generation* says *nails* is an obstacle to anything.

Wearing long acrylic nails was thoroughly normative and unremarkable for Tinu. It was a basic aspect of young, modern femininity. In fact, as I will come back to, Tinu was at first baffled and then bemused by my line of questioning about what she could or could not do or achieve while wearing false nails. She seemed to find my questions a little ridiculous, the answers being, to her, quite self-evident. Just like the capacity that she claimed to be able to not merely walk but run in high heels, cooking and cleaning with false nails were embodied competencies that a "lady" came to possess. A lady was an "appropriate" feminine subject: appropriately subjected, appropriately embodied, appropriately desiring, appropriately self-stylizing, appropriately postfeminist.

Yet from the participants' comments as well as from what they did not say, I would argue that appropriately postfeminist did not mean that one was completely free of the kitchen or, quite importantly, sharing domestic labor and responsibilities with the present or imagined male partners of which the women spoke. Tobi jokingly imagined a hypothetical future marriage in which her husband would be the primary provider and treat her to luxuries. She referenced not only spectacular items of her dress but also "a nice car, something expensive, a Mercedes or something." Discomfited, in retrospect, by the conservatism of my language, I asked Tobi, "And then what are your duties?" What I was trying to ask was how Tobi imagined the relational dynamic of a heterosexual marriage because, what I thought I was hearing was that she was imagining having both posttraditional feminine freedom *and* a traditional male provider, an unlikely combination it seemed to me. Promptly, and in a naturalized manner, Tobi proffered her contribution to the hypothetical marriage in terms of domestic life, if also imagining that she would exercise a class-privileged choice in the detail of the chores that she would consent to undertake:

> Tobi: I will cook; I won't clean.
> Simi: You won't clean?
> Tobi: Yes. You [that is, the future husband] better get someone to clean the house.
> Simi: (in a clarifying tone) But you *will* cook?
> Tobi: I'll cook—that's not a problem. Take care of the kids—we will share it *o*—be contributing to the house. A woman's touch.

Tobi did not include her hypothetical husband in the cooking and cleaning. If a postfeminist woman's place was no longer in the kitchen, the kitchen was still a feminine place, one for women, not men. Having first said that she would look after "the kids," Tobi went back to add and emphasize (*o*) that her husband would "share" this role. Arguably, she was imagining him as a new kind of father, although she did not otherwise represent him as a new kind of man. She then summarized her contribution to her marital home in terms of a vague and essentialist notion of bringing "a woman's touch" to bear. Tobi would or perhaps could not elaborate what this stylized repertoire might actually mean or look like in practice:

> Simi: Which is what?
> Tobi: Woman's touch (*laughs*).
> Simi: As in, which is what?
> Tobi: A woman's touch! Just leave it at that (*laughs*).

While it is important to remember that Tobi was speaking only hypothetically, as well as tongue-in-cheek, what I want to point to is the absence in her projections of anything approaching feminism or its considerations and cautions. Tobi was imagining a marriage in which she would "have everything" in the form of a stylized and assertive feminine freedom *premised* on her husband's primary income—a financial dependency rendered respectable by marriage. The question, from a feminist perspective, is whether such a formula would add up in the manner that Tobi was calculating.

POWERFUL WIVES AND YUMMY MUMMIES

I have noted that Misan embraced certain feminine stereotypes that others, like Funke, rejected outrightly. Saying that she liked "girly stuff," Misan enumerated some examples: "Pink—although it's not my favorite color—but I like *pink*, I like *weddings*, I like *fluffy things*, romantic comedies. I will never watch—I hate action movies. . . . I love watching like all those wedding videos when the man is crying." Here I laughed, and Misan summarized the kind of cultural content that she enjoyed with the remark "All these stupid things." Branding her own tastes stupid, in effect acknowledging that they easily could be seen as such, served to untrouble them. It positioned Misan as not stupid or "silly-girly" really but, much like Sade relaxing into "a Cinderella world" after a hard day at work, a woman purposely embracing and finding pleasure in what she knew were stereotyped feminine things. Misan recounted that having been a "tomboy" and "a boy's girl" when she was younger, her desires and interests had been since captured by the girly, and she had run with it, she explained. She spoke of having taken up the culturally proffered tools where they lay,[27] having told herself, "You know what let me just go with the [girly] stereotype, there's no need trying to force [tomboy]. . . . I actually said I'm going to fit into the stereotype. I'll just focus on being a girl and liking dolls, yeah, you know."

I subsequently asked Misan, who had spoken about a boyfriend, if her "going with the girly-girl" factored into her relationships with men. Misan did not follow what I meant, so I rephrased and further specified the question with reference to another participant, saying, "For instance, there's a woman I interviewed who was saying like 'Oh, in a relationship, like I'm the girl.' So she had very sort of conventional ideas about being the girl and being girly in a relationship." In her reply, Misan referred to the notion, and implicit judgment, that I had introduced about conventionality:

> Misan: Okay, I'm unconventional in that aspect.
> Simi: Unconventional?
> Misan: Yeah, I don't (*pauses*). Em, this is what I think is typical, em, [what] the typical Nigerian girl would be: the man is sort of like, I don't know how to explain it, it's like (*pauses*), they allow the man be the man, make most of the *decisions*, be the financial—
> Simi: Provider?
> Misan: You know, pay for, be the financial provider. Em (*pauses*), I don't do that.

In Misan's opinion, the "typical Nigerian girl" was one who, in the context of a heterosexual relationship, expected and allowed that her partner assume a traditional or stereotypical male role, with the status, power, and control implied and expected. By further implication, this was the type of woman to take up a submissive or subordinate female role. Moving on to differentiate her contrary, "unconventional" mode of heterosexual relating, Misan could not find the words. The exchange below continues directly from where she had said "I don't do that" in the excerpt above:

> Misan: Em, meaning, I feel, how would I say it? Em (*pauses*), hmm. I just feel like, just because (*pauses*). Em, I don't know how to say it now, em, hmm.
> Simi: (*hesitantly*) Hmm, is it more, I mean, I don't know, do you have like, more of a, an idea of equality, I don't know, or partnership?
> Misan: Yes! To me it's more like a partnership. I don't, it's more like a partnership.

Quite striking is that Misan, exceedingly articulate and reflexive across the interview as a whole, in this particular moment seemed to completely lack the discursive resources to name, much less elaborate, relational values like equality or partnership between women and men. There was a gap. We can call the gap the absence of feminism, on the one hand; the kinds of ideas and vocabulary that Misan was looking for, that I eventually ventured, are feminist. But from another angle, we can also see the gap as the presence of postfeminism, as the discursive and ideological hollowing out, unnaming and bypassing that postfeminism represents, which may leave women without a full-enough scope of language, and critique, to name not only their experiences but their hopes and ideals, too.

The other research participant whose position I had summarized to prompt Misan was Sade. Not only was it methodologically problematic for me to have editorialized Sade's position for Misan in the way that I did, from my later close engagement with the transcript of her interview, I came to see that I had misrepresented it. Sade's position was not in fact conventional, and much like Misan she had explicitly differentiated her way of doing femininity in a heterosexual relationship from what she deemed the more common norm in Nigeria. She did so starting from and then applying a number of postfeminist twists to this norm. After Sade had described her hyperstylized mode of doing postfeminist girly in the kitchen, I asked, "What about like in the context of a relationship, in terms of being girly or being feminine?" Sade recalled a past long-term heterosexual relationship, stating:

> Sade: The roles were very well defined. I was the girl; he was the man.
> Simi: In terms of what?
> Sade: Like I mean (*pauses and sighs*), I didn't emasculate him.

Sade did not give examples of the "well-defined" gendered roles that she and this boyfriend had assumed. Her reference to the specter of emasculation was key, though: Emasculation means a loss of masculinity, means a loss, real or perceived, of male power. Sade's reported way of being "the girl" in a heterosexual relationship included not challenging or encroaching upon her male partner's normative gendered power and terrain. Recognizing that this might appear contrary to the status and sensibilities of an empowered woman, Sade continued, "You'd assume that I would be the girl who like, who would wear [the] pants in the house, but in that, in that context, I stepped back, I stepped—only because my life is so (*sighs*) is so *tough* already, like you know, like so I'm just like, yeah (*speaking hypothetically to her male partner*), 'You deal with that.'" Drawing once again on the postfeminist rationality to which she had taken frequent recourse in the interview, in which stylized girliness was "a fantasy of transcendence and evasion, a respite from other areas of experience,"[28] Sade's point was that she had not emasculated her partner with a strategic view to her girly happiness. She had let him wear the "pants" in the relationship, handle the things that an independent woman would normally handle for herself, so that she could have the fun of wearing the skirt! And in any case, she indicated that in performing a seemingly fragile girly who could only "deal" with so much, she was actually wielding the *real power* in the relationship because demanding that her male partner step in to take care of her—stylized care in the hypothetical example she gave, below. It was for all these strategic twists and turns that Sade distinguished her conduct of, and position within, heterosexual relationships from what she thought obtained more commonly in Nigeria: "In Nigeria, the expectations are very different. It is expected that a woman will wait hand and feet on a man here. That's not me (*pauses*). I'm more the reverse. I'm the girl (*puts on a girly voice*) *who should be pampered*. And I want to put my feet up and (*to a hypothetical male partner*) 'You, Mister, massage them.'"

Without denying or dismissing the pleasure that Sade seemed to derive from her girly games with her male partner(s), if we understand fantasy and play as allowing "the exploration of what multiple subjectivities might feel like by allowing us to move between them," we can see how they may easily go awry, or invite unintended consequences.[29] The subject might become stuck in places and positions that it meant to occupy only temporarily or playfully, especially as in the intimate, intersubjective scenarios Sade was describing, when giving the illusion of power to others normatively accustomed to it. Amaka did not brook Sade's kind of play. She foresaw potentially disempowering consequences. Speaking of the importance of maintaining financial independence from men, even in marriage, she explained that her attitude was to make sure to always have her "own shit." This was so that financial dependency would not box her in, such as leading her to put up with behavior that she deemed unacceptable: "I like to have my own shit, so if you talking shit I can just walk off." Amaka also spoke of resisting the prospect of a man trying to change her, claiming that Nigerian men in particular "always want to mold you. . . . [Y]ou meet me this way . . . now all of a sudden you want to mold me into something I'm probably not." This statement was in keeping with her insistence that she would not accept a male partner, including a husband, presuming to police her dress: "I've always said I don't want to be with someone that says, 'Oh, you can't wear your short skirts, no, you can't.' No. I want to be able to wear whatever I want to wear. So if I feel like I'm getting a bit too old to wear something, I feel that should be my own decision and not because I all of a sudden I have a ring on my finger or have a *kid*." Her subsequent remarks suggested that she was not completely opposed to dominant notions of maternal respectability, that mothers should "keep it classy," but rather wanted to be able to exercise her individual choice and discretion in this regard: "Obviously, when I have a kid, it's not that I'll be walking around with booty-booty batty-riders, but hey, what if I feel like wearing one? Shit, that should be my decision (*both laugh*)."

Not "booty-booty batty-riders," the shortest of shorts, but a middle-classed (and, again, "classy") sexy and immaculately feminine aesthetic is now in vogue for the postfeminist mother, such as figured by the "yummy mummy" and the "MILF" (that is, "Mother I'd Like to Fuck").[30] Imogen Tyler writes, too, of the new figure of the "pregnant beauty." She characterizes this as a "highly spectacular and contradictory 'maternal femininity' that combines signifiers of (sexual) freedom, consumption, choice, agency and futurity in a powerful and seductive post-feminist cultural ideal."[31] To these happy signifiers, Tinu added postfeminist embodied competence or know-how, as we discussed how she had dressed when she had been pregnant. Responding "of course" to my question of whether she had been "still wearing heels" during her pregnancy, Tinu added that, in fact, this was "the best time" for such shoes. I remarked, "Like Kim Kardashian"—who was heavily pregnant, and doing pregnant beauty, at the time. Tinu concurred, "Yeah. And the nurses would be like 'This is not good for you! You will lose balance, if anything happens' . . . and luckily and I don't know maybe I took more precaution, I never fell down." She had adeptly performed a new and stylish mode of pregnancy that the nurses monitoring her progress had neither understood nor appreciated. Her reenactment of these women's uncomprehending and unnecessary warnings about doing pregnancy in heels further offset her position as a modern, cosmopolitan, savvy, and certainly not dowdy or matronly maternal figure. Unlike these women, *she* knew that pregnancy was no longer a time for "sensible shoes" but one for continued spectacularity and sexiness.

Adaeze also recalled that pregnancy had not impeded her hyperfeminine stylization: "When I was pregnant, I still dressed up, like still always had on my makeup, my hair was always done. . . . I remember my baby shower I had on heels." She cited her mother's repeated advice that she "shouldn't let go" when she became a wife or mother, meaning not let her appearance and figure slide, which could encourage the waning and wandering of her husband's sexual interest. Adaeze gave an example of the kinds of women she did not want to look like or think like as a wife and mother: women who "put on so much weight after childbirth, after getting married, they've put on so much weight, or they feel that 'Ah, I'm married now, the chase is over, so I don't have to do all that anymore.'" These were not women committed to postfeminist practices of the self or to embodying the position of the yummy mummy, that is, the "mother [and wife] who is sexually attractive and well groomed, and who knows the importance of spending time on herself."[32] Explicitly locating herself within a transnational postfeminist culture and sensibility, Adaeze cited the mediated figure and practice of the celebrity yummy mummy to which she was instead oriented: "You know, the world is smaller, we all see what's going on with everybody in Hollywood and everywhere, and you see these new mothers, [and you think] like 'Er, okay, I need to step it up.'" Adaeze made light of this new feminine biopolitical imperative and the laborious work on self that it entailed: "So even when you're tired and you just think, '*Uuuggh*, I'm just gonna let go,' you remember [the yummy mummy types], *nooo, nooo (laughs)*." In other words, remembering the yummy mummy types served as a reminder, a prompt, that one could not "give up and let go."

In addition to understanding the spectacular figures of the pregnant beauty and yummy mummy as a new site of feminine pleasure and aspiration, and at the very same time one "of feminine performance anxiety and thus ironically a new kind of confinement for women," as Adaeze's joking above confirms, we can see them as fetishes for the less than glamorous subject position and certainly work of motherhood.[33] Adaeze reasoned that if being pregnant had not lessened her glamorous style, becoming a mother had to some extent. She described a certain ideological and practical dilemma between looking after a small child and retaining her "yumminess," or what she termed "spunk": "Imagine you're already up all night with your child, you're tired, the last thing you wanna have to deal with is some shoes [that is, heels] that are, you know—but you don't wanna let go, you don't wanna become a mother and not have that, you know, spunk, but you, you start thinking, okay, this is not practical, my *back* hurts, you know." She gave the further example of how, in her dressing up and appearing, a mother of young children had to take into account new considerations like whether she might have to bend down to pick up her child or suddenly run after him or her. Thus, a maternal subjectivity and habitus included a certain shifting to be "more practical" and "comfortable" in one's dress. Adaeze contrasted this to her younger and child-free self for whom buying heels had been a question of "What do they look like? It didn't matter if they were uncomfortable or not." Motherhood had also somewhat shifted her style, according to June. She joked that she had been "a real chick" before she got married, but the need to take care of a child had demanded changes like no longer affixing false nails, "because I couldn't manage that with making children's food and holding a little baby."

Not so for Tinu. She reported that she had been easily able to take care of her baby with her long acrylic nails, so easily, in fact, that when I first posed the question of whether she had been able to keep wearing her false nails while looking after her baby, Tinu had not seen how or why there was a question to be posed. When she did see what I was trying to get at, she laughed at my apparent naïveté and gave me some advice about my own nails (shabby) to guide me to becoming a "lady" like her. The extract below begins with me attempting to illustrate with examples the question I had just posed to Tinu, which she had not understood, about whether she had found it possible and practical to care for a small baby with her habitual long acrylic nails:

> Simi: You had a small baby, you're carrying her, changing diapers, with the nails?
> Tinu: Why not?! Why? Are you serious? (*laughs*)
> Simi: I don't know now! [Note: "now" said in the colloquial Nigerian sense, here lending emphasis]
> Tinu: Please go and fix your nails (*laughs and grabs my hands*). . . . [A]s a lady you shouldn't be caught . . . with such.

To prove to me that long nails were not an impediment to practical tasks like cleaning oneself or caring for a baby, next, without warning, Tinu stuck one of her long manicured nails into the top of my left ear! From where she was positioned, what Tinu saw in me was a young Nigerian woman needing instruction and intervention, being inappropriately fashioned and subjected for "this our *generation*," as she went on to call it, or for what this book has been arguing are, for some but not all of us in Nigeria and beyond, post-feminist times.

CONCLUSION

A NEW FASHION FOR FEMINISM?

In the eight years that I have been working on the research in this book, fashions have changed, as they do. The weave, for example, which featured so prominently in the research participants' self-styling, is less popular with black women the world over than it used to be. For many, the thing to do nowadays is "go natural." Billed "the natural hair movement" by its adherents, a billing that casts the new fashion as more than a fad, young black women are flocking enthusiastically to social media especially, as well as off-line meet-ups, to forge new aesthetics, practices, communities, and even enterprises around their natural hair.[1] Feminism, too, has become fashionable. As Sarah Banet-Weiser put it in 2018, surveying the Anglo-American popular cultural landscape, "It feels as if everywhere you turn, there is an expression of feminism—on a T-shirt, in a movie, in the lyrics of a pop song, in an inspirational Instagram post, in an awards ceremony speech."[2]

An important turning point, in Catherine Rottenberg's estimation, was the 2013 publication of the self-help book *Lean In: Women, Work, and the Will to Lead* by Sheryl Sandberg, chief operating officer of Facebook.[3] *Lean In* sought to advise professional women on how to advance in the workplace, particularly when juggling family responsibilities at the same time. Rottenberg reads the much-publicized and -editorialized text as helping to launch a new style or brand of feminism that she calls "neoliberal feminism." Unlike postfeminism, neoliberal feminism acknowledges rather than disavows the persistence of gender inequality in the world of work, for even the most "high-powered" of women, but proposes highly individuated and entrepreneurial strategies for them to push onward and upward, much as this book has argued that postfeminism also does. Rottenberg further ventures that because neoliberal feminism does not offer a structural and, we could say, "angry" critique of women's status, it has helped to make the notion and language of "feminism" more broadly acceptable and even popular.[4]

A "popular feminism," to use Banet-Weiser's conceptual term, certainly seemed to explode into the mass-mediated mainstream in 2014, with celebrities lining up to declare themselves on side, for instance.[5] Most crucial, in my view, was Beyoncé, who is perhaps the single most popular female celebrity on the planet contemporarily, with fans spanning vast demographics and locations, such that any stage on which she performs and pronounces is effectively global. In what has since become a much-cited and -remediated scene from the 2014 annual MTV music awards, Beyoncé concluded the performance of her song "Flawless," which samples from the 2012 TEDx Talk by Nigerian novelist Chimamanda Ngozi Adichie, "We Should All Be Feminists," by standing tall and triumphant on a darkened stage, in front of a towering, bright white sign of the word, in all caps, "FEMINIST." The image, the spectacle of it, exemplifies Banet-Weiser's contention that popular feminism operates and circulates, and has currency, within a hypermediated "economy of visibility," in which the seeing, naming, and claiming, and also "liking" of feminism become the said feminism, suffice as the politics.

As it so happens, 2014 was also a highly significant year for intersecting feminisms, and economies of feminist visibility, in and concerning Nigeria specifically. In mid-April, 276 teenage girls were abducted from their secondary school in Chibok, in the northeast of the country, by the Islamic fundamentalist terrorist group Boko Haram. It was not the first time, and has not been the last, that Boko Haram has seized girls and young women against their will. Opposed to what it deems "Western education," and engaged in an insurgent cross-border campaign against the Nigerian state since 2009, the group uses and further traffics its female abductees as sex and domestic slaves. Some have also been forced into carrying out suicide bombings. Boko Haram's violence has not been trained on women's bodies alone. Thousands of boys and young men have been forcibly conscripted into its ranks, and just two months before Chibok the group slaughtered scores of boys—the reported casualty numbers range from about twenty-four to sixty—on their school grounds, which they also razed. All this is in addition to periodic indiscriminate acts of violence, most often bombings, against the larger public.

The atrocities of Boko Haram were not new to Nigerians, then, by the time of the abduction of the Chibok girls, as they came to be called. However, the scale of this particular event, and the utterly apathetic response of the Nigerian government, effectively treating the girls as disposable, led to a sustained and outraged feminist campaign on the ground—one that is still ongoing as of 2019. Entitled "Bring Back Our Girls," the central demand of the campaign was that the state deploy its military and intelligence assets to secure the safe return of the Chibok girls. The activism went viral internationally, in hashtag form, shortly after its inception; "#BringBackOurGirls" (#BBOG) was tweeted and retweeted *more than two million times within one month*, including by ultra-high-profile global figures like Michelle Obama, who was at the time still first lady of the United States. Obama later added, "In these girls, Barack and I see our own daughters." With these powerful words, as well as in the broader enthusiastic recitation in the West of the proprietary phrase "our girls," dominant Western visions of normative girlhood and its futures were universalized and naturalized, and the particular intersectional conditions of the girls' daily lives in Chibok, without which their abduction cannot be understood, were further removed from consideration.[6] These conditions, violences really, include extreme rural poverty and worsening ecological degradation across the West African Sahel, ethnoreligious tensions within Nigeria that trace directly and legibly back to British imperial design, and the heightened state of global militarism incited by, and massively profitable for, the West, America especially.[7] This last factor renders it all the more pertinent and painfully ironic to consider that there were calls from various quarters for the U.S. military-industrial complex to intervene on behalf of the Chibok girls and in a new terrain of the "war on terror."

The #BBOG campaign could gain the swift and solid traction that it did in the West, and then, as Mary Maxfield points out, be abandoned just as swiftly, because it corresponded with and reconfirmed established rationalities and visions there about the immiserated collective state of African girls and women, as well as the feared "Muslim terrorist."[8] We can understand the popular Western campaign for the Chibok girls, then, as an instantiation of what could be called imperial postfeminism, or "missionary girl power," in Özlem Sensoy and Elizabeth Marshall's formulation, in which the putative present feminist empowerment of some is invoked and mobilized performatively and, as Banet-Weiser might add, visibly—retweeting, liking, "favoriting," posting sad emojis and selfies, and so forth—for the future empowerment of inversely imagined others. I discussed this dynamic in the introduction to the book, when I argued that a key part of how postfeminism hails and seems natural or obvious for the Western girl is through representations of her Southern counterpart as in need of rescue, which therefore serve to distinguish and distance the Western girl as empowered, agentic, and free, able to come to the rescue. But here it becomes necessary to recall the closely related contention, also in the book's introductory discussion, that it is equally through logics and structures of distinction and distantiation that postfeminism interpellates and makes sense in the global South. Where I am going with this is to point out that, for the sort or type of Nigerian women who are the subjects of this book, from the kinds of Nigerian zones that they inhabit, Chibok is also *worlds away*. "London" is closer, or zones of "London," to be more exact.

The women in *Fashioning Postfeminism* see and hold themselves at a distance, outside the prevailing or normative gender order in Nigeria, instead in a transnational zone of empowered exception. I use exception in Aihwa Ong's broad sense of a biopolitical state of "extraordinary departure," whether this is a state of extraordinary privilege or extraordinary dispossession, "having it all" or "having nothing at all."[9] With this let me briefly assert that, even for a state as weak and insecure as Nigeria, victims of spectacular masculinist violence and terror like the Chibok girls are also in the realm of exception—of the most horrific sort, needless to say. I want to underscore this first to not lose sight of the severity of what happened at Chibok and elsewhere where Boko Haram has abducted and otherwise grievously targeted girls and women. This is not a normal or average state of affairs for Nigeria's female citizens. I also want to make clear that the argument or point in this book is not that the research participants' sense of themselves as what I have called "already empowered" was about, or contingent upon, such extremes as Chibok, even as we can imagine that the events there and others like it would probably buttress the women's view that they are doing just fine. Rather, as heard in the accounts and experiences that the book details, it was in relation and contradistinction to both actual others and imagined types from their everyday lives that the women considered themselves exceptional, empowered. These others and types ranged from the almost certainly underpaid and overworked domestic and beauty workers on whom they relied, to the mothers and grandmothers whose "traditional values" could sometimes pose a problem, to the "froufrou" girly-girls whom one was likely to bump into here or there in Lagos, who gave them all a troubled reputation.

Hence it is that the book argues that the women's sense of their own exception rested simultaneously on their material or class privilege and on their dispositions and sensibilities, which are, of course, themselves classed effects. The women almost never framed or explained their postfeminist self-positioning in material terms, though, as a matter of money. In their view, it was their know-how, and even more their can-do, their attitudes and mentalities, that set them apart. Exception lay in doing spectacular postfeminist feminine beauty for and by oneself, and as a matter of utmost urgency and agency, because "knowing" that this beauty promised feminine happiness and power, "knowing," furthermore, that beauty's promise was not what it would do on the outside, intersubjectively, for the external gaze, but that it would work and boost on the inside, where, postfeminism says, its subjects' most salient barriers are to be found. Consider the following remarks by one of the interview participants, which encapsulate the line of thinking that for the "already empowered" woman, spectacular femininity and the internal self-confidence and esteem it generates suffice, resolve whatever remains to be resolved: "I consider [looking good] one of the biggest or most effective 'pick-me-up[s]' you can, you can have. . . . If you have somebody who has self-esteem issues, who has issues with this, 'Oh, my husband is cheating' or something, something, start with a makeover. . . . There's nothing that can't be fixed with a little more happiness."

The "killjoy critique" that *Fashioning Postfeminism* mounts is quite simply that postfeminism is and tells a lie. In media representations perhaps, on our screens, under fictive or highly staged conditions, it may look persuasive, like it works. But for women in the flesh, in the "real world," postfeminism does not do what it says.[10] It *cannot*. The "intervening conditions" required for a performative to engender itself have not been met, which, in the case of postfeminism, would be for women to be postpatriarchy.[11] The problem, however, is that postfeminism asks women to proceed as if they have indeed left patriarchal power behind. To make themselves in its image, to be or become its subjects, postfeminism asks women to make its seductive image true, to materialize the image. And it does not ask that they do so by, say, working on the world to change their place and prospects within it, such as through an insistent and "unhappy" politics like feminism. Instead, women are invited to work on themselves: on how they move through life, the face they show, the color of their lips, the style of their stride, and how they *feel* about it all. Via intense bodily, psychic, and affective labors, asked of black women in extra measure, women are invited *to will themselves individual exceptions* to the very nonperformativity of postfeminism.

For those who try, day in and day out, such as the women in the book, it is a cruelly optimistic, disappointing, and even bewildering experience, even as there may be real and deep pleasures along the way. It hurts that postfeminism proves impossible to inhabit. In fact, it hurts to even try to inhabit it, as the book has also shown. The inevitable failure or nonperformativity of postfeminism is productive, nonetheless. It constitutes an ideological dilemma for its would-be subjects, a discursive gap or disjunct, a wound, where politics may enter or emerge, where complaint and critique may begin to fester and eventually erupt, where solidarities may be sutured. We can understand some of the bubbling up of #MeToo in 2017 in this way, for example. In the most spectacular and spectacularized enunciations of the phrase and nascent movement, such as by A-list Hollywood celebrities, in effect what we saw was women who really looked to have it made, some of whom may well have disavowed feminism not too long before, coming forward to reveal that, in fact, all is not well, that things are not as they appeared. *Lean In*, too: the most basic premise and purpose of the book is to tell women that hurdles, barriers, and problems that they may have thought, or been assured, were surmounted are still stubbornly in place. The same confessional logic, one of belated and regretful realization, is manifest in the title alone of Anne-Marie Slaughter's 2012 article "Why Women Still Can't Have It All," which Rottenberg also identifies as a root text of neoliberal feminism.[12] This title suggests that previously one might have thought otherwise, that women could have it all. Slaughter cops to this within the piece:

> Suddenly, finally, the penny dropped. . . . I'd been the one telling young women at my lectures that you can have it all and do it all, regardless of what field you are in. Which means I'd been part, albeit unwittingly, of making millions of women feel that they are to blame if they cannot manage to rise up the ladder as fast as men and also have a family and an active home life (and be thin and beautiful to boot).[13]

The penny dropped that postfeminism is a lie and that even women's consent and subjection to its "violent ethos of self-determination,"[14] even their straining and striving, will not make it true.

Thus, postfeminism, I submit, is grounds for new or renewed feminisms. The question is feminisms of what kind, that look and feel like, and do and demand, what exactly? The continuities of postfeminism with both neoliberal and popular feminisms are quite clear. Among other things, all three formations rely on highly individualized logics and repertoires and, wedded firmly to consumerism, invite women to look both deep within and outward to the market for what they might need. They promote "happiness" and "go-getting" rather than justice or liberation as the end or aim. Media friendly, they are oriented toward the spectacular over and above the structural and attached to normative femininity.[15] While there is not and has never been a singular or agreed answer to what feminism is or should be, we face a heightened new challenge in the current conjuncture in the fact that, increasingly trendy, crowd-pleasing, and sexy, both the word and its substance are becoming more and more hollow. Thus, while I agree with Chimamanda Ngozi Adichie—and, laterally, Beyoncé—that we *should* all be feminists, that is to say ideally, obviously, because feminism is a good thing, under conditions of global white supremacist capitalist patriarchy, we *cannot* all be, not if the subject position and its politics are to mean, much less try to effect, much. I agree with Clare Hemmings in her contention that we need to reclaim feminism as a "minority pursuit"[16]—a strident and angry one, I would add. If we are to ever really get "post-" past the intersectional injustices and violence that constitute our historicized presents, and foretell worse to come, feminism cannot be happy, cannot be popular, cannot be fashionable.

NOTES

INTRODUCTION: A NEW STYLE OF FEMININITY

1. Projansky, *Spectacular Girls*.

2. See, for example, Hopkins, "Girl Power-Dressing"; Pramaggiore and Negra, "Keeping Up"; Parameswaran, "Global Queens."

3. The concept of the feminine masquerade originates in psychoanalysis in the work of Joan Riviere, "Womanliness as Masquerade." It has been most taken up in feminist psychoanalytic, film, and literary theory—for example, Emily S. Apter, *Feminizing the Fetish*; Mary Ann Doane, "Masquerade Reconsidered"; Luce Irigaray, *This Sex Which Is Not One*; and interdisciplinary feminist scholarship on gender and sexual identity, cultural representation, and fashion, including Mary Russo, *The Female Grotesque*; Efrat Tseëlon, *The Masque of Femininity*; and Carole-Anne Tyler, "The Feminine Look." While Riviere and others drawing on her, including Angela McRobbie in *The Aftermath of Feminism*, see the masquerade as a self-disempowering subject, others, like Luce Irigaray and Mary Ann Doane, read the masquerade (or the miming of femininity) as subversive.

4. Some feminist scholars and writers like Susan Faludi in *Backlash* and Tania Modleski in *Feminism without Women* have understood postfeminism as a kind of linear backlash against feminism, "in effect delivering us back into a prefeminist world," according to Modleski (3). Others, like Charlotte Brunsdon in "Feminism, Postfeminism," argue that the term should be used to signify a neutral periodization of that which came after the so-called second wave of Western feminism. There is also a third understanding and use of the term to refer to the intersection of feminism with poststructuralism and postcolonial theory. For instance, in her book *Postfeminisms*, Ann Brooks uses the term to designate the "conceptual shift within feminism from debates about equality to . . . difference" (4). See Gill, "Postfeminist Media Culture," for an overview of different conceptualizations of the term.

5. Gill, "Postfeminist Media Culture"; McRobbie, *Aftermath of Feminism*.

6. Gill, "Affective, Cultural and Psychic Life," 611.

7. Lazar, "Discover the Power," 505.

8. McRobbie, "Notes on the Perfect."

9. McRobbie, *Aftermath of Feminism*, 67. Others who have written on the spectacularly feminine as a mediated phenomenon include Evans and Riley, "Immaculate Consumption"; and Hopkins, "Girl Power-Dressing."

10. Ahmed, *The Promise of Happiness*.

11. Berlant, "Cruel Optimism."

12. Judith Butler, *Psychic Life of Power*.

13. Other book-length, ethnographic (rather than textual) research on what it means to be a woman in a postfeminist age include *Repudiating Postfeminism* by Christina Scharff; *Girls' Feminist Blogging in a Postfeminist Age* by Jessalynn Keller; and *Postfeminist Education?* by Jessica Ringrose.

14. McRobbie, *Aftermath of Feminism*, 11.

15. Mustafa, "Portraits of Modernity," 178.

16. Dogbe, "Unraveled Yarns," 382.

17. Ismail, "From 'Area-Boyism' to 'Junctions and Bases,'" 91.

18. Mbembe and Nuttall, "Writing the World," 348.

19. Shih, "Towards an Ethics," 95; Mohanty, "Under Western Eyes."

20. Shih, "Towards an Ethics," 108–9.

21. McRobbie, *Aftermath of Feminism*, 66–70; Wilkes, "Colluding with Neoliberalism," 22, 24; Tasker and Negra, "Introduction," 2; Jess Butler, "For White Girls Only?," 47–48.

22. Tasker and Negra, "Introduction"; Jess Butler, "For White Girls Only?," 48–50 (emphases added).

23. I also read Beyoncé as a postfeminist figure in this book, although in the time that I have been researching and writing it she explicitly declared herself a feminist. I come back to this in the conclusion of the book, where I discuss the emergence of new popular feminisms.

24. Chatman, "Pregnancy, Then It's 'Back to Business,'" 930 (emphasis in the original).

25. McRobbie, *Aftermath of Feminism*, 70, 71.

26. McRobbie, *Aftermath of Feminism*; Gill, "Postfeminist Media Culture" and "Culture and Subjectivity." McRobbie, for instance, writes of postfeminism as interpellative, inviting women to come forward as its new subjects on condition of renouncing feminism.

27. An address is also made to men. On postfeminist masculinities, see, for example, Hamad, *Postfeminism and Paternity*; and O'Neill, *Seduction*.

28. Judith Butler, *Excitable Speech*, 33

29. Gill, "Postfeminist Media Culture."

30. McRobbie, *Aftermath of Feminism*, 63.

31. Tate, *Black Beauty*.

32. Jess Butler, "For White Girls Only?," 48.

33. McRobbie, *Aftermath of Feminism*, 67.

34. Joseph, "'Tyra Banks Is Fat'"; Springer, "Divas."

35. See also Lazar, "Discover the Power." In her analysis of postfeminist beauty advertisements in Singapore, Lazar argues that where white models are used, Singaporean women are being invited to identify *with* these women, not being excluded. Or, in other words, postfeminism is not being represented as exclusively white; whiteness is being represented as universal. Other visual strategies in the beauty ads to create the effect of a multiracial postfeminism are the use of globally iconic black celebrities such as Beyoncé, as well as pan-Asian models.

36. Joseph, "'Tyra Banks Is Fat,'" 249.

37. In her book *Repudiating Feminism*, Christina Scharff also gets at this point in a different direction than I have taken here, in her key finding that part of how young British and German women repudiate and disidentify from feminism is by displacing its continued need to other women in other places—for instance, via what she calls the "trope of the oppressed Muslim woman."

38. A host of postcolonial and transnational feminist cultural scholars make this point. See, for example, Ahmed, *Strange Encounters*; Grewal, *Transnational America*; Nguyen, *Gift of Freedom*.

39. Grewal, *Transnational America*, 63.

40. See, for example, Bent, "Different Girl Effect"; Calkin, "Post-Feminist Spectatorship"; Koffman and Gill, "Revolution"; Sensoy and Marshall, "Missionary Girl Power"; Switzer, "(Post)Feminist Development Fables"; and Wilson, "'Race,' Gender and Neoliberalism."

41. Switzer, "(Post)Feminist Development Fables."

42. Nguyen, *Gift of Freedom*, 45.

43. Mama, cited in Salo, "Talking about Feminism in Africa," 59.

44. Win, "Not Very Poor," 82.

45. McRobbie, *Aftermath of Feminism* and "Top Girls?"

46. McRobbie, "Top Girls?," 733–34.

47. McRobbie, *Aftermath of Feminism*, 89.

48. Chen, "Shanghai(ed) Babies," 215.

49. On postfeminism in Singapore, see Lazar, "Discover the Power," "Entitled to Consume," and "Right to Be Beautiful"; in Japan, see Gwynne, "Japan"; in Russia, see Salmenniemi and Adamson, "New Heroines"; in Kenya, see Ligaga, "Presence, Agency and Popularity"; and in South Africa, see Bradfield, "Society's Emerging Femininities," and Iqani, *Consumption, Media and the Global South*.

50. For a fuller discussion, see Dosekun, "For Western Girls Only?"

51. Lazar, "Discover the Power" and "Entitled to Consume."

52. Grewal, *Transnational America*.

53. Kaplan and Grewal, "Transnational Feminist Cultural Studies," 440 (emphasis in the original).

54. Alexander and Mohanty, "Cartographies," 24. A feminist transnational approach can also entail thinking about women in dissimilar but interrelated or mutually

constitutive contexts around the world, such as women connected by consumer commodity chains. See, for example, Priti Ramamurthy, "Material Consumers."

55. Hegde, introduction to *Circuits of Visibility*, 1.

56. Appadurai, *Modernity at Large*; Hegde, introduction to *Circuits of Visibility*; Mankekar, "Media and Mobility."

57. Mankekar, "Media and Mobility," 149.

58. Chen, "Shanghai(ed) Babies"; In "Discover the Power," Lazar writes in similar terms of a postfeminist "global consumer sisterhood . . . , premised upon the consumption of goods of 'empowerment'" (515).

59. Mankekar, "Media and Mobility," 153.

60. Shih, *Visuality and Identity*, 44.

61. Ong, *Neoliberalism as Exception*, 14.

62. The insight, and formulation, that the hybrid is not posthegemonic comes from Marwan Kraidy in "Hybridity in Cultural Globalization" and *Hybridity*. On the broader points here, see also Ang, "Culture and Communication"; Appadurai, *Modernity at Large*; Grewal, *Transnational America*; Hegde, *Circuits of Visibility*; and Ong, *Neoliberalism as Exception*.

63. In "Consumption in the City," Dejmanee suggests and maps different temporal phases of postfeminism in the West, for example. Picking up on a thread of Dejmanee's argument, as well as Diane Negra's exegesis of a number of films in *What a Girl Wants?*, I would venture that more in the United States than the United Kingdom there is a certain inflection of postfeminism with conservative, even evangelical, femininities. See "Warrior Chicks" by Jenkins and Marti for a discussion of an instantiation of postfeminist evangelical Christian femininities. The point here is that postfeminism is not a static or monolithic cultural formation in the West or elsewhere.

64. Gwynne, "Japan," 326, 327.

65. See, for example, Freeman, *Entrepreneurial Selves*; Grewal, *Transnational America*; and Ong, *Neoliberalism as Exception*.

66. Giraldo, "Coloniality at Work," 162.

67. Chen, "Shanghai(ed) Babies," 223.

68. Appadurai, *Modernity at Large*, 30.

69. Sassen, "Spatialities and Temporalities," 215.

70. Amin, "Spatialities of Globalisation."

71. See, for example, Grewal, *Transnational America*; Parameswaran, "Global Queens"; Reddy, "Global Indian Woman" and "Feminist Cosmopolitics"; and P. Butler and Desai, "Manolos, Marriage, and Mantras."

72. See Dosekun, "For Western Girls Only?" for a more concerted discussion of what I see as the particular analytic value of both the concept and the term *postfeminism* for understanding certain new styles of femininity in the global South.

73. P. Butler and Desai, "Manolos, Marriage, and Mantras," 2.

74. Shome and Hegde, "Challenge of Globalization," 178.

75. Mbembe and Nuttall, "Writing the World," 348.

76. Shih, *Visuality and Identity*, 43.

77. Browne, *Feminism, Time, and Nonlinear History*, 39.

78. Mbembe, "African Modes of Self-Writing," is the primary source of the ideas here, as well as Nguyen's observation in *Gift of Freedom*, that the imperialist liberal invitation to coevality, while an act of violence and subjection, is therein also subjectifying, "actuating persons as free" (17).

79. Hegde, "View from Elsewhere," 273.

80. Conor, *Spectacular Modern Woman*, 256. I am borrowing here from Conor's phrasing of the question she poses of the 1920s Australian "modern woman."

81. Wetherell, "Step Too Far," 668. See also Davies and Harré, "Positioning."

82. Pillow, "Confession, Catharsis, or Cure?"

83. Lather, "Fertile Obsessions," 675.

84. Judith Butler, *Excitable Speech*.

85. See Dosekun, "'Hey, You Stylized Woman There,'" for further uncomfortable reflexive discussion about the research project and especially the recruitment methods that I used.

86. Judith Butler, "Performative Acts," 521.

87. Judith Butler, *Excitable Speech*, 38.

88. See, for example, Edley, "Analysing Masculinity"; Wetherell, "Positioning"; and Wetherell and Edley, "Negotiating Hegemonic Masculinity."

89. Wetherell, "Positioning."

90. Gill, "Critical Respect," 77 (emphasis in the original).

91. Gonick and Hladki, "Who Are the Participants?," 289.

92. Britzman, "'Question of Belief,'" 232.

CHAPTER 1. CONTEXTUAL CROSSROADS: AFRICAN WOMEN IN THE WORLD OF THINGS

1. Grewal, *Transnational America*.

2. All names are pseudonyms chosen by me. I use a mix of randomly distributed Nigerian names of different ethnic origin, and English names, to reflect the range of the women's real names.

3. All emphases in direct quotes from the interviews are as I heard and transcribed them.

4. See, for example, Falola and Heaton, *A History of Nigeria*.

5. Mbembe and Nuttall, "Writing the World," 348.

6. The study of dress (and also of Western modernity) has often distinguished Western "fashion" from the "nonfashion" of non-Western "costume" and so on, where the former implies self-conscious and individualized dressing up, stylistic change, and consumption for their own sake, in a word "modernity," while the latter implies aesthetic status and dressing for functionality and group orientation, as dictated by "tradition." Joanne Entwistle, for example, in the preface to the latest edition of

The Fashioned Body, reiterates her earlier position that fashion "must be historically located within western modernity" and that "to argue that fashion can be found everywhere and at other historical moments is Eurocentric: it is a view that imposes particular western characteristics onto non-western places" (15–16). In *The Face of Fashion*, Jennifer Craik argues that this kind of "approach does a disservice to nonwestern styles of dress and fails to appreciate [their] subtleties . . . [and instead] merely confirms the assumptions of European philosophy, specifically, the distinction between western cultures as civilised and other cultures as pre-civilised" (18–19). Others who extend the concept and category of fashion to non-Western dress include Allman, *Fashioning Africa*; Kondo, *About Face*; Niessen, Leshkowich, and Jones, *Re-Orienting Fashion*; and Rovine, *African Fashion, Global Style*.

7. See, for example, Allman, *Fashioning Africa*; Gott, "Asante Hightimers"; Hendrickson, *Clothing and Difference*; Rabine, *Global Circulation*; and Sylvanus, *Patterns in Circulation*.

8. Edoh, "Redrawing Power?"; Sylvanus, "Fabric of Africanity" and *Patterns in Circulation*.

9. Lowe, *Intimacies of Four Continents*.

10. Edoh, "Redrawing Power?," 258.

11. Sylvanus, "Fabric of Africanity," 210.

12. For example, Bakare-Yusuf, "Nudity and Morality"; Byfield, "Dress and Politics"; Coly, "Un/Clothing African Womanhood"; John L. Comaroff and Jean Comaroff, *Of Revelation and Revolution*; Diawara, "Sixties in Bamako"; Hansen, "Dressing Dangerously"; Hay, "Changes in Clothing"; and Ivaska, *Cultured States*.

13. Rabine, *Global Circulation*, 29.

14. Byfield, "Dress and Politics."

15. As Jean Allman argues in her introduction to the key edited collection *Fashioning Africa*, on and through the dressed body in Africa, "tradition and modernity are constructed simultaneously; they are mutually constitutive" (5).

16. For visual examples of this, see @AsoEbiBella on Instagram.

17. Chow, "Where Have All the Natives Gone?," 324.

18. Mbembe, "African Modes of Self-Writing," 272 (emphasis in the original).

19. Hansen, *Salaula*, 24, 15.

20. Hall, "Old and New Identities," 67.

21. Mbembe, "African Modes of Self-Writing," 242.

22. Shih, *Visuality and Identity*, 43.

23. Thomas, "Modern Girl and Racial Respectability"; Weinbaum et al., *Modern Girl around the World*.

24. Weinbaum et al., *Modern Girl around the World*, 10; Grewal, *Transnational America*.

25. See, for example, Diawara, "Sixties in Bamako"; Ford, *Liberated Threads*; Ivaska, *Cultured States*.

26. Diawara, "Sixties in Bamako."

27. Elam and Jackson, *Black Cultural Traffic*.

28. On these and further examples, see Diawara, "Sixties in Bamako"; Ford, "'Afro Look'" and *Liberated Threads*; McAndrew, "Twentieth-Century Triangle Trade"; Thomas, "Modern Girl and Racial Respectability."

29. Thomas, "Modern Girl and Racial Respectability," 110–11.

30. McAndrew, "Twentieth-Century Triangle Trade," 798. That the African American beauty entrepreneurs were also thereby marketing "America" and consumer capitalism, in Cold War times they attracted U.S. government interest and backing for their forays into Africa.

31. Diawara, "Sixties in Bamako."

32. Ivaska, *Cultured States*, 5–6.

33. See, for example, Bakare-Yusuf, "Nudity and Morality"; Ivaska, "Anti-Mini Militants" and *Cultured States*; Mougoué, "African Women Do Not Look Good in Wigs"; and Tamale, "'Keep Your Eyes off My Thighs.'"

34. Ivaska, "Anti-Mini Militants."

35. Tamale, "'Keep Your Eyes off My Thighs,'" 83.

36. Yuval-Davis, *Gender and Nation*, 45.

37. For more detail on some of these cases, see Hansen, "Dressing Dangerously"; Ivaska, "Anti-Mini Militants"; Pereira and Ibrahim, "On the Bodies of Women"; and Tamale, "'Keep Your Eyes off My Thighs.'"

38. See Pereira and Ibrahim, "On the Bodies of Women."

39. For an overview of this case in Nigeria, see Bakare-Yusuf, "Nudity and Morality"; Pereira, "Setting Agendas"; and Pereira and Ibrahim, "On the Bodies of Women."

40. Bakare-Yusuf, "Nudity and Morality," 122.

41. Dogbe, "Unraveled Yarns," 378.

42. Nuttall, "Stylizing the Self," 432. See also Foucault, *The History of Sexuality*, 2:10–11.

43. As of 2014, according to the Lagos State government's website. Note that Lagos is the name of both the city and the federal state in which the city is located.

44. Nigerians comprise more than two hundred ethnic groups that speak at least four hundred distinct languages and are roughly divided between Islam and Christianity. To accommodate this internal diversity, a product of arbitrary colonial borders, and a precipitate of the brutal civil war between 1967 and 1970, Nigeria operates a federal political structure and is now subdivided into thirty-six states plus the federal capital territory of Abuja.

45. Mann, *Slavery and the Birth of an African City*, 40.

46. Olaniyan, *Arrest the Music!*, 89.

47. O. Okome, "Nollywood, Lagos."

48. Krings and Okome, *Global Nollywood*, 1. Definitive statistics for the largely informal industry are hard to come by, but Nollywood is widely reported to be the third-largest film industry in the world by revenue after Hollywood and Bollywood and the second largest by volume of output after Bollywood.

49. Cordwell, "Art and Aesthetics," 58. See also Boyer, "Yoruba Cloths"; and Oyeniyi, "Dress and Identity in Yorubaland."

50. Bascom, "Social Status, Wealth and Individual Differences"; Boyer, "Yoruba Cloths."

51. Adesokan, "Anticipating Nollywood," 103.

52. Haynes, "Neoliberalism, Nollywood and Lagos," 61.

53. Ismail, "From 'Area-Boyism' to 'Junctions and Bases,'" 91.

54. Adesokan, "Anticipating Nollywood"; Nwafor, "Spectacle of Aso Ebi"; O. Okome, "Nollywood, Lagos."

55. Nwafor, "Spectacle of Aso Ebi," 53.

56. Osaghae, *Crippled Giant.*

57. See, for example, Falola and Heaton, *A History of Nigeria*; and Osaghae, *Crippled Giant.*

58. UNDP, Human Development Indices and Indicators, 2018 Statistical Update, http://hdr.undp.org/sites/default/files/2018_human_development_statistical_update.pdf.

59. Pereira, "Configuring 'Global,' 'National,' and 'Local,'" 786.

60. A. Apter, *Pan-African Nation,* 22.

61. Newell cited in Ligaga, "Mapping Emerging Constructions," 250.

62. Unigwe, *On Black Sisters Street,* 46.

63. Mohammed and Madunagu, "WIN," 103. For more on how feminism is popularly delegitimated or qualified (or both) in Africa, see, for example, Dosekun, "Defending Feminism in Africa"; Essof, "African Feminisms"; Mohammed and Madunagu, "WIN"; and Salo, "Talking about Feminism in Africa." Questions of whether there is or are African feminism(s), if so what they do or should look like particularly in relation to Western feminisms, have also been taken up in scholarly discussions. In addition to the foregoing sources, see, for example, Lewis, "Introduction: African Feminisms"; Mikell, *African Feminism*; and Nnaemeka, "Nego-Feminism."

64. See, for example, Chuku, "Igbo Women and Political Participation"; Geiger, Allman, and Musisi, *Women in African Colonial Histories*; George, *Making Modern Girls*; Hassim, *Women's Organizations*; Ifeka-Moller, "Female Militancy and Colonial Revolt"; Johnson-Odim, "Actions Louder than Words" and "'For Their Freedoms'"; Johnson-Odim and Mba, *For Women and the Nation*; Madunagu, "Nigerian Feminist Movement"; Mba, *Nigerian Women Mobilized*; and Mohammed and Madunagu, "WIN."

65. Mama, "Editorial," 1.

66. Johnson-Odim, "Actions Louder than Words," 82.

67. Johnson-Odim, "Actions Louder than Words" and "'For Their Freedoms.'"

68. In relation to Nigeria specifically, see, for example, Chuku, "Igbo Women and Political Participation"; Ifeka-Moller, "Female Militancy and Colonial Revolt"; George, *Making Modern Girls*; Johnson, "Grassroots Organizing"; Mann, *Marrying Well*; Oyěwùmí, *Invention of Women.*

69. Chuku, "Igbo Women and Political Participation," 88.

70. For example, Chuku, "Igbo Women and Political Participation"; Ifeka-Moller, "Female Militancy and Colonial Revolt"; and Mba, *Nigerian Women Mobilized*.

71. Johnson, "Grassroots Organizing," 2.

72. Byfield, "Dress and Politics" and "Taxation"; Johnson-Odim and Mba, *For Women and the Nation*.

73. Byfield, "Taxation," 270.

74. Pereira, "Domesticating Women?," 81.

75. Chuku, "Igbo Women and Political Participation," 82.

76. Nigeria experienced a sustained period of military rule from 1966 to 1999, with the exception of a brief interlude between 1979 and 1983.

77. M. O. Okome, "Gendered States," 111.

78. Madunagu, "Nigerian Feminist Movement," 666.

79. See Abdullah, "'Transition Politics'"; Mama, "Feminism or Femocracy?" and "Khaki in the Family"; and Soetan, "Feminist Civil Society Organizations."

80. Mama, "Khaki in the Family"; Pereira, "Appropriating 'Gender' and 'Empowerment.'"

81. Wilson, "Towards a Radical Re-appropriation."

82. Pereira, "Appropriating 'Gender' and 'Empowerment,'" 45.

83. See Pereira, "Understanding Women's Experiences," for an excellent overview of the range of issues women face in Nigeria.

CHAPTER 2. CHOOSING IT ALL: FROM PLEASURE TO SELF-CONFIDENCE TO PAIN

1. Ahmed, *The Promise of Happiness*.

2. Favaro, "'Just Be Confident Girls!'"

3. In "The Confidence Cult(ure)," Gill and Orgad call self-confidence "the new imperative of our time" (324), while Banet-Weiser writes of the veritable market for self-confidence in "'Confidence You Can Carry!'" See also Gill and Elias, "Awaken Your Incredible"; Gill and Orgad, "The Confidence Cult(ure)" and "Confidence Culture"; and Favaro, "'Just Be Confident Girls!'"

4. Coleman and Figueroa, "Past and Future Perfect?"

5. Craig, "Race, Beauty, and the Tangled Knot," 160.

6. Jarrín, *The Biopolitics of Beauty*, 13.

7. Judith Butler, "Giving an Account," 28.

8. I refer to myself as Simi in the interview excerpts as this is how I introduced and named myself in the field.

9. Foucault, *Use of Pleasure*, 5.

10. Roughly, at the rate that obtained at the time of my fieldwork in early 2013, namely, N140–50 to US$1.

11. Månsson, "Drinking as a Feminine Practice," 58.

12. Ahmed, "Collective Feelings."

13. Judith Butler, *Excitable Speech*, 154–55.

14. See, for example, Banet-Weiser and Portwood-Stacer, "'I Just Want to Be Me Again!'"; Bartky, "Foucault, Femininity"; Bordo, *Unbearable Weight*; Figueroa, "Displaced Looks"; Gimlin, *Body Work*; Patton, "Hey Girl"; and Tate, "Black Beauty."

15. Coleman and Figueroa, "Past and Future Perfect?"

16. Berlant, "Cruel Optimism," 20. Jarrín, *Biopolitics of Beauty*, and Nguyen, "Biopower of Beauty," also conceptualize beauty as promising things and argue, as I also endeavor in this book, that the promissory nature of beauty, including that it is therefore future oriented, is part of how it comes to function as a form of biopower.

17. Lazar, "Right to Be Beautiful," 38.

18. See Durham, "'Check on It.'"

19. Jackson and Scott cited in Gill, "Empowerment/Sexism," 37. See also Lazar, "Discover the Power."

20. Skeggs cited in Frith, Raisborough, and Klein, "C'mon Girlfriend."

21. McRobbie, *Aftermath of Feminism*, 63.

22. Gill, "Culture and Subjectivity."

23. Banet-Weiser, "Am I Pretty or Ugly?," 94.

24. Bartky, "Foucault, Femininity," 74.

25. Judith Butler, *Psychic Life of Power*, 21.

26. Winch, *Girlfriends and Postfeminist Sisterhood*, 22.

27. Negra, *What a Girl Wants?*, 152.

28. Davies, Browne, et al., "Constituting the Feminist Subject"; Petersen, "Passionately Attached."

29. Gill, "Culture and Subjectivity," 441.

30. Joseph, "'Tyra Banks Is Fat,'" 248, 239.

31. Berlant, "Cruel Optimism," 21.

32. Berlant, "Cruel Optimism," 21.

33. Berlant, "Cruel Optimism," 20 (emphasis in the original).

34. Judith Butler, *Gender Trouble*.

35. Scharff, *Repudiating Feminism*.

36. Gill and Elias, "'Awaken Your Incredible.'"

37. Ahmed, *The Promise of Happiness*, 45, 59.

38. In *Repudiating Feminism*, for example, Scharff hears this sentiment from her research participants who, in positioning themselves as postfeminist, describe and distance feminists as "hard-core," "angry" women and so on.

CHAPTER 3. "I'M WORKING, YOU KNOW": THE SERIOUS BUSINESS OF SPECTACULARITY

1. Davies, Flemmen, et al., "Working on the Ground," 298.

2. Lazar, "Entitled to Consume," 372.

3. That women earn independent wages does not fully answer the question, in any case: there is still scope to inquire how exactly they budget, plan, possibly borrow

to achieve postfeminist consumerist standards and lifestyles, and to consider their limits, that is, what they cannot afford or choose to forego. The "ordinary women" in A. Evans and Riley's article "Immaculate Consumption" provide an indirect example of the points I am getting at; with some regret, they position the immaculate beauty practices of feminine celebrities as beyond their budgets.

4. For the purposes of this discussion I am using this term to refer not only or strictly to relationships between women and men that are sexually consummated, but also those that remain at the level of romance, flirtation, and suggestion as well. Tsitsi Masvawure, for example, in "'I Just Need to Be Flashy on Campus'" details some of the strategies young Zimbabwean women use to avoid having sex with men with whom they are in transactional sexualized and romantic engagements.

5. Dobson, "Performative Shamelessness."

6. Trouillot cited in Freeman, *Entrepreneurial Selves*, 4.

7. Dejmanee, "Consumption in the City," 131.

8. Rottenberg, "Rise of Neoliberal Feminism," 422.

9. See Berry, "Zombie Commodity."

10. Brown, "Neo-liberalism."

11. Banet-Weiser, *Authentic™*, 75.

12. MAC is a global makeup brand. At the time of my fieldwork, the first MAC store in Nigeria was about to open in an elite Lagos mall where I approached prospective participants and eventually recruited two.

13. Judith Butler, *Gender Trouble*, 177. Butler puts the point conversely, stating that gendered subjects are "never fully self-styled, for styles have a history, and those histories condition and limit the possibilities."

14. McNay, "Gender, Habitus and the Field," 97.

15. Berlant, "Cruel Optimism," 20 (emphasis in the original).

16. Lazar, "Entitled to Consume."

17. Binkley, "Perilous Freedoms," 351.

18. For example, Cahill, "Feminist Pleasure"; Conor, *Spectacular Modern Woman*; Craig, "Race, Beauty, and the Tangled Knot"; Davis, *Reshaping the Female Body*; Elias, Gill, and Scharff, *Aesthetic Labour*; Gimlin, *Body Work*; and Mustafa, "Eros, Beauty and Crisis."

19. Elias, Gill, and Scharff, *Aesthetic Labour*.

20. George, *Making Modern Girls*, 41; Mann, *Marrying Well*.

21. Lindsay, "Domesticity and Difference," 786–87.

22. Dogbe, "Unraveled Yarns," 381; Sylvanus, *Patterns in Circulation*.

23. Wetherell, "Positioning and Interpretative Repertoires."

24. On practices and the relative prevalence of transactional heterosex in various postcolonial urban African contexts, see, for example, Hunter, "Materiality of Everyday Sex" and *Love in the Time of AIDS*; Leclerc-Madlala, "Transactional Sex"; Masvawure, "'I Just Need to Be Flashy on Campus'"; and Shefer, Clowes, and Vergnani, "Narratives of Transactional Sex." More pertinent for the present discussion is

work that variously concerns or references not the empirical happening of transactional sex, but imaginations and suspicions that it is happening and that it accounts for how young women come to consume. On this, see, for example, Bakare-Yusuf, "Nudity and Morality"; Ivaska, "Anti-Mini Militants"; Ligaga, "Mapping Emerging Constructions"; Odejide, "'What Can a Woman Do?'"; and Thomas, "Modern Girl and Racial Respectability."

25. Leclerc-Madlala, "Transactional Sex"; Hunter, *Love in the Time of AIDS*; Odejide, "'What Can a Woman Do?,'" 52; Shefer, Clowes, and Vergnani, "Narratives of Transactional Sex," 436.

26. As Bakare-Yusuf notes in her critique of both the text and the underpinning logics of the 2007 proposed "indecent dressing" bill in Nigeria, the focus and blame is on women and there is no "sense in which male desire itself should be circumscribed, or that men should be held to account (either morally or within the law) for their desires [and actions] in specific circumstances" ("Nudity and Morality," 125).

27. O. Okome, "Nollywood, Lagos," 181. See also Newell, "Constructions of Nigerian Women."

28. Wetherell, "Positioning and Interpretative Repertoires," 404.

29. Lazar, "Entitled to Consume."

30. Tasker and Negra, "Introduction," 3.

31. Byrne, "Reciting the Self," 30.

32. Lazar, "Entitled to Consume," 374.

33. See, for example, Nwafor, "Spectacle of Aso Ebi."

34. Lazar, "Entitled to Consume"; McRobbie, *Aftermath of Feminism*.

35. See, for instance, Negra's discussion of movies like *13 Going on 30* in *What a Girl Wants?*

CHAPTER 4. GLOBALLY BLACK, "NAIJA," AND FABULOUS: ASSERTING AUTHENTIC SELVES

1. Adichie cited in Kellaway, Kate. "Chimamanda Ngozi Adichie: 'My New Novel Is about Love, Race . . . and Hair,'" *Guardian UK*, April 6, 2013, www.theguardian.com/theobserver/2013/apr/07/chimamanda-ngozi-adichie-americanah-interview.

2. Mougoué, "African Women Do Not Look Good in Wigs,"16.

3. hooks, *Black Looks*, 71.

4. C. Thompson, "Black Women," 855.

5. Nyamnjoh and Fuh, "Africans Consuming Hair," 59.

6. Tate, "Not All the Women," 195.

7. Tate, *Black Beauty: Aesthetics, Stylization* and "Not All the Women."

8. Tate, *Black Beauty*, 143 (emphasis in the original).

9. Campt, *Other Germans*, 179.

10. Browne, *Feminism, Time, and Nonlinear History*, 38–44.

11. Tate, *Black Beauty*, 47 (emphasis in the original).

12. It is beyond the scope of the present discussion, but I would also argue that the fact that black women are avidly consuming what is marketed as hair from places like Brazil, India, and Vietnam, which is to say hair marketed as originating from bodies of color, further complexifies notions that what black women are desiring and aspiring toward is or must be whiteness. Chika gestured toward this when she said that wearing a weave did not mean she wanted to be "European" or "Asian."

13. Mercer, "Black Hair/Style Politics," 37 (emphasis added).

14. In addition to Tate, *Black Beauty*; Mercer, "Black Hair/Style Politics"; and Craig, "Decline and Fall of the Conk," whom I have cited, others like Deborah Grayson in "Is it Fake?" and Samantha Pinho in "Afro-aesthetics in Brazil" also variously argue about the need to move beyond reading black women's hair in terms of an emulation of whiteness. The list of black scholars taking this position is, as I have said, really quite short.

15. C. Thompson, "Black Women."

16. Tate, *Black Beauty*, 26. In the article "Black Beauty," Tate also notes that, for some black women, black antiracist politics also potentially compound this culturally instituted melancholy because they promote and delimit "correct" ways of fashioning resistant blackness.

17. Nyamnjoh, Durham, and Fokwang, "Domestication of Hair," 99.

18. My experience included that most hairdressers simply did not know what to do with my hair and would gather around curiously to discuss it and ask me questions, and to watch and learn as, after asking for it to be washed, I would resort to styling it myself.

19. Nzegwu, "Colonial Racism," 142.

20. Nzegwu, "Colonial Racism," 142.

21. As Pierre argues in *The Predicament of Blackness*, postcolonial African societies, too, are structured by global white supremacy, a consideration relatively overlooked in African studies, and to understand racialization there demands contention with, among others, "the various transnational political and cultural significations associated with constructions of 'Blackness'" (1).

22. See, for example, hooks, *Black Looks*; Tate, *Black Beauty*; and C. Thompson, "Black Women."

23. Erasmus, "'Oe! My Hare Gaan Huistoe.'"

24. C. Thompson, "Black Women," 855.

25. Petersen, "Passionately Attached," 55–56.

26. I have not gone into detail in the body of the chapter because it is well rehearsed in black and other feminist scholarship; in a nutshell, the politics of black hair dates back to the enslavement of black people predominantly in the Americas, the colonization of Africa, and concurrent emergence of so-called race sciences. In all this, dominant racist ideologies constructed and stigmatized the look and texture of "black hair" as inferior to that of "white hair," including constructing hierarchies of types of the former, the "softer" and "wavier" the better. Black feminists have also

shown how such constructs are gendered, intersecting for black women with hege-monic normalizations and representations of feminine beauty, and indeed femininity itself, as white, for which long hair is normative. It is out of these historical contexts that black women have come to be broadly orientated away from "natural hair," al-though again it is also important that black hair-alteration practices are also about class, social mobility, respectability politics, and other logics of distinction *within* black communities.

27. Ahmed, *The Promise of Happiness*, 159.

28. Chiluwa, "Assessing the Nigerianness," 54.

29. Pandey, "Code Alteration in Nigerian English."

30. Fair, "Remaking Fashion," 13.

31. Ahmed, *Strange Encounters*.

32. Conradson and McKay, "Translocal Subjectivities," 168.

33. See McKay, "Migration and Masquerade," for an elaboration of this point in rela-tion to women's transnational mobility, and McNay, "Gender, Habitus and the Field" and *Gender and Agency*, for a more theoretical discussion building on Bourdieu.

34. Mohanty, "Women Workers," 5.

35. Grewal, *Transnational America*, 38.

36. "Glossy" as opposed to Nollywood, which tends to have lower production values but is, nonetheless, the single largest cultural export in and from Africa.

37. See, for example, Bradfield, "Society's Emerging Femininities"; Laden, "'Mak-ing the Paper Speak Well'"; Nuttall, "Stylizing the Self"; Odhiambo, "Black Female Body"; and Sanger, "New Women, Old Messages?"

38. Laden, "'Making the Paper Speak Well,'" 543.

39. Odhiambo, "Black Female Body," 76.

40. Ang, "Culture and Communication," 250.

41. For ethnographic case studies about the fact that the entry of new transna-tional media and consumer cultures into local spaces, specifically in the non-Western world, does not simply amount to cultural homogenization, see, for example, Kraidy, "Global, Local, and Hybrid"; and Salo, "Negotiating Gender and Personhood."

42. Pramaggiore and Negra, "Keeping Up," 79.

43. McKay, "Migration and Masquerade," 45.

44. A. Evans, Riley, and Shankar, "Technologies of Sexiness," 114.

45. Gill, "Critical Respect," 72.

46. Dobson, "'Sexy' and 'Laddish' Girls."

47. For example, Attwood, "Fashion and Passion"; Devereux, "'Last Night, I Did a Striptease for My Husband'"; Donaghue and Whitehead, "Spinning the Pole"; A. Evans, Riley, and Shankar, "Postfeminist Heterotopias"; and Gill, "Mediated Intimacy."

48. Gill, "Mediated Intimacy," 365 (emphasis in the original).

49. Work that variously concerns the relative panics in the West about the sexu-alization of culture, as well as feminist scholarly debates on how to broach it, espe-cially girls' sexual agency, includes Attwood, "Sexed Up"; Dobson, "Performative

Shamelessness"; Duits and Van Zoonen, "Headscarves and Porno-Chic"; Egan, *Becoming Sexual*; Gavey, "Beyond 'Empowerment'?"; Gill, "Critical Respect"; Jackson, Vares, and Gill, "'Playboy Mansion Image'"; Ringrose and Renold, "Teen Girls."

50. I. Tyler, "'Chav Mum Chav Scum.'"

51. Harris, *Future Girl*.

52. Lutwama-Rukundo, "Skimpy Fashion," 58.

53. See, for instance, Tamale, "'Keep Your Eyes off My Thighs'"; and Bakare-Yusuf, "Nudity and Morality."

54. See Coly, "Un/Clothing African Womanhood," for an excellent analysis of how the un/clothed African female body has functioned as a rhetorical device, and site of angst, in colonial, anticolonial, and postcolonial discourses.

55. Bakare-Yusuf, "Nudity and Morality," 121.

56. Allman, "'Let Your Fashion Be in Line'"; Bakare-Yusuf, "Nudity and Morality"; Coly, "Un/Clothing African Womanhood"; John L. Comaroff and Jean Comaroff, *Of Revelation and Revolution*.

57. Coly makes a particularly clear case for this in "Un/Clothing African Womanhood," drawing on Fanon to show what is often the "coloniality of anticolonial resistance" (14).

58. Vats and Nishime, "Containment as Neocolonial Visual Rhetoric," 423. Others making similar arguments include Ang, *On Not Speaking Chinese*; and Chow, "Where Have All the Natives Gone?" and *The Protestant Ethnic and the Spirit of Capitalism*, in which she writes of "coercive mimeticism" that the ethnicized subject faces, which is to reproduce and perform the stereotyped view of itself.

59. Vats and Nishime, "Containment as Neocolonial Visual Rhetoric," 441.

CHAPTER 5. "NOT THAT KINDA GIRL": RESIGNIFYING HYPERFEMININITY FOR POSTFEMINIST TIMES

1. In Riviere's piece "Womanliness as a Masquerade," the masquerade, said to be one of her patients, is a woman who is a competent professional yet systematically undermines herself through her own behavior, with "compulsive ogling and coquetting" when in the presence of her male colleagues (305).

2. I say "unambiguously agentic" because, by the end of Riviere's theoretical propositions, it is unclear if masquerading is simply the feminine condition, or pathological, or strategic, or somehow all of the above. On the ambiguities in Riviere's account of the masquerade, see Heath, "Joan Riviere and the Masquerade."

3. Irigaray, *This Sex Which Is Not One*, 76. See also Doane, "Masquerade Reconsidered."

4. Scharff finds this concern to repudiate association with the subject position in her ethnographic study *Repudiating Feminism*.

5. McRobbie, *Aftermath of Feminism*.

6. Conor, *Spectacular Modern Woman*.

7. On the stereotypes, see for instance, Holland, *Alternative Femininities*; Holland and Harpin, "Who Is the 'Girly' Girl?"; Reay, "'Spice Girls,' 'Nice Girls'"; and Stern, "What Is Femme?"

8. Tate, *Black Beauty*.

9. Busia, "Women and the Dynamics of Representation," 107; Hobson, "Black Beauty."

10. Tate, *Black Beauty*, 22.

11. Paechter, "Masculine Femininities," 257.

12. See Ismail, "From 'Area-Boyism' to 'Junctions and Bases.'"

13. McRobbie, *Aftermath of Feminism*.

14. Nadesan and Trethewey, "Performing the Enterprising Subject," 223.

15. Entwistle and Wissinger, "Keeping Up Appearances"; Entwistle, "Fashioning the Career Woman"; Nadesan and Trethewey, "Performing the Enterprising Subject."

16. Conor, *Spectacular Modern Woman*.

17. Feher, "Self-Appreciation."

18. Banet-Weiser, *Authentic*™, 56.

19. Scheper, "'Of La Baker, I Am a Disciple'"; Springer, "Divas, Evil Black Bitches, and Bitter Black Women."

20. Gill and Donaghue, "As If Postfeminism Had Come True."

21. Entwistle, "Fashioning the Career Woman."

22. Balogun, "Cultural and Cosmopolitan,"366. See also Busia, "Women and the Dynamics of Representation"; and Odejide, "'What Can a Woman Do?'"

23. Negra, *What a Girl Wants?*, 132.

24. Ang cited in Hollows, "Feeling Like a Domestic Goddess," 190.

25. Hollows, "Feeling Like a Domestic Goddess."

26. As Sarah Sharma puts it in "It Changes Space and Time," labor may contribute to constitution and "maintenance of someone else's experience of time" (75).

27. Judith Butler, *Gender Trouble*, 185.

28. Tasker and Negra, "Introduction," 18.

29. Hollows, "Feeling Like a Domestic Goddess," 195.

30. Littler, "Rise of the 'Yummy Mummy'"; I. Tyler, "Pregnant Beauty."

31. I. Tyler, "Pregnant Beauty," 23.

32. Littler, "Rise of the 'Yummy Mummy,'" 227.

33. I. Tyler, "Pregnant Beauty," 29.

CONCLUSION: A NEW FASHION FOR FEMINISM?

1. Neil and Mbilishaka, "'Hey Curlfriends!'"; Norwood, "Decolonizing My Hair."

2. Banet-Weiser, *Empowered*, 1.

3. Rottenberg, *Rise of Neoliberal Feminism*.

4. Banet-Weiser, Gill, and Rottenberg, "Postfeminism, Popular Feminism and Neoliberal Feminism?"

5. See, for example, Hamad and Taylor, "Introduction." See also Banet-Weiser, *Empowered.*

6. Berents, "Hashtagging Girlhood"; Maxfield, "History Retweeting Itself."

7. Berents, "Hashtagging Girlhood."

8. Maxfield, "History Retweeting Itself." See also Berents, "Hashtagging Girlhood"; and Loken, "#BringBackOurGirls."

9. Ong, *Neoliberalism as Exception,* 5.

10. There is a methodological point to be made here, too, about the relative insights that textual versus ethnographic approaches may offer us to understand mediated subjectivities. Both approaches are necessary and complementary, in my view.

11. Judith Butler, "Performative Agency," 151.

12. Rottenberg, *Rise of Neoliberal Feminism.*

13. Slaughter, "Why Women Still Can't Have It All."

14. Favaro, "'Just Be Confident Girls!,'" 289.

15. See, for example, Banet-Weiser, Gill, and Rottenberg, "Postfeminism, Popular Feminism and Neoliberal Feminism?"; Gill, "Post-postfeminism?"; and Hemmings, "Resisting Popular Feminisms."

16. Hemmings, "Resisting Popular Feminisms," 973.

BIBLIOGRAPHY

Abdullah, Hussaina. "'Transition Politics' and the Challenge of Gender in Nigeria." *Review of African Political Economy* 20, no. 56 (1993): 27–41.

Adebanwi, Wale, and Ebenezer Obadare. "Introducing Nigeria at Fifty: The Nation in Narration." *Journal of Contemporary African Studies* 28, no. 4 (2010): 379–405.

Adesokan, Akin. "Anticipating Nollywood: Lagos circa 1996." *Social Dynamics* 37, no. 1 (2011): 96–110.

Ahmed, Sara. "Affective Economies." *Social Text* 22, no. 2 (2004): 117–39.

———. "Collective Feelings; or, The Impressions Left by Others." *Theory, Culture & Society* 21, no. 2 (2004): 25–42.

———. *The Promise of Happiness*. Durham, NC: Duke University Press, 2010.

———. *Strange Encounters: Embodied Others in Post-Coloniality*. London: Routledge, 2000.

Alexander, Jacqui, and Chandra Mohanty. "Cartographies of Knowledge and Power: Transnational Feminism as Radical Praxis." In *Critical Transnational Feminist Practice*, edited by Amanda Lock Swarr and Richa Nagar, 23–45. Albany: State University of New York Press.

Allan, Alexandra Jane. "The Importance of Being a 'Lady': Hyper-femininity and Heterosexuality in the Private, Single-Sex Primary School." *Gender and Education* 21, no. 2 (2009): 145–58.

Allen, Amy. "Power Trouble: Performativity as Critical Theory." *Constellations* 5, no. 4 (1998): 456–71.

Allman, Jean Marie, ed. *Fashioning Africa: Power and the Politics of Dress*. Bloomington: Indiana University Press, 2004.

———. "Fashioning Africa: Power and the Politics of Dress." In *Fashioning Africa: Power and the Politics of Dress*, edited by Jean Marie Allman, 1–10. Bloomington: Indiana University Press, 2004.

———. "'Let Your Fashion Be in Line with Our Ghanaian Costume': Nation, Gender, and the Politics of Clothing in Nkrumah's Ghana." In *Fashioning Africa: Power and the Politics of Dress*, edited by Jean Marie Allman, 144–65. Bloomington: Indiana University Press, 2004.

Althusser, Louis. "Ideology and Ideological State Apparatuses." In *Lenin and Philosophy and Other Essays*, translated by Ben Brewster, 127–88. London: New Left Books, 1971.

Amin, Ash. "Spatialities of Globalisation." *Environment and Planning A* 34, no. 3 (2002): 385–99.

Andrews, Molly. "Feminist Research with Non-Feminist and Anti-Feminist Women: Meeting the Challenge." *Feminism & Psychology* 12, no. 1 (2002): 55–77.

Ang, Ien. "Culture and Communication: Towards an Ethnographic Critique of Media Consumption in the Transnational Media System." *European Journal of Communication* 5, no. 2 (1990): 239–60.

———. *Desperately Seeking the Audience*. London: Routledge, 2006.

———. "Doing Cultural Studies at the Crossroads: Local/Global Negotiations." *European Journal of Cultural Studies* 1, no. 1 (1998): 13–31.

———. "I'm a Feminist but ... 'Other' Women and Postnational Feminism." In *Feminist Postcolonial Theory: A Reader*, edited by Reina Lewis and Sara Mills, 190–206. Edinburgh: Edinburgh University Press, 2003.

———. *Living Room Wars: Rethinking Media Audiences for a Postmodern World*. London: Routledge, 1996.

———. *On Not Speaking Chinese: Living between Asia and the West*. London: Routledge, 2001.

———. *Watching Dallas: Soap Opera and the Melodramatic Imagination*. London: Methuen, 1985.

Appadurai, Arjun. "Grassroots Globalization and the Research Imagination." *Public Culture* 12, no. 1 (2000): 1–19.

———. *Modernity at Large: Cultural Dimensions of Globalization*. Vol. 1. Minneapolis: University of Minnesota Press, 1996.

Apter, Andrew. *The Pan-African Nation: Oil and the Spectacle of Culture in Nigeria*. Chicago: University of Chicago Press, 2008.

Apter, Emily S. *Feminizing the Fetish: Psychoanalysis and Narrative Obsession in Turn-of-the-Century France*. Ithaca, NY: Cornell University Press, 1991.

Arnfred, Signe, ed. *Re-thinking Sexualities in Africa*. Uppsala: Nordic Africa Institute, 2004.

Arthurs, Jane. "*Sex and the City* and Consumer Culture: Remediating Postfeminist Drama." *Feminist Media Studies* 3, no. 1 (2003): 83–98.

Attwood, Feona. "Fashion and Passion: Marketing Sex to Women." *Sexualities* 8, no. 4 (2005): 392–406.

———. "Sexed Up: Theorizing the Sexualization of Culture." *Sexualities* 9, no. 1 (2006): 77–94.

Bakare-Yusuf, Bibi. "Nudity and Morality: Legislating Women's Bodies and Dress in Nigeria." In *African Sexualities: A Reader*, edited by Sylvia Tamale, 116–29. Cape Town: Pambazuka Press, 2011.

Balogun, Oluwakemi M. "Cultural and Cosmopolitan: Idealized Femininity and Embodied Nationalism in Nigerian Beauty Pageants." *Gender & Society* 26, no. 3 (2012): 357–81.

Banet-Weiser, Sarah. "Am I Pretty or Ugly? Girls and the Market for Self-Esteem." *Girlhood Studies* 7, no. 1 (2014): 83–101.

———. *Authentic™: The Politics of Ambivalence in a Brand Culture*. New York: New York University Press, 2012.

———. "'Confidence You Can Carry!': Girls in Crisis and the Market for Girls' Empowerment Organisations." *Continuum: Journal of Media and Cultural Studies* 29, no. 2 (2015): 182–93.

———. *Empowered: Popular Feminism and Popular Misogyny*. Durham, NC: Duke University Press, 2018.

———. *The Most Beautiful Girl in the World: Beauty Pageants and National Identity*. Berkeley: University of California Press, 1999.

———. "What's Your Flava? Race and Postfeminism in Media Culture." In *Interrogating Postfeminism: Gender and the Politics of Popular Culture*, edited by Yvonne Tasker and Diane Negra, 201–26. Durham, NC: Duke University Press, 2007.

Banet-Weiser, Sarah, and Laura Portwood-Stacer. "'I Just Want to Be Me Again!': Beauty Pageants, Reality Television and Post-Feminism." *Feminist Theory* 7, no. 2 (2006): 255–72.

———. "The Traffic in Feminism: An Introduction to the Commentary and Criticism on Popular Feminism." *Feminist Media Studies* 17, no. 5 (2017): 884–88.

Banet-Weiser, Sarah, Rosalind Gill, and Catherine Rottenberg. "Postfeminism, Popular Feminism and Neoliberal Feminism? Sarah Banet-Weiser, Rosalind Gill and Catherine Rottenberg in Conversation." *Feminist Theory* (2019): 1–22.

Banks, Ingrid. *Hair Matters: Beauty, Power, and Black Women's Consciousness*. New York: New York University Press, 2000.

Barnes, Ruth, and Joanne Bubolz Eicher, eds. *Dress and Gender: Making and Meaning in Cultural Contexts*. Vol. 2. New York: Berg, 1992.

Bartky, Sandra Lee. "Foucault, Femininity, and the Modernization of Patriarchal Power." In *Femininity and Domination: Studies in the Phenomenology of Oppression*, 93–111. London: Routledge, 1990.

Barvosa-Carter, Edwina. "Strange Tempest: Agency, Poststructuralism, and the Shape of Feminist Politics to Come." *International Journal of Sexuality and Gender Studies* 6, no. 1–2 (2001): 123–37.

Bascom, William R. "Social Status, Wealth and Individual Differences among the Yoruba." *American Anthropologist* 53, no. 4 (1951): 490–505.

Baumgardner, Jennifer, and Amy Richards. "Feminism and Femininity; or, How We Learned to Stop Worrying and Love the Thong." In *All about the Girl: Cul-*

ture, Power, and Identity, edited by Anita Harris, 59–67. London: Routledge, 2004.

Bell, Vikki. "Performativity and Belonging: An Introduction." *Theory, Culture & Society* 16, no. 2 (1999): 1–10.

Benhabib, Seyla. "Feminism and Postmodernism: An Uneasy Alliance." In *Feminist Contentions: A Philosophical Exchange*, edited by Seyla Benhabib, 17–34. London: Routledge, 1995.

———, ed. *Feminist Contentions: A Philosophical Exchange*. London: Routledge, 1995.

Bent, Emily. "A Different Girl Effect: Producing Political Girlhoods in the 'Invest in Girls' Climate." *Sociological Studies of Children and Youth* 16, no. 1 (2013): 3–20.

Berents, Helen. "Hashtagging Girlhood: #IAmMalala, #BringBackOurGirls and Gendering Representations of Global Politics." *International Feminist Journal of Politics* 18, no. 4 (2016): 513–27.

Berlant, Lauren. "Cruel Optimism." *Differences* 17, no. 3 (2006): 20–36.

Berry, Esther R. "The Zombie Commodity: Hair and the Politics of Its Globalization." *Postcolonial Studies* 11, no. 1 (2008): 63–84.

Bhabha, Homi. "Of Mimicry and Man." In *Tensions in Empire: Colonial Cultures in a Bourgeois World*, edited by Frederick Cooper and Ann Laura Stoley, 152–60. Berkeley: University of California Press, 1997.

Binkley, Sam. *Happiness as Enterprise: An Essay on Neoliberal Life*. New York: State University of New York Press, 2014.

———. "Happiness, Positive Psychology and the Program of Neoliberal Governmentality." *Subjectivity* 4, no. 4 (2011): 371–94.

———. "The Perilous Freedoms of Consumption: Toward a Theory of the Conduct of Consumer Conduct." *Journal for Cultural Research* 10, no. 4 (2006): 343–62.

Blue, Morgan Genevieve. "The Best of Both Worlds? Youth, Gender, and a Postfeminist Sensibility in Disney's Hannah Montana." *Feminist Media Studies* 13, no. 4 (2013): 660–75.

Bollen, Jonathan James. "Dressing Up and Growing Up: Rehearsals on the Threshold of Intelligibility: A Response to Affrica Taylor." In *Judith Butler in Conversation: Analyzing the Texts and Talk of Everyday Life*, edited by Bronwyn Davies, 217–34. London: Routledge, 2008.

Bordo, Susan. *Unbearable Weight: Feminism, Western Culture and the Body*. Berkeley: University of California Press, 1993.

Bose, Purnima. "From Humanitarian Intervention to the Beautifying Mission: Afghan Women and Beauty without Borders." *Genders*, no. 51 (2010): n.p.

Bourdieu, Pierre. *Outline of a Theory of Practice*. Vol. 16. Cambridge: Cambridge University Press, 1977.

———. *The Logic of Practice*. Stanford, CA: Stanford University Press, 1990.

Boyer, Ruth M. "Yoruba Cloths with Regal Names." *African Arts* 16, no. 2 (1983): 42–98.

Bradfield, Shelley-Jean. "Society's Emerging Femininities: Neoliberal, Postfeminist, and Hybrid Identities on Television in South Africa." In *The Routledge Companion to Media and Gender*, edited by Cynthia Carter, Linda Steiner, and Lisa McLaughlin, 280–89. London: Routledge, 2014.

Braun, Virginia. "'The Women Are Doing It for Themselves': The Rhetoric of Choice and Agency around Female Genital 'Cosmetic Surgery.'" *Australian Feminist Studies* 24, no. 60 (2009): 233–49.

Breckenridge, Carol Appadurai. *Consuming Modernity: Public Culture in a South Asian World*. Minneapolis: University of Minnesota Press, 1995.

Britzman, Deborah P. "'The Question of Belief': Writing Poststructural Ethnography." *International Journal of Qualitative Studies in Education* 8, no. 3 (1995): 229–38.

Broekhuizen, Francien, and Adrienne Evans. "Pain, Pleasure and Bridal Beauty: Mapping Postfeminist Bridal Perfection." *Journal of Gender Studies* 25, no. 3 (2016): 335–48.

Brooks, Ann. *Postfeminisms: Feminism, Cultural Theory and Cultural Forms*. London: Routledge, 2002.

Brown, Wendy. "Neo-liberalism and the End of Liberal Democracy." *Theory & Event* 7, no. 1 (2003).

Browne, Victoria. *Feminism, Time, and Nonlinear History*. New York: Palgrave Macmillan, 2014.

Brunsdon, Charlotte. "Feminism, Postfeminism, Martha, Martha, and Nigella." *Cinema Journal* 44, no. 2 (2005): 110–16.

Bryce, Jane. "Signs of Femininity, Symptoms of Malaise: Contextualizing Figurations of 'Woman' in Nollywood." *Research in African Literatures* 43, no. 4 (2012): 71–87.

Budgeon, Shelley. "Identity as an Embodied Event." *Body & Society* 9, no. 1 (2003): 35–55.

Budgeon, Shelley, and Dawn H. Currie. "From Feminism to Postfeminism: Women's Liberation in Fashion Magazines." *Women's Studies International Forum* 18, no. 2 (1995): 173–86.

Burman, Erica, and Ian Parker. *Discourse Analytic Research: Repertoires and Readings of Texts in Action*. London: Routledge, 1993.

Burns, Maree Leeann. "Bodies That Speak: Examining the Dialogues in Research Interactions." *Qualitative Research in Psychology* 3, no. 1 (2006): 3–18.

———. "I. Interviewing: Embodied Communication." *Feminism & Psychology* 13, no. 2 (2003): 229–36.

Burns-Ardolino, Wendy. "Reading Woman: Displacing the Foundations of Femininity." *Hypatia* 18, no. 3 (2003): 42–59.

Busia, Abena P. A. "Women and the Dynamics of Representation: Of Cooking, Cars, and Gendered Culture." *Feminist Africa* 16 (2012): 98–117.

Butler, Jess. "For White Girls Only? Postfeminism and the Politics of Inclusion." *Feminist Formations* 25, no. 1 (2013): 35–58.

Butler, Judith. *Bodies That Matter: On the Discursive Limits of Sex.* London: Routledge, 2011.

———. "Contingent Foundations: Feminism and the Question of 'Postmodernism.'" In *Feminist Contentions: A Philosophical Exchange,* edited by Seyla Benhabib, 35–57. New York and London: Routledge, 1995.

———. "Critically Queer." *GLQ: A Journal of Lesbian and Gay Studies* 1, no. 1 (1993): 17–32.

———. "Endangered/Endangering: Schematic Racism and White Paranoia." In *Reading Rodney King/Reading Urban Uprising,* edited by Robert Gooding-Williams, 15–22. London: Routledge, 1993.

———. *Excitable Speech: A Politics of the Performative.* London: Routledge, 1997.

———. *Gender Trouble: Feminism and the Subversion of Identity.* London: Routledge, 1999.

———. "Giving an Account of Oneself." *Diacritics* 31, no. 4 (2001): 22–40.

———. *Giving an Account of Oneself.* Oxford: Oxford University Press, 2005.

———. "Performative Acts and Gender Constitution: An Essay in Phenomenology and Feminist Theory." *Theatre Journal* 40, no. 4 (1988): 519–31.

———. "Performative Agency." *Journal of Cultural Economy* 3, no. 2 (2010): 147–61.

———. *The Psychic Life of Power: Theories in Subjection.* Stanford, CA: Stanford University Press, 1997.

———. *Undoing Gender.* London: Routledge, 2004.

Butler, Pamela, and Jigna Desai. "Manolos, Marriage, and Mantras: Chick-Lit Criticism and Transnational Feminism." *Meridians: Feminism, Race, Transnationalism* 8, no. 2 (2008): 1–31.

Byfield, Judith A. "Dress and Politics in Post–World War II Abeokuta (Western Nigeria)." In *Fashioning Africa: Power and the Politics of Dress,* edited by Jean Marie Allman, 31–49. Bloomington: Indiana University Press, 2004.

———. "Taxation, Women, and the Colonial State: Egba Women's Tax Revolt." *Meridians* 3, no. 2 (2003): 250–77.

Byrd, Ayana, and Lori Tharps. *Hair Story: Untangling the Roots of Black Hair in America.* New York: Macmillan, 2014.

Byrne, Bridget. "Reciting the Self: Narrative Representations of the Self in Qualitative Interviews." *Feminist Theory* 4, no. 1 (2003): 29–49.

Cahill, Ann J. "Feminist Pleasure and Feminine Beautification." *Hypatia* 18, no. 4 (2003): 42–64.

Calefato, Patrizia. "Fashion as Cultural Translation: Knowledge, Constrictions and Transgressions on/of the Female Body." *Social Semiotics* 20, no. 4 (2010): 343–55.

Calkin, Sydney. "Post-Feminist Spectatorship and the Girl Effect: 'Go Ahead, Really Imagine Her.'" *Third World Quarterly* 36, no. 4 (2015): 654–69.

Campt, Tina Marie. *Other Germans: Black Germans and the Politics of Race, Gender, and Memory in the Third Reich.* Ann Arbor: University of Michigan Press, 2004.

Chakrabarty, Dipesh. *Provincializing Europe: Postcolonial Thought and Historical Difference*. Princeton, NJ: Princeton University Press, 2000.

Chatman, Dayna. "Pregnancy, Then It's 'Back to Business': Beyoncé, Black Femininity, and the Politics of a Post-feminist Gender Regime." *Feminist Media Studies* 15, no. 6 (2015): 926–41.

Cheah, Pheng, and Bruce Robbins. *Cosmopolitics: Thinking and Feeling beyond the Nation*. Minneapolis: University of Minnesota Press, 1998.

Chen, Eva. "Shanghai(ed) Babies: Geopolitics, Biopolitics and the Global Chick Lit." *Feminist Media Studies* 12, no. 2 (2012): 214–28.

Chiluwa, Innocent. "Assessing the Nigerianness of SMS Text-Messages in English." *English Today* 24, no. 1 (2008): 51–56.

Chow, Rey. "Chineseness as Theoretical Problem." *Boundary 2* 25, no. 3 (1998): 1–24.

———. *The Protestant Ethnic and the Spirit of Capitalism*. New York: Columbia University Press, 2002.

———. "Where Have All the Natives Gone?" In *Feminist Postcolonial Theory: A Reader*, edited by Reina Lewis and Sara Mills, 324–49. Edinburgh: Edinburgh University Press, 2003.

Chuku, Gloria. "Igbo Women and Political Participation in Nigeria, 1800s–2005." *International Journal of African Historical Studies* 42, no. 1 (2009): 81–103.

Coleman, Rebecca, and Mónica Moreno Figueroa. "Past and Future Perfect? Beauty, Affect and Hope." *Journal for Cultural Research* 14, no. 4 (2010): 357–73.

Collins, Patricia. *Black Feminist Thought: Knowledge, Consciousness and the Politics of Empowerment*. London: Routledge, 2000.

Coly, Ayo A. "Un/Clothing African Womanhood: Colonial Statements and Postcolonial Discourses of the African Female Body." *Journal of Contemporary African Studies* 33, no. 1 (2015): 12–26.

Comaroff, Jean, and John L. Comaroff. *Modernity and Its Malcontents: Ritual and Power in Postcolonial Africa*. Chicago: University of Chicago Press, 1993.

———. "Theory from the South; or, How Euro-America Is Evolving toward Africa." *Anthropological Forum* 22, no. 2 (2012): 113–31.

Comaroff, John L., and Jean Comaroff. *Of Revelation and Revolution*. Vol. 2, *The Dialectics of Modernity on a South African Frontier*. Chicago: University of Chicago Press, 2009.

Conor, Liz. *The Spectacular Modern Woman: Feminine Visibility in the 1920s*. Bloomington: Indiana University Press, 2004.

Conradson, David, and Deirdre McKay. "Translocal Subjectivities: Mobility, Connection, Emotion." *Mobilities* 2, no. 2 (2007): 167–74.

Cordwell, Justine M. "The Art and Aesthetics of the Yoruba." *African Arts* 16, no. 2 (1983): 56–100.

Cornwall, Andrea, and Jenny Edwards. "Introduction: Negotiating Empowerment." In *Feminisms, Empowerment and Development: Changing Women's Lives*, edited by Jenny Edwards and Andrea Cornwall, 1–37. London: Zed Books, 2014.

Cornwall, Andrea, Jasmine Gideon, and Kalpana Wilson. "Introduction: Reclaiming Feminism: Gender and Neoliberalism." *IDS Bulletin* 39, no. 6 (2008): 1–9.

Craft-Fairchild, Catherine. *Masquerade and Gender: Disguise and Female Identity in Eighteenth-Century Fictions by Women*. University Park: Pennsylvania State University Press, 2010.

Craig, Maxine Leeds. *Ain't I a Beauty Queen? Black Women, Beauty, and the Politics of Race*. Oxford: Oxford University Press, 2002.

——. "The Decline and Fall of the Conk; or, How to Read a Process." *Fashion Theory* 1, no. 4 (1997): 399–419.

——. "Race, Beauty, and the Tangled Knot of a Guilty Pleasure." *Feminist Theory* 7, no. 2 (2006): 159–77.

Craik, Jennifer. *The Face of Fashion: Cultural Studies in Fashion*. London: Routledge, 2003.

Crang, Philip, Claire Dwyer, and Peter Jackson. "Transnationalism and the Spaces of Commodity Culture." *Progress in Human Geography* 27, no. 4 (2003): 438–56.

Cruikshank, Barbara. "Revolutions Within: Self-Government and Self-Esteem." *Economy and Society* 22, no. 3 (1993): 327–44.

Cvajner, Martina. "Hyper-femininity as Decency: Beauty, Womanhood and Respect in Emigration." *Ethnography* 12, no. 3 (2011): 356–74.

Davies, Bronwyn. "Subjectification: The Relevance of Butler's Analysis for Education." *British Journal of Sociology of Education* 27, no. 4 (2006): 425–38.

——. "The Concept of Agency: A Feminist Poststructuralist Analysis." *Social Analysis: The International Journal of Social and Cultural Practice*, no. 30 (1991): 42–53.

——. "The Problem of Desire." *Social Problems* 37, no. 4 (1990): 501–16.

Davies, Bronwyn, Jenny Browne, Susanne Gannon, Eileen Honan, Cath Laws, Babette Mueller-Rockstroh, and Eva Bendix Petersen. "The Ambivalent Practices of Reflexivity." *Qualitative Inquiry* 10, no. 3 (2004): 360–89.

Davies, Bronwyn, Jenny Browne, Susanne Gannon, Eileen Honan, and Margaret Somerville. "Embodied Women at Work in Neoliberal Times and Places." *Gender, Work & Organization* 12, no. 4 (2005): 343–62.

Davies, Bronwyn, Jenny Browne, Susanne Gannon, Lekkie Hopkins, Helen McCann, and Monne Wihlborg. "Constituting the Feminist Subject in Poststructuralist Discourse." *Feminism & Psychology* 16, no. 1 (2006): 87–103.

Davies, Bronwyn, Suzy Dormer, Sue Gannon, Cath Laws, Sharn Rocco, Hillevi Lenz Taguchi, and Helen McCann. "Becoming Schoolgirls: The Ambivalent Project of Subjectification." *Gender and Education* 13, no. 2 (2001): 167–82.

Davies, Bronwyn, Anne Britt Flemmen, Susanne Gannon, Cath Laws, and Barbara Watson. "Working on the Ground—a Collective Biography of Feminine Subjectivities: Mapping the Traces of Power and Knowledge." *Social Semiotics* 12, no. 3 (2002): 291–313.

Davies, Bronwyn, and Susanne Gannon. "Feminism/Poststructuralism." In *Research Methods in the Social Sciences*, edited by Bridget Somekh, and Cathy Lewin, 318–25. London: Sage, 2005.

Davies, Bronwyn, and Rom Harré. "Positioning: The Discursive Production of Selves." *Journal for the Theory of Social Behaviour* 20, no. 1 (1990): 43–63.

Davis, Kathy. *Reshaping the Female Body: The Dilemma of Cosmetic Surgery.* London: Routledge, 2013.

Dejmanee, Tisha. "Consumption in the City: The Turn to Interiority in Contemporary Postfeminist Television." *European Journal of Cultural Studies* 19, no. 2 (2016): 119–33.

Devereux, Cecily. "'Last Night, I Did a Striptease for My Husband': Erotic Dance and the Representation of 'Everyday' Femininity." *Feminist Media Studies* 12, no. 3 (2012): 317–34.

Diawara, Manthia. "The Sixties in Bamako: Malick Sidibé and James Brown." In *Malick Sidibé: Photographs*, edited by Andre Magnin, 8–22. Gothenburg: Hasselblad Centre, 2004.

Doane, Mary Ann. "Film and the Masquerade: Theorising the Female Spectator." *Screen* 23, nos. 3–4 (1982): 74–88.

———. "Masquerade Reconsidered: Further Thoughts on the Female Spectator." *Discourse* 11, no. 1 (1988): 42–54.

———. "Theorising the Female Spectator." *Hollywood: Cultural Dimensions: Ideology, Identity and Cultural Industry Studies* 4 (2004): 95–110.

Dobson, Amy Shields. "Performative Shamelessness on Young Women's Social Network Sites: Shielding the Self and Resisting Gender Melancholia." *Feminism & Psychology* 24, no. 1 (2014): 97–114.

———. "'Sexy' and 'Laddish' Girls: Unpacking Complicity between Two Cultural Imag(inations)es of Young Femininity." *Feminist Media Studies* 14, no. 2 (2014): 253–69.

Dogbe, Esi. "Unraveled Yarns: Dress, Consumption, and Women's Bodies in Ghanaian Culture." *Fashion Theory* 7, nos. 3–4 (2003): 377–95.

———. "Warped Identities: Dress in Popular West African Video Films." *African Identities* 1, no. 1 (2003): 95–117.

Donaghue, Ngaire, Tim Kurz, and Kally Whitehead. "Spinning the Pole: A Discursive Analysis of the Websites of Recreational Pole Dancing Studios." *Feminism & Psychology* 21, no. 4 (2011): 443–57.

Donham, Donald L. "On Being Modern in a Capitalist World: Some Conceptual and Comparative Issues." In *Critically Modern: Alternatives, Alterities, Anthropologies*, edited by Bruce Knauft, 241–57. Bloomington: Indiana University Press, 2002.

Dormer, Susan, and Bronwyn Davies. "Desiring Women and the (Im)Possibility of Being." *Australian Psychologist* 36, no. 1 (2001): 4–9.

Dosekun, Simidele. "Defending Feminism in Africa." *Postamble* 3 (2007): 41–47.

———. "For Western Girls Only? Post-feminism as Transnational Culture." *Feminist Media Studies* 15, no. 6 (2015): 960–75.

———. "'Hey, You Stylized Woman There': An Uncomfortable Reflexive Account of Performative Practices in the Field." *Qualitative Inquiry* 21, no. 5 (2015): 436–44.

Duits, Linda, and Liesbet Van Zoonen. "Headscarves and Porno-Chic: Disciplining Girls' Bodies in the European Multicultural Society." *European Journal of Women's Studies* 13, no. 2 (2006): 103–17.

Durham, Aisha. "'Check On It': Beyoncé, Southern Booty, and Black Femininities in Music Video." *Feminist Media Studies* 12, no. 1 (2012): 35–49.

Edley, Nigel. "Analysing Masculinity: Interpretative Repertoires, Ideological Dilemmas and Subject Positions." In *Discourse as Data: A Guide for Analysis*, edited by Margaret Wetherell, Stephanie Taylor, and Simeon Yates, 189–228. Milton Keynes: Open University Press, 2001.

Edley, Nigel, and Margaret Wetherell. "Jekyll and Hyde: Men's Constructions of Feminism and Feminists." *Feminism & Psychology* 11, no. 4 (2001): 439–57.

———. "Jockeying for Position: The Construction of Masculine Identities." *Discourse & Society* 8, no. 2 (1997): 203–17.

Edoh, M. Amah. "Redrawing Power? Dutch Wax Cloth and the Politics of 'Good Design.'" *Journal of Design History* 29, no. 3 (2016): 258–72.

Egan, R. Danielle. *Becoming Sexual: A Critical Appraisal of the Sexualization of Girls.* Cambridge: Polity Press, 2013.

Eicher, Joanne B., and Mary E. Higgins Roach. "Definition and Classification of Dress: Implications for Analysis of Gender Roles." In *Dress and Gender: Making and Meaning*, edited by Ruth Barnes and Joanne B. Eicher, 8–28. Oxford: Berg, 1992.

Elam, Harry Justin, and Kennell A. Jackson, eds. *Black Cultural Traffic: Crossroads in Global Performance and Popular Culture*. Ann Arbor: University of Michigan Press, 2005.

Elias, Ana Sofia, Rosalind Gill, and Christina Scharff. "Aesthetic Labour: Beauty Politics in Neoliberalism." In *Aesthetic Labour: Beauty Politics in Neoliberalism*, edited by Ana Elias, Rosalind Gill, and Christina Scharff, 3–49. London: Palgrave Macmillan, 2017.

Elias, Ana Sofia, and Rosalind Gill. "Beauty Surveillance: The Digital Self-Monitoring Cultures of Neoliberalism." *European Journal of Cultural Studies* (2017).

Elias, Juanita. "Davos Woman to the Rescue of Global Capitalism: Postfeminist Politics and Competitiveness Promotion at the World Economic Forum." *International Political Sociology* 7, no. 2 (2013): 152–69.

Entwistle, Joanne. "Fashion and the Fleshy Body: Dress as Embodied Practice." *Fashion Theory* 4, no. 3 (2000): 323–47.

———. "Fashioning the Career Woman: Power Dressing as a Strategy of Consumption." In *All the World and Her Husband: Women in 20th Century Consumer Culture*, edited by Margaret Andrews and Molly Talbot, 224–38. London: Cassell, 2000.

———. *The Fashioned Body: Fashion, Dress and Modern Social Theory.* Cambridge: Polity Press, 2000.

Entwistle, Joanne, and Elizabeth B. Wilson, eds. *Body Dressing.* Oxford: Berg, 2001.

Entwistle, Joanne, and Elizabeth Wissinger. "Keeping Up Appearances: Aesthetic Labour in the Fashion Modelling Industries of London and New York." *Sociological Review* 54, no. 4 (2006): 774–94.

Erasmus, Zmitri. "Hair Politics." In *Senses of Culture: South African Cultural Studies*, edited by Sarah Nuttall and Cheryl-Ann Michael, 380–92. Oxford: Oxford University Press, 2000.

———. "'Oe! My Hare Gaan Huistoe': Hair-Styling as Black Cultural Practice." *Agenda* 13, no. 32 (1997): 11–16.

Essof, Shireen. "African Feminisms: Histories, Applications and Prospects." *Agenda* 16, no. 50 (2001): 124–27.

Evans, Adrienne, and Sarah Riley. "Immaculate Consumption: Negotiating the Sex Symbol in Postfeminist Celebrity Culture." *Journal of Gender Studies* 22, no. 3 (2013): 268–81.

Evans, Adrienne, Sarah Riley, and Avi Shankar. "Postfeminist Heterotopias: Negotiating 'Safe' and 'Seedy' in the British Sex Shop Space." *European Journal of Women's Studies* 17, no. 3 (2010): 211–29.

———. "Technologies of Sexiness: Theorizing Women's Engagement in the Sexualization of Culture." *Feminism & Psychology* 20, no. 1 (2010): 114–31.

Evans, Caroline, and Minna Thornton. "Fashion, Representation, Femininity." *Feminist Review*, no. 38 (1991): 48–66.

Fabian, Johannes. *Time and the Other: How Anthropology Makes Its Object*. New York: Columbia University Press, 2014.

Fair, Laura. "Remaking Fashion in the Paris of the Indian Ocean: Dress, Performance and the Cultural Construction of a Cosmopolitan Zanzibari Identity." In *Fashioning Africa: Power and the Politics of Dress*, edited by Jean Marie Allman, 13–30. Bloomington: Indiana University Press, 2004.

Falola, Toyin, and Matthew M. Heaton. *A History of Nigeria*. Cambridge: Cambridge University Press, 2008.

Faludi, Susan. *Backlash: America's Undeclared War against Women*. New York: Anchor / Doubleday Books, 1992.

Favaro, Laura. "'Just Be Confident Girls!': Confidence Chic as Neoliberal Governmentality." In *Aesthetic Labour: Beauty Politics in Neoliberalism*, edited by Ana Elias, Rosalind Gill, and Christina Scharff, 283–99. London: Palgrave Macmillan, 2017.

Feher, Michel. "Self-Appreciation; or, The Aspirations of Human Capital." *Public Culture* 21, no. 1 (2009): 21–41.

Figueroa, Mónica G. Moreno. "Displaced Looks: The Lived Experience of Beauty and Racism." *Feminist Theory* 14, no. 2 (2013): 137–51.

Fleetwood, Nicole R. *Troubling Vision: Performance, Visuality, and Blackness*. Chicago: University of Chicago Press, 2011.

Ford, Tanisha. "The 'Afro Look' and Global Black Consciousness." *Nka Journal of Contemporary African Art*, no. 37 (2015): 28–37.

———. *Liberated Threads: Black Women, Style, and the Global Politics of Soul*. Chapel Hill: University of North Carolina Press, 2015.

———. "Soul Generation: Radical Fashion, Beauty, and the Transnational Black Liberation Movement, 1954–1980." *Journal of Pan African Studies* 5, no. 1 (2012): 294.

Foucault, Michel. *Technologies of the Self: A Seminar with Michel Foucault.* Edited by Luther H. Martin, Huck Gutman, and Patrick H. Hutton. London: Tavistock Publishing, 1988.

——. *The History of Sexuality.* Vol. 1, *An Introduction.* New York: Vintage Books, 1990.

——. *The History of Sexuality.* Vol. 2, *The Use of Pleasure.* New York: Vintage Books, 1990.

——. *The History of Sexuality.* Vol. 3, *The Care of the Self.* London: Penguin Books, 1990.

Fraser, Nancy. "False Antitheses: A Response to Seyla Benhabib and Judith Butler." In *Feminist Contentions: A Philosophical Exchange,* edited by Seyla Benhabib, 59–74. London: Routledge, 1995.

Freeman, Carla. "Embodying and Affecting Neoliberalism." In *A Companion to the Anthropology of the Body and Embodiment,* edited by Frances Mascia-Lees, 353–69. Malden, MA: Wiley Blackwell, 2011.

——. *Entrepreneurial Selves: Neoliberal Respectability and the Making of a Caribbean Middle Class.* Durham, NC: Duke University Press, 2014.

——. "Is Local: Global as Feminine: Masculine? Rethinking the Gender of Globalization." *Signs: Journal of Women in Culture and Society* 26, no. 4 (2001): 1007–37.

Frith, Hannah, Jayne Raisborough, and Orly Klein. "C'mon Girlfriend: Sisterhood, Sexuality and the Space of the Benign in Makeover TV." *International Journal of Cultural Studies* 13, no. 5 (2010): 471–89.

Gaonkar, Dilip Parameshwar. "On Alternative Modernities." *Public Culture* 11, no. 1 (1999): 1–18.

Gavey, Nicola. "Beyond 'Empowerment'? Sexuality in a Sexist World." *Sex Roles* 66, nos. 11–12 (2012): 718–24.

——. "Feminist Poststructuralism and Discourse Analysis: Contributions to Feminist Psychology." *Psychology of Women Quarterly* 13, no. 4 (1989): 459–75.

——. "Feminist Poststructuralism and Discourse Analysis Revisited." *Psychology of Women Quarterly* 35, no. 1 (2011): 183–88.

Geiger, Susan, Jean Marie Allman, and Nakanyike Musisi. *Women in African Colonial Histories.* Bloomington: Indiana University Press, 2002.

Giraldo, Isis. "Coloniality at Work: Decolonial Critique and the Postfeminist Regime." *Feminist Theory* 17, no. 2 (2016): 157–73.

Giroux, Henry A. "Beyond the Biopolitics of Disposability: Rethinking Neoliberalism in the New Gilded Age." *Social Identities* 14, no. 5 (2008): 587–620.

George, Abosede A. *Making Modern Girls: A History of Girlhood, Labor, and Social Development in Colonial Lagos.* Athens: Ohio University Press, 2014.

Gerhard, Jane. "Sex and the City: Carrie Bradshaw's Queer Postfeminism." *Feminist Media Studies* 5, no. 1 (2005): 37–49.

Gikandi, Simon. "Globalization and the Claims of Postcoloniality." *South Atlantic Quarterly* 100, no. 3 (2001): 627–58.

Gilbert, Jeremy. "What Kind of Thing Is 'Neoliberalism'?" *New Formations* 80, no. 80 (2013): 7–22.

Gill, Rosalind. "The Affective, Cultural and Psychic Life of Postfeminism: A Postfeminist Sensibility 10 Years On." *European Journal of Cultural Studies* 20, no. 6 (2017): 606–26.

———. "Beyond the 'Sexualization of Culture' Thesis: An Intersectional Analysis of 'Sixpacks,' 'Midriffs' and 'Hot Lesbians' in Advertising." *Sexualities* 12, no. 2 (2009): 137–60.

———. "Critical Respect: The Difficulties and Dilemmas of Agency and 'Choice' for Feminism: A Reply to Duits and van Zoonen." *European Journal of Women's Studies* 14, no. 1 (2007): 69–80.

———. "Culture and Subjectivity in Neoliberal and Postfeminist Times." *Subjectivity* 25, no. 1 (2008): 432–45.

———. "Empowerment/Sexism: Figuring Female Sexual Agency in Contemporary Advertising." *Feminism & Psychology* 18, no. 1 (2008): 35–60.

———. "From Sexual Objectification to Sexual Subjectification: The Resexualisation of Women's Bodies in the Media." *Feminist Media Studies* 3, no. 1 (2003): 100–106.

———. "Media, Empowerment and the 'Sexualization of Culture' Debates." *Sex Roles* 66, nos. 11–12 (2012): 736–45.

———. "Mediated Intimacy and Postfeminism: A Discourse Analytic Examination of Sex and Relationships Advice in a Women's Magazine." *Discourse & Communication* 3, no. 4 (2009): 345–69.

———. "Postfeminist Media Culture: Elements of a Sensibility." *European Journal of Cultural Studies* 10, no. 2 (2007): 147–66.

———. "Post-postfeminism? New Feminist Visibilities in Postfeminist Times." *Feminist Media Studies* 16, no. 4 (2016): 610–30.

———. "Sexism Reloaded; or, It's Time to Get Angry Again!" *Feminist Media Studies* 11, no. 01 (2011): 61–71.

Gill, Rosalind, and Ngaire Donaghue. "As If Postfeminism Had Come True: The Turn to Agency in Cultural Studies of 'Sexualisation.'" In *Gender, Agency, and Coercion*, edited by Sumi Madhok, Anne Phillips, and Kalpana Wilson, 240–58. Basingstoke: Palgrave Macmillan, 2013.

Gill, Rosalind, and Ana Sofia Elias. "'Awaken Your Incredible': Love Your Body Discourses and Postfeminist Contradictions." *International Journal of Media & Cultural Politics* 10, no. 2 (2014): 179–88.

Gill, Rosalind, and Shani Orgad. "The Confidence Cult(ure)." *Australian Feminist Studies* 30, no. 86 (2015): 324–44.

———. "Confidence Culture and the Remaking of Feminism." *New Formations: A Journal of Culture, Theory and Politics* 91 (2017): 16–34.

Gill, Rosalind, and Christina Scharff, eds. *New Femininities: Postfeminism, Neoliberalism and Subjectivity*. Basingstoke: Palgrave Macmillan, 2011.

Gilroy, Paul. *The Black Atlantic: Modernity and Double Consciousness*. Cambridge, MA: Harvard University Press, 1993.

Gimlin, Debra. *Body Work: Beauty and Self-Image in American Culture*. Berkeley: University of California Press, 2002.

Gonick, Marnina. "Old Plots and New Identities: Ambivalent Femininities in Late Modernity." *Discourse: Studies in the Cultural Politics of Education* 25, no. 2 (2004): 189–209.

Gonick, Marnina, and Janice Hladki. "Who Are the Participants? Rethinking Representational Practices and Writing with Heterotopic Possibility in Qualitative Inquiry." *International Journal of Qualitative Studies in Education* 18, no. 3 (2005): 285–304.

Gonick, Marnina, Emma Renold, Jessica Ringrose, and Lisa Weems. "Rethinking Agency and Resistance: What Comes after Girl Power?" *Girlhood Studies* 2, no. 2 (2009): 1–9.

Gott, Suzanne. "Asante Hightimers and the Fashionable Display of Women's Wealth in Contemporary Ghana." *Fashion Theory* 13, no. 2 (2009): 141–76.

———. "The Ghanaian Kaba: Fashion That Sustains Culture." In *Contemporary African Fashion*, edited by Suzanne Gott and Kristyne Loughran, 11–27. Bloomington: Indiana University Press, 2010.

Gott, Suzanne, and Kristyne Loughran, eds. *Contemporary African Fashion*. Bloomington: Indiana University Press, 2010.

Gqola, Pumla Dineo. "A Peculiar Place for a Feminist? The New South African Woman, True Love Magazine and Lebo (Gang) Mashile." *Safundi* 17, no. 2 (2016): 119–36.

Grayson, Deborah R. "Is It Fake? Black Women's Hair as Spectacle and Spec(tac)ular." *Camera Obscura* 12, no. 3 (1995): 12–31.

Grewal, Inderpal. *Transnational America: Feminisms, Diasporas, Neoliberalisms*. Durham, NC: Duke University Press, 2005.

Grewal, Inderpal, and Caren Kaplan. "Global Identities: Theorizing Transnational Studies of Sexuality." *GLQ: A Journal of Lesbian and Gay Studies* 7, no. 4 (2001): 663–79.

———. "Introduction: Transnational Feminist Practices and Questions of Postmodernity." In *Scattered Hegemonies: Postmodernity and Transnational Feminist Practices*, edited by Inderpal Grewal and Caren Kaplan, 1–30. Minneapolis: University of Minnesota Press, 1994.

———, eds. *Scattered Hegemonies: Postmodernity and Transnational Feminist Practices*. Minneapolis: University of Minnesota Press, 1994.

———. "Warrior Marks: Global Womanism's Neo-Colonial Discourse in a Multicultural Context." *Camera Obscura* 13, no. 3 (1996): 4–33.

Gwynne, Joel. "Japan, Postfeminism and the Consumption of Sexual(ised) Schoolgirls in Male-Authored Contemporary Manga." *Feminist Theory* 14, no. 3 (2013): 325–43.

Hall, Stuart. "Culture, Community, Nation." *Cultural Studies* 7, no. 3 (1993): 349–63.

———. "Introduction: Who Needs "Identity." In *Questions of Cultural Identity*, edited by Stuart Hall and Paul Du Gay, 1–17. London: Sage, 1996.

———. "Old and New Identities, Old and New Ethnicities." In *Culture, Globalization and the World-System: Contemporary Conditions for the Representation of Identity*, 41–68. Minneapolis: University of Minnesota Press, 1997.

———. "What Is This 'Black' in Black Popular Culture?" *Social Justice* 20, nos. 1–2 (1993): 104–14.

———. "When Was 'the Post-colonial'? Thinking at the Limit." In *The Postcolonial Question*, edited by Iain Chambers and Lidia Curti, 242–60. London: Routledge, 1996.

Hall, Stuart, and Paul Du Gay, eds. *Questions of Cultural Identity*. London: Sage, 1996.

Halse, Christine, and Anne Honey. "Unraveling Ethics: Illuminating the Moral Dilemmas of Research Ethics." *Signs: Journal of Women in Culture and Society* 30, no. 4 (2005): 2141–62.

Hamad, Hannah. *Postfeminism and Paternity in Contemporary US Film: Framing Fatherhood*. New York and Abingdon: Routledge, 2013.

Hamad, Hannah, and Anthea Taylor. "Introduction: Feminism and Contemporary Celebrity Culture." *Celebrity Studies* 6, no. 1 (2015): 124–27.

Hansen, Karen Tranberg. "Dressing Dangerously: Miniskirts, Gender Relations, and Sexuality in Zambia." In *Fashioning Africa: Power and the Politics of Dress*, edited by Jean Marie Allman, 166–85. Bloomington: Indiana University Press, 2004.

———. "Fashioning: Zambian Moments." *Journal of Material Culture* 8, no. 3 (2003): 301–9.

———. *Salaula: The World of Secondhand Clothing and Zambia*. Chicago: University of Chicago Press, 2000.

———. "The World in Dress: Anthropological Perspectives on Clothing, Fashion, and Culture." *Annual Review of Anthropology* 33 (2004): 369–92.

Harris, Anita. *Future Girl: Young Women in the Twenty-First Century*. New York: Routledge, 2004.

Hasinoff, Amy Adele. "Fashioning Race for the Free Market on America's Next Top Model." *Critical Studies in Media Communication* 25, no. 3 (2008): 324–43.

Hassim, Shireen. *Women's Organizations and Democracy in South Africa: Contesting Authority*. Madison: University of Wisconsin Press, 2006.

Hatef, Azeta. "From under the Veil to under the Knife: Women, Cosmetic Surgery, and the Politics of Choice in Afghanistan." *Feminist Media Studies* (2017): 1–17.

Hawkesworth, Mary. "The Semiotics of Premature Burial: Feminism in a Postfeminist Age." *Signs: Journal of Women in Culture and Society* 29, no. 4 (2004): 961–85.

Hay, Margaret. "Changes in Clothing and Struggles over Identity in Colonial Western Kenya." In *Fashioning Africa: Power and the Politics of Dress*, edited by Jean Marie Allman, 67–83. Bloomington: Indiana University Press, 2004.

Haynes, Jonathan. "Neoliberalism, Nollywood and Lagos." In *Global Cinematic Cities: New Landscapes of Film and Media*, edited by Johan Andersson and Lawrence Webb, 59–76. New York: Columbia University Press, 2016.

——. "Nollywood in Lagos, Lagos in Nollywood Films." *Africa Today* 54, no. 2 (2007): 131–50.

Heath, Stephen. "Joan Riviere and the Masquerade." In *Formations of Fantasy*, edited by Victor Burgin, James Donald, and Cora Kaplan, 45–61. London: Routledge, 1986.

Hegde, Radha S. "A View from Elsewhere: Locating Difference and the Politics of Representation from a Transnational Feminist Perspective." *Communication Theory* 8, no. 3 (1998): 271–97.

——, ed. *Circuits of Visibility: Gender and Transnational Media Cultures*. New York: New York University Press, 2011.

Hemmings, Clare. "Resisting Popular Feminisms: Gender, Sexuality and the Lure of the Modern." *Gender, Place & Culture* 25, no. 7 (2018): 963–77.

——. "Affective Solidarity: Feminist Reflexivity and Political Transformation." *Feminist Theory* 13, no. 2 (2012): 147–61.

——. "Invoking Affect: Cultural Theory and the Ontological Turn." *Cultural Studies* 19, no. 5 (2005): 548–67.

——. "Telling Feminist Stories." *Feminist Theory* 6, no. 2 (2005): 115–39.

——. *Why Stories Matter: The Political Grammar of Feminist Theory*. Durham, NC: Duke University Press, 2011.

Hendrickson, Hildi. *Clothing and Difference: Embodied Identities in Colonial and Post-Colonial Africa*. Durham, NC: Duke University Press, 1996.

Hennessy, Rosemary. "Queer Visibility in Commodity Culture." *Cultural Critique*, no. 29 (1994): 31–76.

Hey, Valerie. "The Girl in the Mirror: The Psychic Economy of Class in the Discourse of Girlhood Studies." *Girlhood Studies* 2, no. 2 (2009): 10–32.

Hoad, Neville. "World Piece: What the Miss World Pageant Can Teach about Globalization." *Cultural Critique* 58, no. 1 (2004): 56–81.

Hobson, Janell. "Black Beauty and Digital Spaces: The New Visibility Politics." *Ada: A Journal of Gender, New Media, and Technology*, no. 10 (2016).

——. *Venus in the Dark: Blackness and Beauty in Popular Culture*. New York: Routledge, 2005.

Hodgson, Dorothy L., and Sheryl A. McCurdy, eds. *"Wicked" Women and the Reconfiguration of Gender in Africa*. Portsmouth: Heinemann, 2001.

Holland, Samantha. *Alternative Femininities: Body, Age and Identity*. Oxford: Berg, 2004.

Holland, Samantha, and Julie Harpin. "Who Is the 'Girly' Girl? Tomboys, Hyperfemininity and Gender." *Journal of Gender Studies* 24, no. 3 (2015): 293–309.

Hollows, Joanne. "Feeling like a Domestic Goddess: Postfeminism and Cooking." *European Journal of Cultural Studies* 6, no. 2 (2003): 179–202.

hooks, bell. *Black Looks: Race and Representation*. Boston: South End Press, 1992.

——. "Straightening Our Hair." In *Tenderheaded: A Comb-Bending Collection of Hair Stories*, edited by Pamela Johnson and Juliette Harris, 111–15. New York: Pocket Books, 2001.

Hopkins, Susan. "Girl Power-Dressing: Fashion, Feminism and Neoliberalism with Beckham, Beyoncé and Trump." *Celebrity Studies* 9, no 1. (2017): 1–6.

Horn, Jessica. "Re-righting the Sexual Body." *Feminist Africa* 6 (2006): 7–19.

Hoskins, Marie, and Jo-Anne Stoltz. "Fear of Offending: Disclosing Researcher Discomfort When Engaging in Analysis." *Qualitative Research* 5, no. 1 (2005): 95–111.

Hua, Julietta. "'Gucci Geishas' and Post-Feminism." *Women's Studies in Communication* 32, no. 1 (2009): 63–88.

Hunter, Mark. "The Materiality of Everyday Sex: Thinking beyond 'Prostitution.'" *African Studies* 61, no. 1 (2002): 99–120.

Ifeka-Moller, Caroline. "Female Militancy and Colonial Revolt: The Women's War of 1929, Eastern Nigeria." In *Perceiving Women*, edited by Shirley Ardener, 127–57. New York: John Wiley and Sons, 1975.

Iqani, Mehita. *Consumption, Media and the Global South: Aspiration Contested.* Basingstoke: Palgrave Macmillan, 2016.

Irigaray, Luce. *This Sex Which Is Not One.* Ithaca, NY: Cornell University Press, 1985.

Ismail, Olawale. "From 'Area-Boyism' to 'Junctions and Bases': Youth Social Formation and the Micro Structures of Violence in Lagos Island." In *State Fragility, State Formation, and Human Security in Nigeria*, edited by Mojubaolu Okome, 87–109. New York: Palgrave Macmillan, 2013.

Ivaska, Andrew. "'Anti-Mini Militants Meet Modern Misses': Urban Style, Gender and the Politics of 'National Culture' in 1960s Dar Es Salaam, Tanzania." In *Fashioning Africa: Power and the Politics of Dress*, edited by Jean Marie Allman, 104–21. Bloomington: Indiana University Press, 2004.

———. *Cultured States: Youth, Gender, and Modern Style in 1960s Dar Es Salaam.* Durham, NC: Duke University Press, 2011.

Jackson, Alecia Youngblood. "Performativity Identified." *Qualitative Inquiry* 10, no. 5 (2004): 673–90.

Jackson, Sue, and Tiina Vares. "'Perfect Skin,' 'Pretty Skinny': Girls' Embodied Identities and Post-feminist Popular Culture." *Journal of Gender Studies* 24, no. 3 (2015): 347–60.

Jackson, Sue, Tiina Vares, and Rosalind Gill. "'The Whole Playboy Mansion Image': Girls' Fashioning and Fashioned Selves within a Postfeminist Culture." *Feminism & Psychology* 23, no. 2 (2013): 143–62.

Jacobs, Sean. "Big Brother, Africa Is Watching." *Media, Culture & Society* 29, no. 6 (2007): 851–68.

Jarrín, Alvaro. *The Biopolitics of Beauty: Cosmetic Citizenship and Affective Capital in Brazil.* Berkeley: University of California Press, 2017.

Jenkins, Kathleen E., and Gerardo Marti. "Warrior Chicks: Youthful Aging in a Postfeminist Prosperity Discourse." *Journal for the Scientific Study of Religion* 51, no. 2 (2012): 241–56.

Johnson, Cheryl P. "Grassroots Organizing: Women in Anticolonial Activity in Southwestern Nigeria." *African Studies Review* 25, nos. 2–3 (1982): 137–57.

Johnson-Odim, Cheryl. "Actions Louder than Words: The Historical Task of Defining Feminist Consciousness in Colonial West Africa." In *Nation, Empire, Colony: Historicizing Gender and Race*, edited by Ruth Roach Pierson and Nupur Chaudhuri, 77–93. Bloomington: Indiana University Press, 1998.

———. "'For Their Freedoms': The Anti-imperialist and International Feminist Activity of Funmilayo Ransome-Kuti of Nigeria." *Women's Studies International Forum* 32 (2009): 51–59.

Johnson-Odim, Cheryl, and Nina Emma Mba. *For Women and the Nation: Funmilayo Ransome-Kuti of Nigeria*. Urbana: University of Illinois Press, 1997.

Joseph, Ralina L. "'Tyra Banks Is Fat': Reading (Post-)racism and (Post-)feminism in the New Millennium." *Critical Studies in Media Communication* 26, no. 3 (2009): 237–54.

Kaplan, Caren. "'A World without Boundaries': The Body Shop's Trans/National Geographics." *Social Text*, no. 43 (1995): 45–66.

———. "Hillary Rodham Clinton's Orient: Cosmopolitan Travel and Global Feminist Subjects." *Meridians: Feminism, Race, Transnationalism* 2, no. 1 (2001): 219–40.

Kaplan, Caren, and Inderpal Grewal. "Transnational Feminist Cultural Studies: Beyond the Marxism/Poststructuralism/Feminism Divides." *Positions* 2, no. 2 (1994): 430–55.

Kauppinen, Kati. "'Full Power despite Stress': A Discourse Analytical Examination of the Interconnectedness of Postfeminism and Neoliberalism in the Domain of Work in an International Women's Magazine." *Discourse & Communication* 7, no. 2 (2013): 133–51.

Kehily, Mary Jane, and Anoop Nayak. "Global Femininities: Consumption, Culture and the Significance of Place." *Discourse: Studies in the Cultural Politics of Education* 29, no. 3 (2008): 325–42.

Keller, Jessalynn. *Girls' Feminist Blogging in a Postfeminist Age*. New York and London: Routledge, 2016.

———. "Fiercely Real? Tyra Banks and the Making of New Media Celebrity." *Feminist Media Studies* 14, no. 1 (2014): 147–64.

Knauft, Bruce M., ed. *Critically Modern: Alternatives, Alterities, Anthropologies*. Bloomington: Indiana University Press, 2002.

Koffman, Ofra, and Rosalind Gill. "'The Revolution Will Be Led by a 12-Year-Old Girl': Girl Power and Global Biopolitics." *Feminist Review* 105, no. 1 (2013): 83–102.

Koffman, Ofra, Shani Orgad, and Rosalind Gill. "Girl Power and 'Selfie Humanitarianism.'" *Continuum* 29, no. 2 (2015): 157–68.

Kondo, Dorinne. *About Face: Performing Race in Fashion and Theater*. London: Routledge, 2014.

Kraidy, Marwan. "The Global, the Local, and the Hybrid: A Native Ethnography of Glocalization." *Critical Studies in Mass Communication* 16, no. 4 (1999): 456–76.

———. "Glocalisation: An International Communication Framework?" *Journal of International Communication* 9, no. 2 (2003): 29–49.

———. *Hybridity; or, The Cultural Logic of Globalization*. Philadelphia: Temple University Press, 2017.

———. "Hybridity in Cultural Globalization." *Communication Theory* 12, no. 3 (2002): 316–39.

Krings, Matthias, and Onookome Okome. *Global Nollywood: The Transnational Dimensions of an African Video Film Industry*. Bloomington: Indiana University Press, 2013.

Laden, Sonja. "'Making the Paper Speak Well'; or, The Pace of Change in Consumer Magazines for Black South Africans." *Poetics Today* 22, no. 2 (2001): 515–48.

———. "Who's Afraid of a Black Bourgeoisie? Consumer Magazines for Black South Africans as an Apparatus of Change." *Journal of Consumer Culture* 3, no. 2 (2003): 191–216.

Lakämper, Judith. "Affective Dissonance, Neoliberal Postfeminism and the Foreclosure of Solidarity." *Feminist Theory* 18, no. 2 (2017): 119–35.

Larner, Wendy. "Neo-Liberalism: Policy, Ideology, Governmentality." *Studies in Political Economy* 63, no. 1 (2000): 5–25.

Lather, Patti. "Fertile Obsession: Validity after Poststructuralism." *Sociological Quarterly* 34, no. 4 (1993): 673–93.

———. "Postbook: Working the Ruins of Feminist Ethnography." *Signs: Journal of Women in Culture and Society* 27, no. 1 (2001): 199–227.

Lazar, Michelle M. "'Discover the Power of Femininity!': Analyzing Global 'Power Femininity' in Local Advertising." *Feminist Media Studies* 6, no. 4 (2006): 505–17.

———. "Entitled to Consume: Postfeminist Femininity and a Culture of Post-Critique." *Discourse & Communication* 3, no. 4 (2009): 371–400.

———. "Feminist Critical Discourse Analysis: Articulating a Feminist Discourse Praxis." *Critical Discourse Studies* 4, no. 2 (2007): 141–64.

———. "The Right to Be Beautiful: Postfeminist Identity and Consumer Beauty Advertising." In *New Femininities: Postfeminism, Neoliberalism and Subjectivity*, edited by Rosalind Gill and Christina Scharff, 37–51. Basingstoke: Palgrave Macmillan, 2011.

Leclerc-Madlala, Suzanne. "Transactional Sex and the Pursuit of Modernity." *Social Dynamics* 29, no. 2 (2003): 213–33.

Leissle, Kristy. "Cosmopolitan Cocoa Farmers: Refashioning Africa in Divine Chocolate Advertisements." *Journal of African Cultural Studies* 24, no. 2 (2012): 121–39.

Leve, Michelle, Lisa Rubin, and Andrea Pusic. "Cosmetic Surgery and Neoliberalisms: Managing Risk and Responsibility." *Feminism & Psychology* 22, no. 1 (2012): 122–41.

Lewis, Desiree. "Introduction: African Feminisms." *Agenda* 50 (2001): 4–10.

Ligaga, Dina. "Mapping Emerging Constructions of Good Time Girls in Kenyan Popular Media." *Journal of African Cultural Studies* 26, no. 3 (2014): 249–61.

———. "Presence, Agency and Popularity: Kenyan 'Socialites,' Femininities and Digital Media." *Eastern African Literary and Cultural Studies* 2, nos. 3–4 (2016): 111–23.

Littler, Jo. "The Rise of the 'Yummy Mummy': Popular Conservatism and the Neoliberal Maternal in Contemporary British Culture." *Communication, Culture & Critique* 6, no. 2 (2013): 227–43.

Lindsay, Lisa A. "Domesticity and Difference: Male Breadwinners, Working Women, and Colonial Citizenship in the 1945 Nigerian General Strike." *American Historical Review* 104, no. 3 (1999): 783–812.

Loken, Meredith. "#BringBackOurGirls and the Invisibility of Imperialism." *Feminist Media Studies* 14, no. 6 (2014): 1100–1101.

Lowe, Lisa. *The Intimacies of Four Continents*. Durham, NC: Duke University Press, 2015.

Lunga, Violet. "Of Hair Identities: Stretching Postcolonial Cultural Identities." In *Africa and Europe: En/countering Myths: Essays on Literature and Cultural Politics*, edited by Carlotta von Maltzan, 103–17. Frankfurt: Peter Lang, 2004.

Lutwama-Rukundo, Evelyn. "Skimpy Fashion and Sexuality in Sheebah Karungi's Performances." *Feminist Africa* 21 (2016): 52–62.

Machelidon, Véronique. "Masquerade: A Feminine or Feminist Strategy?" In *Psychoanalyses/Feminisms*, edited by Peter Rudnytsky and Andrew Gordon, 103–20. Albany: State University of New York Press, 2000.

Madhok, Sumi, Anne Phillips, Kalpana Wilson, and Clare Hemmings, eds. *Gender, Agency, and Coercion*. Basingstoke: Palgrave Macmillan, 2013.

Madunagu, Bene E. "The Nigerian Feminist Movement: Lessons from Women in Nigeria, WIN." *Review of African Political Economy* 35, no. 118 (2008): 666–73.

Mama, Amina. "Editorial." *Feminist Africa* 5 (2005): 1–16.

———. "Feminism or Femocracy? State Feminism and Democratisation in Nigeria." *Africa Development/Afrique et Développement* (1995): 37–58.

———. "Khaki in the Family: Gender Discourses and Militarism in Nigeria." *African Studies Review* 41, no. 2 (1998): 1–18.

———. "What Does It Mean to Do Feminist Research in African Contexts?" *Feminist Review* 98, no. 1 (2011): e4–e20.

Mankekar, Purnima. "Media and Mobility in a Transnational World." In *The Media and Social Theory*, edited by Desmond Hesmondhalgh and Jason Toynbee, 1:145–58. London: Routledge, 2008.

Mann, Kristin. *Marrying Well: Marriage, Status, and Social Change among the Educated Elite in Colonial Lagos*. Cambridge: Cambridge University Press, 1985.

———. *Slavery and the Birth of an African City: Lagos, 1760–1900*. Bloomington: Indiana University Press, 2007.

———. "The Dangers of Dependence: Christian Marriage among Elite Women in Lagos Colony, 1880–1915." *Journal of African History* 24, no. 1 (1983): 37–56.

———. "Women, Landed Property, and the Accumulation of Wealth in Early Colonial Lagos." *Signs: Journal of Women in Culture and Society* 16, no. 4 (1991): 682–706.

Månsson, Elinor. "Drinking as a Feminine Practice: Post-Feminist Images of Women's Drinking in Swedish Women's Magazines." *Feminist Media Studies* 14, no. 1 (2014): 56–72.

Masilela, Ntongela. "The 'Black Atlantic' and African Modernity in South Africa." *Research in African Literatures* 27, no. 4 (1996): 88–96.

Masvawure, Tsitsi. "'I Just Need to Be Flashy on Campus': Female Students and Transactional Sex at a University in Zimbabwe." *Culture, Health & Sexuality* 12, no. 8 (2010): 857–70.

Maxfield, Mary. "History Retweeting Itself: Imperial Feminist Appropriations of 'Bring Back Our Girls.'" *Feminist Media Studies* 16, no. 5 (2016): 886–900.

Mba, Nina Emma. *Nigerian Women Mobilized: Women's Political Activity in Southern Nigeria, 1900–1965*. Berkeley: University of California Press, 1982.

Mbembe, Achille. "Aesthetics of Superfluity." *Public Culture* 16, no. 3 (2004): 373–405.

———. "African Modes of Self-Writing." *Public Culture* 14, no. 1 (2002): 239–73.

Mbembe, Achille, and Sarah Nuttall. "Writing the World from an African Metropolis." *Public Culture* 16, no. 3 (2004): 347–72.

McAndrew, Malia. "A Twentieth-Century Triangle Trade: Selling Black Beauty at Home and Abroad, 1945–1965." *Enterprise & Society* 11, no. 4 (2010): 784–810.

McClintock, Anne. *Imperial Leather: Race, Gender, and Sexuality in the Colonial Contest*. New York: Routledge, 1995.

McIntosh, Marjorie. *Yoruba Women, Work, and Social Change*. Bloomington: Indiana University Press, 2009.

McKay, Deirdre. "Migration and Masquerade: Gender and Habitus in the Philippines." In *Geography Research Forum* (Keele University) 21 (2001): 44–56.

McLarney, Ellen. "The Burqa in Vogue: Fashioning Afghanistan." *Journal of Middle East Women's Studies* 5, no. 1 (2009): 1–23.

McNay, Lois. "Agency and Experience: Gender as a Lived Relation." *Sociological Review* 52, no. 2 (2004): 175–90.

———. "Agency, Anticipation and Indeterminacy in Feminist Theory." *Feminist Theory* 4, no. 2 (2003): 139–48.

———. *Foucault and Feminism: Power, Gender and the Self*. Cambridge: Polity Press, 2013.

———. "Gender, Habitus and the Field: Pierre Bourdieu and the Limits of Reflexivity." *Theory, Culture & Society* 16, no. 1 (1999): 95–117.

———. *Gender and Agency: Reconfiguring the Subject in Feminist and Social Theory*. Cambridge: Polity Press, 2013.

———. "Self as Enterprise: Dilemmas of Control and Resistance in Foucault's *The Birth of Biopolitics*." *Theory, Culture & Society* 26, no. 6 (2009): 55–77.

———. "Subject, Psyche and Agency: The Work of Judith Butler." *Theory, Culture & Society* 16, no. 2 (1999): 175–93.

———. "The Foucauldian Body and the Exclusion of Experience." *Hypatia* 6, no. 3 (1991): 125–39.

McRobbie, Angela. "Notes on the Perfect: Competitive Femininity in Neoliberal Times." *Australian Feminist Studies* 30, no. 83 (2015): 3–20.

———. *The Aftermath of Feminism: Gender, Culture and Social Change*. London: Sage, 2009.

———. "Top Girls? Young Women and the Post-feminist Sexual Contract." *Cultural Studies* 21, nos. 4–5 (2007): 718–37.

Mercer, Kobena. "Black Hair/Style Politics." *New Formations: A Journal of Culture, Theory and Politics* 3 (1987): 33–54.

Metzger, Sean. *Chinese Looks: Fashion, Performance, Race.* Bloomington: Indiana University Press, 2014.

Mikell, Gwendolyn. *African Feminism: The Politics of Survival in Sub-Saharan Africa.* Philadelphia: University of Pennsylvania Press, 1997.

Millen, Dianne. "Some Methodological and Epistemological Issues Raised by Doing Feminist Research on Non-Feminist Women." *Sociological Research Online* (1997).

Modleski, Tania. *Feminism without Women: Culture and Criticism in a "Postfeminist" Age.* London: Routledge, 2014.

Mohammed, Altine, and Bene Madunagu. "WIN: A Militant Approach to the Mobilisation of Women." *Review of African Political Economy* 37 (1986): 103–5.

Mohanty, Chandra Talpade. "Under Western Eyes: Feminist Scholarship and Colonial Discourses." *Feminist Review*, no. 30 (1988): 61–88.

———. "'Under Western Eyes' Revisited: Feminist Solidarity through Anticapitalist Struggles." *Signs: Journal of Women in Culture and Society* 28, no. 2 (2003): 499–535.

———. "Women Workers and Capitalist Scripts: Ideologies of Domination, Common Interests, and the Politics of Solidarity." In *Feminist Genealogies, Colonial Legacies, Democratic Futures*, edited by Jacqui Alexander and Chandra Talpade Mohanty, 3–29. London: Routledge, 1997.

Molz, Jennie. "Cosmopolitanism and Consumption." In *The Ashgate Research Companion to Cosmopolitanism*, edited by Maria Rovisco and Magdalena Nowicka, 33–52. Surrey: Ashgate, 2011.

Montrelay, Michele. "Inquiry into Femininity." *M/F* 1 (1978): 86–99.

Motsemme, Nthabiseng. "Distinguishing Beauty, Creating Distinctions: The Politics and Poetics of Dress among Young Black Women." *Agenda* 17, no. 57 (2003): 12–19.

Mougoué, Jacqueline-Bethel. "African Women Do Not Look Good in Wigs: Gender, Beauty Rituals and Cultural Identity in Anglophone Cameroon, 1961–1972." *Feminist Africa* 21 (2016): 7–22.

Mulvey, Laura. "Visual Pleasure and Narrative Cinema." In *The Feminism and Visual Culture Reader*, edited by Amelia Jones, 44–53. New York and London: Routledge, 2003.

Munshi, Shoma. "Wife/Mother/Daughter-in-Law: Multiple Avatars of Homemaker in 1990s Indian Advertising." *Media, Culture & Society* 20, no. 4 (1998): 573–91.

———. "'Women of Substance': Commodification and Fetishization in Contemporary Advertising within the Indian 'Urbanscape.'" *Social Semiotics* 7, no. 1 (1997): 37–51.

Murphy, Michelle. "The Girl: Mergers of Feminism and Finance in Neoliberal Times." *Scholar and Feminist Online* 11, no. 2 (2013).

Mustafa, Hudita Nura. "Eros, Beauty and Crisis: Notes from Senegal." *Feminist Africa* 6 (2006): 20–32.

———. "Portraits of Modernity: Fashioning Selves in Dakarois Popular Photography." In *Images and Empires: Visuality in Colonial and Postcolonial Africa*, edited by Paul Stuart Landau and Deborah D. Kaspin, 172–92. Berkeley: University of California Press, 2002.

———. "Ruins and Spectacles: Fashion and City Life in Contemporary Senegal." *Nka Journal of Contemporary African Art*, no. 15 (2001): 47–53.

———. "Sartorial Ecumenes: African Styles in a Social and Economic Context." In *The Art of African Fashion*, edited by Els van der Plas and Marlous Willensen, 13–48. Trenton, NJ, and The Hague: Prince Claus Fund/Africa World Press, 1998.

Nadesan, Majia Holmer, and Angela Trethewey. "Performing the Enterprising Subject: Gendered Strategies for Success(?)." *Text and Performance Quarterly* 20, no. 3 (2000): 223–50.

Nayak, Anoop, and Mary Jane Kehily. "Gender Undone: Subversion, Regulation and Embodiment in the Work of Judith Butler." *British Journal of Sociology of Education* 27, no. 4 (2006): 459–72.

Negra, Diane. *What a Girl Wants? Fantasizing the Reclamation of Self in Postfeminism.* London: Routledge, 2009.

Neil, Latisha, and Afiya Mbilishaka. "'Hey Curlfriends!': Hair Care and Self-Care Messaging on YouTube by Black Women Natural Hair Vloggers." *Journal of Black Studies* 50, no. 2 (2019): 156–77.

Newell, Stephanie. "Constructions of Nigerian Women in Popular Literatures by Men." *African Languages and Cultures* 9, no. 2 (1996): 169–88.

Nguyen, Mimi Thi. "The Biopower of Beauty: Humanitarian Imperialisms and Global Feminisms in an Age of Terror." *Signs: Journal of Women in Culture and Society* 36, no. 2 (2011): 359–83.

———. *The Gift of Freedom: War, Debt, and Other Refugee Passages.* Durham, NC: Duke University Press, 2012.

Niessen, Sandra, Ann Marie Leshkowich, and Carla Jones, eds. *Re-Orienting Fashion: The Globalization of Asian Dress.* Oxford: Bloomsbury Academic, 2003.

Nnaemeka, Obioma. "Nego-Feminism: Theorizing, Practicing, and Pruning Africa's Way." *Signs: Journal of Women in Culture and Society* 29, no. 2 (2004): 357–85.

Norwood, Carolette R. "Decolonizing My Hair, Unshackling My Curls: An Autoethnography on What Makes My Natural Hair Journey a Black Feminist Statement." *International Feminist Journal of Politics* 20, no. 1 (2018): 69–84.

Nuttall, Sarah, "Introduction: Rethinking Beauty." In *Beautiful/Ugly: African and Diaspora Aesthetics*, edited by Sarah Nuttall, 1–27. Durham, NC: Duke University Press, 2006.

———. "Stylizing the Self: The Y Generation in Rosebank, Johannesburg." *Public Culture* 16, no. 3 (2004): 430–52.

Nuttall, Sarah, and Achille Mbembe. "A Blasé Attitude: A Response to Michael Watts." *Public Culture* 17, no. 1 (2005): 193–202.

Nwafor, Okechukwu. "Of Mutuality and Copying: Fashioning Aso Ebi through Fashion Magazines in Lagos." *Fashion Theory* 16, no. 4 (2012): 493–520.

———. "The Spectacle of Aso Ebi in Lagos, 1990–2008." *Postcolonial Studies* 14, no. 1 (2011): 45–62.

Nyamnjoh, Francis, Deborah Durham, and Jude Fokwang. "The Domestication of Hair and Modernised Consciousness in Cameroon: A Critique in the Context of Globalisation." *Identity, Culture and Politics* 3, no. 2 (2002): 98–124.

Nyamnjoh, Francis, and Divine Fuh. "Africans Consuming Hair, Africans Consumed by Hair." *Africa Insight* 44, no. 1 (2014): 52–68.

Nzegwu, Nkiru. "Colonial Racism: Sweeping out Africa with Mother Europe's Broom." In *Racism and Philosophy*, edited by Susan Babbitt and Sue Campbell, 124–56. Ithaca, NY: Cornell University Press, 1999.

Odejide, Abiola. "'What Can a Woman Do?': Being Women in a Nigerian University." *Feminist Africa* 8 (2007): 42–59.

Odhiambo, Tom. "The Black Female Body as a 'Consumer and a Consumable' in Current *Drum* and *True Love* Magazines in South Africa." *African Studies* 67, no. 1 (2008): 71–80.

Okome, Mojúbàolú Olúfúnké. "Gendered States: Women's Civil Society Activism in Nigerian Politics." In *Contesting the Nigerian State: Civil Society and the Contradictions of Self-Organization*, edited by Mojúbàolú Olúfúnké Okome, 109–55. New York: Palgrave Macmillan, 2013.

Okome, Onookome. "Nollywood, Lagos, and the Good-Time Woman." *Research in African Literatures* 43, no. 4 (2012): 166–86.

Ojakangas, Mika. "Impossible Dialogue on Bio-Power: Agamben and Foucault." *Foucault Studies*, no. 2 (2005): 5–28.

Olaniyan, Tejumola. *Arrest the Music! Fela and His Rebel Art and Politics*. Bloomington: Indiana University Press, 2004.

Olofintuade, Ayodele. "Female in Nigeria: Profile." *Feminist Africa* 22 (2018): 163–73.

O'Neill, Rachel. *Seduction: Men, Masculinity and Mediated Intimacy*. Cambridge: Polity Press, 2018.

Ong, Aihwa. *Flexible Citizenship: The Cultural Logics of Transnationality*. Durham, NC: Duke University Press, 1999.

———. *Neoliberalism as Exception: Mutations in Citizenship and Sovereignty*. Durham, NC: Duke University Press, 2006.

Osaghae, Eghosa E. *Crippled Giant: Nigeria since Independence*. Bloomington: Indiana University Press, 1998.

Oyeniyi, Bukola Adeyemi. "Dress and Identity in Yorubaland, 1880–1980." PhD diss., Universiteit Leiden, 2012.

Oyěwùmí, Oyèrónke. *The Invention of Women: Making an African Sense of Western Gender Discourses*. Minneapolis: University of Minnesota Press, 1997.

Paechter, Carrie. "Masculine Femininities/Feminine Masculinities: Power, Identities and Gender." *Gender and Education* 18, no. 3 (2006): 253–63.

———. "Tomboys and Girly-Girls: Embodied Femininities in Primary Schools." *Discourse: Studies in the Cultural Politics of Education* 31, no. 2 (2010): 221–35.

Pandey, Anita. "The Pragmatics of Code Alteration in Nigerian English." *Studies in the Linguistic Sciences* 25, no. 1 (1995): 75–117.

Parameswaran, Radhika. "Global Queens, National Celebrities: Tales of Feminine Triumph in Post-liberalization India." *Critical Studies in Media Communication* 21, no. 4 (2004): 346–70.

Parkins, Ilya. "Fashion as Methodology: Rewriting the Time of Women's Modernity." *Time & Society* 19, no. 1 (2010): 98–119.

Patton, Tracey Owens. "Hey Girl, Am I More than My Hair? African American Women and Their Struggles with Beauty, Body Image, and Hair." *NWSA Journal* 18, no. 2 (2006): 24–51.

Pereira, Charmaine. "Appropriating 'Gender' and 'Empowerment': The Resignification of Feminist Ideas in Nigeria's Neoliberal Reform Programme." *IDS Bulletin* 39, no. 6 (2008): 42–50.

———. "Configuring 'Global,' 'National,' and 'Local' in Governance Agendas and Women's Struggles in Nigeria." *Social Research: An International Quarterly* 69, no. 3 (2002): 781–804.

———. "Domesticating Women? Gender, Religion and the State in Nigeria under Colonial and Military Rule." *African Identities* 3, no. 1 (2005): 69–94.

———. "National Council of Women's Societies and the State, 1985–1993: The Use of Discourses of Womanhood by the NCWS." In *Identity Transformation and Identity Politics under Structural Adjustment in Nigeria*, edited by Attahiru Jega, 109–33. Uppsala: Nordiska Afrikainstitutet and Centre for Research and Documentation, 2000.

———. "Setting Agendas for Feminist Thought and Practice in Nigeria." *Signs: Journal of Women in Culture and Society* 34, no. 2 (2009): 263–69.

———. "Understanding Women's Experiences of Citizenship in Nigeria." In *Gender, Economies and Entitlements in Africa*, 87–110. Codesria Gender Series, vol. 2. Dakar: Council for the Development of Social Science Research in Africa, 2004.

Pereira, Charmaine, and Jibrin Ibrahim. "On the Bodies of Women: The Common Ground between Islam and Christianity in Nigeria." *Third World Quarterly* 31, no. 6 (2010): 921–37.

Petersen, Eva Bendix. "Passionately Attached: Academic Subjects of Desire." In *Judith Butler in Conversation: Analysing the Texts and Talk of Everyday Life*, edited by Bronwyn Davies, 55–68. London: Routledge, 2008.

Pham, Minh-Ha T. "The Right to Fashion in the Age of Terrorism." *Signs: Journal of Women in Culture and Society* 36, no. 2 (2011): 385–410.

Pierre, Jemima. *The Predicament of Blackness: Postcolonial Ghana and the Politics of Race*. Chicago: University of Chicago Press, 2012.

Pillow, Wanda. "Confession, Catharsis, or Cure? Rethinking the Uses of Reflexivity as Methodological Power in Qualitative Research." *International Journal of Qualitative Studies in Education* 16, no. 2 (2003): 175–96.

Pinho, Patricia. "Afro-aesthetics in Brazil." In *Beautiful Ugly: African and Diaspora Aesthetics*, edited by Sarah Nuttall, 266–89. Durham, NC: Duke University Press, 2006.

Piot, Charles. "Atlantic Aporias: Africa and Gilroy's Black Atlantic." *South Atlantic Quarterly* 100, no. 1 (2001): 155–70.

Pomerantz, Shauna, Rebecca Raby, and Andrea Stefanik. "Girls Run the World? Caught between Sexism and Postfeminism in School." *Gender & Society* 27, no. 2 (2013): 185–207.

Pramaggiore, Maria, and Diane Negra. "Keeping Up with the Aspirations: Commercial Family Values and the Kardashian Brand." In *Reality Gendervision: Sexuality and Gender on Transatlantic Reality Television*, edited by Brenda Weber, 76–96. Durham, NC: Duke University Press, 2014.

Projansky, Sarah. *Spectacular Girls: Media Fascination and Celebrity Culture*. New York: New York University Press, 2014.

Rabine, Leslie W. *The Global Circulation of African Fashion*. Oxford: Berg, 2002.

Ramamurthy, Priti. "Material Consumers, Fabricating Subjects: Perplexity, Global Connectivity Discourses, and Transnational Feminist Research." *Cultural Anthropology* 18, no. 4 (2003): 524–50.

Read, Jason. "A Genealogy of Homo-Economicus: Neoliberalism and the Production of Subjectivity." *Foucault Studies* (2009): 25–36.

Reay, Diane. "'Spice Girls,' 'Nice Girls,' 'Girlies,' and 'Tomboys': Gender Discourses, Girls' Cultures and Femininities in the Primary Classroom." *Gender and Education* 13, no. 2 (2001): 153–66.

Reddy, Vanita. "Jhumpa Lahiri's Feminist Cosmopolitics and the Transnational Beauty Assemblage." *Meridians: Feminism, Race, Transnationalism* 11, no. 2 (2013): 29–59.

———. "The Nationalization of the Global Indian Woman: Geographies of Beauty in Femina." *South Asian Popular Culture* 4, no. 1 (2006): 61–85.

Rifkin, Mark. *Beyond Settler Time: Temporal Sovereignty and Indigenous Self-Determination*. Durham, NC: Duke University Press, 2017.

Ringrose, Jessica. *Postfeminist Education? Girls and the Sexual Politics of Schooling*. London: Routledge, 2013.

Ringrose, Jessica, and Emma Renold. "Teen Girls, Working-Class Femininity and Resistance: Retheorising Fantasy and Desire in Educational Contexts of Heterosexualised Violence." *International Journal of Inclusive Education* 16, no. 4 (2012): 461–77.

Riviere, Joan. "Womanliness as a Masquerade." *International Journal of Psychology* 10 (1929): 303–13.

Rooks, Noliwe M. *Hair Raising: Beauty, Culture, and African American Women*. New Brunswick, NJ: Rutgers University Press, 1996.

Rose, Nikolas. *Governing the Soul: The Shaping of the Private Self*. London: Routledge, 1990.

———. *Inventing Our Selves: Psychology, Power, and Personhood*. Cambridge: Cambridge University Press, 1998.

Rottenberg, Catherine. *The Rise of Neoliberal Feminism*. Oxford: Oxford University Press, 2018.

———. "Happiness and the Liberal Imagination: How Superwoman Became Balanced." *Feminist Studies* 40, no. 1 (2014): 144–68.

———. "The Rise of Neoliberal Feminism." *Cultural Studies* 28, no. 3 (2014): 418–37.

Rovine, Victoria L. *African Fashion, Global Style: Histories, Innovations, and Ideas You Can Wear*. Bloomington: Indiana University Press, 2015.

Russo, Mary J. *The Female Grotesque: Risk, Excess, and Modernity*. London: Routledge, 1994.

Salmenniemi, Suvi, and Maria Adamson. "New Heroines of Labour: Domesticating Post-feminism and Neoliberal Capitalism in Russia." *Sociology* 49, no. 1 (2015): 88–105.

Salo, Elaine. "Negotiating Gender and Personhood in the New South Africa: Adolescent Women and Gangsters in Manenberg Township on the Cape Flats." *European Journal of Cultural Studies* 6, no. 3 (2003): 345–65.

———. "Talking about Feminism in Africa." *Agenda* 16, no. 50 (2001): 58–63.

Sanger, Nadia. "New Women, Old Messages? Constructions of Femininities, Race and Hypersexualised Bodies in Selected South African Magazines, 2003–2006." *Social Dynamics* 35, no. 1 (2009): 137–48.

Sassen, Saskia. "Spatialities and Temporalities of the Global: Elements for a Theorization." *Public Culture* 12, no. 1 (2000): 215–32.

Scharff, Christina. *Repudiating Feminism: Young Women in a Neoliberal World*. Surrey: Ashgate, 2012.

———. "The Psychic Life of Neoliberalism: Mapping the Contours of Entrepreneurial Subjectivity." *Theory, Culture & Society* 33, no. 6 (2016): 107–22.

Scheld, Suzanne. "Youth Cosmopolitanism: Clothing, the City and Globalization in Dakar, Senegal." *City & Society* 19, no. 2 (2007): 232–53.

Scheper, Jeanne. "'Of La Baker, I Am a Disciple': The Diva Politics of Reception." *Camera Obscura: Feminism, Culture, and Media Studies* 22, no. 2 (65) (2007): 73–101.

Scott, Joan W. "The Evidence of Experience." *Critical Inquiry* 17, no. 4 (1991): 773–97.

Sensoy, Özlem, and Elizabeth Marshall. "Missionary Girl Power: Saving the 'Third World' One Girl at a Time." *Gender and Education* 22, no. 3 (2010): 295–311.

Sharma, Sarah. "It Changes Space and Time: Introducing Power-Chronography." In *Communication Matters: Materialist Approaches to Media, Mobility and Networks*, edited by Jeremy Packer and Stephen Crofts Wiley, 66–77. London: Routledge, 2011.

Shefer, Tamara, Lindsay Clowes, and Tania Vergnani. "Narratives of Transactional Sex on a University Campus." *Culture, Health & Sexuality* 14, no. 4 (2012): 435–47.

Shih, Shu-mei. "Towards an Ethics of Transnational Encounters; or, 'When' Does a 'Chinese' Woman Become a 'Feminist'?" *Differences* 13, no. 2 (2002): 90–126.

———. *Visuality and Identity: Sinophone Articulations across the Pacific*. Vol. 2. Berkeley: University of California Press, 2007.

Shome, Raka. "Postcolonial Interventions in the Rhetorical Canon: An 'Other' View." *Communication Theory* 6, no. 1 (1996): 40–59.

——. "Space Matters: The Power and Practice of Space." *Communication Theory* 13, no. 1 (2003): 39–56.

——. "Transnational Feminism and Communication Studies." *Communication Review* 9, no. 4 (2006): 255–67.

Shome, Raka, and Radha Hegde. "Culture, Communication, and the Challenge of Globalization." *Critical Studies in Media Communication* 19, no. 2 (2002): 172–89.

——. "Postcolonial Approaches to Communication: Charting the Terrain, Engaging the Intersections." *Communication Theory* 12, no. 3 (2002): 249–70.

Skeggs, Beverley. "The Making of Class and Gender through Visualizing Moral Subject Formation." *Sociology* 39, no. 5 (2005): 965–82.

——. *Formations of Class & Gender: Becoming Respectable.* Vol. 51. London: Sage, 1997.

Slack, Jennifer Daryl. "The Theory and Method of Articulation in Cultural Studies." In *Stuart Hall: Critical Dialogues in Cultural Studies,* edited by David Morley and Kuan-Hsing Chen, 112–27. London: Routledge, 1996.

Slaughter, Anne-Marie. "Why Women Still Can't Have It All." *Atlantic,* July–August 2012. www.theatlantic.com/magazine/archive/2012/07/why-women-still-cant-have -it-all/309020/.

Soetan, Funmi. "Feminist Civil Society Organizations and Democratization in Nigeria." In *Contesting the Nigerian State: Civil Society and the Contradictions of Self-Organization,* edited by Mojúbàolú Olúfúnké Okome, 157–172. New York: Palgrave Macmillan, 2013.

Springer, Kimberly. "Divas, Evil Black Bitches, and Bitter Black Women: African-American Women in Postfeminist and Post–Civil Rights Popular Culture." In *Interrogating Postfeminism: Gender and the Politics of Popular Culture,* edited by Yvonne Tasker and Diane Negra, 249–76. Durham, NC: Duke University Press, 2007.

Stern, Katherine. "What Is Femme? The Phenomenology of the Powder Room." *Women: A Cultural Review* 8, no. 2 (1997): 183–96.

Stuart, Avelie, and Ngaire Donaghue. "Choosing to Conform: The Discursive Complexities of Choice in Relation to Feminine Beauty Practices." *Feminism & Psychology* 22, no. 1 (2012): 98–121.

Sullivan, Katie Rose, and Helen Delaney. "A Femininity That 'Giveth and Taketh Away': The Prosperity Gospel and Postfeminism in the Neoliberal Economy." *Human Relations* 70, no. 7 (2016): 836–59.

Switzer, Heather. "(Post)Feminist Development Fables: The Girl Effect and the Production of Sexual Subjects." *Feminist Theory* 14, no. 3 (2013): 345–60.

Sylvanus, Nina. "The Fabric of Africanity: Tracing the Global Threads of Authenticity." *Anthropological Theory* 7, no. 2 (2007): 201–16.

——. *Patterns in Circulation: Cloth, Gender, and Materiality in West Africa.* Chicago: University of Chicago Press, 2016.

Tamale, Sylvia. "Profile—'Keep Your Eyes off My Thighs': A Feminist Analysis of Uganda's 'Miniskirt Law.'" *Feminist Africa* 21 (2016): 83–90.

———. "Researching and Theorising Sexualities in Africa." In *African Sexualities: A Reader*, edited by Sylvia Tamale, 11–36. Cape Town: Pambazuka Press, 2011.

———, ed. *Researching and Theorising Sexualities in Africa*. Cape Town: Pambazuka Press, 2011.

Tasker, Yvonne, and Diane Negra. "Introduction: Feminist Politics and Postfeminist Culture." In *Interrogating Postfeminism: Gender and the Politics of Popular Culture*, edited by Yvonne Tasker and Diane Negra, 1–25. Durham, NC: Duke University Press, 2007.

Tate, Shirley. *Black Beauty: Aesthetics, Stylization*. Surrey: Ashgate, 2009.

———. "Black Beauty: Shade, Hair and Anti-racist Aesthetics." *Ethnic and Racial Studies* 30, no. 2 (2007): 300–319.

———. "Not All the Women Want to Be White: Decolonizing Beauty Studies." In *Decolonizing European Sociology: Transdisciplinary Approaches*, 195–223. Surrey: Ashgate, 2010.

Thomas, Lynn M. "The Modern Girl and Racial Respectability in 1930s South Africa." In *The Modern Girl around the World: Consumption, Modernity, and Globalization*, edited by Alys Eve Weinbaum, Lynn M. Thomas, Priti Ramamurthy, Uta G. Poiger, Madeleine Yue Dong, and Tani E. Barlow, 96–119. Durham, NC: Duke University Press, 2008.

Thompson, Cheryl. "Black Women, Beauty, and Hair as a Matter of Being." *Women's Studies* 38, no. 8 (2009): 831–56.

Thompson, Mary. "'Learn Something from This!': The Problem of Optional Ethnicity on America's Next Top Model." *Feminist Media Studies* 10, no. 3 (2010): 335–52.

Thornham, Sue, and Feng Pengpeng. "'Just a Slogan': Individualism, Post-feminism, and Female Subjectivity in Consumerist China." *Feminist Media Studies* 10, no. 2 (2010): 195–211.

Tomaselli, Keyan G. "Blue Is Hot, Red Is Cold: Doing Reverse Cultural Studies in Africa." *Cultural Studies? Critical Methodologies* 1, no. 3 (2001): 283–318.

———. "Cultural Studies in Africa: Positioning Difference." *Critical Arts* 13, no. 1 (1999): 1–14.

———. "Recovering Praxis—Cultural Studies in Africa: The Unnaming Continues (Reply to Wright, 1998 and McNeil, 1998)." *European Journal of Cultural Studies* 1, no. 3 (1998): 387–402.

Tseëlon, Efrat. *The Masque of Femininity: The Presentation of Woman in Everyday Life*. London: Sage, 1995.

Tyler, Carole-Anne. "The Feminine Look." In *Theory between the Disciplines: Authority/Vision/Politics*, edited by Martin Kreiswirth and Mark A. Cheetham, 191–212. Ann Arbor: University of Michigan Press, 1990.

Tyler, Imogen. "'Chav Mum Chav Scum' Class Disgust in Contemporary Britain." *Feminist Media Studies* 8, no. 1 (2008): 17–34.

———. "Pregnant Beauty: Maternal Femininities under Neoliberalism." In *New Femininities: Postfeminism, Neoliberalism and Subjectivity*, edited by Rosalind Gill and Christina Scharff, 21–36. Basingstoke: Palgrave Macmillan, 2011.

Unigwe, Chika. *On Black Sisters Street: A Novel*. New York: Random House, 2011. E-book.

Vats, Anjali, and LeiLani Nishime. "Containment as Neocolonial Visual Rhetoric: Fashion, Yellowface, and Karl Lagerfeld's 'Idea of China.'" *Quarterly Journal of Speech* 99, no. 4 (2013): 423–47.

Walker, Lisa M. "How to Recognize a Lesbian: The Cultural Politics of Looking Like What You Are." *Signs: Journal of Women in Culture and Society* 18, no. 4 (1993): 866–90.

Weber, Brenda, ed. *Reality Gendervision: Sexuality and Gender on Transatlantic Reality Television*. Durham, NC: Duke University Press, 2014.

Weinbaum, Alys Eve, Lynn M. Thomas, Priti Ramamurthy, Uta G. Poiger, Madeleine Yue Dong, and Tani E. Barlow, eds. *The Modern Girl around the World: Consumption, Modernity, and Globalization*. Durham, NC: Duke University Press, 2008.

Wetherell, Margaret. "A Step Too Far: Discursive Psychology, Linguistic Ethnography and Questions of Identity." *Journal of Sociolinguistics* 11, no. 5 (2007): 661–81.

———. "Positioning and Interpretative Repertoires: Conversation Analysis and Post-structuralism in Dialogue." *Discourse & Society* 9, no. 3 (1998): 387–412.

Wetherell, Margaret, and Nigel Edley. "Negotiating Hegemonic Masculinity: Imaginary Positions and Psycho-Discursive Practices." *Feminism & Psychology* 9, no. 3 (1999): 335–56.

Wilkes, Karen. "Colluding with Neo-Liberalism: Post-feminist Subjectivities, Whiteness and Expressions of Entitlement." *Feminist Review* 110, no. 1 (2015): 18–33.

Wilson, Kalpana. "'Race,' Gender and Neoliberalism: Changing Visual Representations in Development." *Third World Quarterly* 32, no. 2 (2011): 315–31.

———. "Towards a Radical Re-appropriation: Gender, Development and Neoliberal Feminism." *Development and Change* 46, no. 4 (2015): 803–32.

Win, Everjoice. "Not Very Poor, Powerless or Pregnant: The African Woman Forgotten by Development." In *Feminisms in Development: Contradictions, Contestations and Challenges*, edited by Andrea Cornwall, Elizabeth Harrison, and Ann Whitehead, 79–85. London: Zed Books, 2007.

Winch, Alison. *Girlfriends and Postfeminist Sisterhood*. Basingstoke: Palgrave Macmillan, 2013.

Yuval-Davis, Nira. *Gender and Nation: SAGE Publications*. London: Sage, 1997.

Zeleza, Paul Tiyambe. "Rewriting the African Diaspora: Beyond the Black Atlantic." *African Affairs* 104, no. 414 (2005): 35–68.

INDEX

SIMIDELE DOSEKUN is an assistant professor in media and communications at the London School of Economics and Political Science.

DISSIDENT FEMINISMS

The University of Illinois Press
is a founding member of the
Association of University Presses.

———————————————————————

Composed in 10.5/13 Minion Pro
with Trend Rh Sans display
by Lisa Connery
at the University of Illinois Press
Cover designed by Jennifer S. Fisher
Cover illustration: karelnoppe/Adobe Stock

University of Illinois Press
1325 South Oak Street
Champaign, IL 61820-6903
www.press.uillinois.edu

Printed by Printforce, United Kingdom